OCT 27 1989

$9.95

AN EGYPTIAN GRAMMAR

with Chrestomathy and Glossary

SAMUEL A. B. MERCER

Professor Emeritus
of Semitic Languages and Egyptology
Trinity College, University of Toronto

FREDERICK UNGAR PUBLISHING CO.
NEW YORK

Republished 1961
by arrangement with the author

Third Printing, 1978

Printed in the United States of America

ISBN 0-8044-0353-8
Library of Congress Catalog Card No. 61-13636

TO

THE MEMORY OF

SIR GASTON MASPERO

SCHOLAR TEACHER AND FRIEND

THIS BOOK IS DEDICATED

BY THE AUTHOR

PREFACE

THIS book is intended for beginners. Experience in teaching Oriental languages has taught me that the beginner needs a textbook which is both simple and also supplied with exercises. Hitherto, so far as I know, only three such books, on Egyptian, have appeared in any modern language. They are: BUDGE's *Easy Lessons in Egyptian Hieroglyphics*, whose method from a pedagogical standpoint I consider to be entirely wrong; Miss MURRAY's *Elementary Egyptian Grammar*, which has practically no exercises; and MERCER-ROEDER, *Short Egyptian Grammar,* which is now out of print. The larger grammars are reference books and unsuited for the use of beginners.

This book has been designed primarily for use in colleges, seminaries, and universities, and is meant to provide for an academic year's work of three hours a week. The needs of the private student were also kept in mind. Egyptian is difficult. Nor have compilers of Egyptian grammars done much to make it attractive to the student. It is with this in mind that I have prepared this little book. I have divided the grammar into chapters or lessons, and supplied each chapter with copious exercises. I am sure that if the student works through these lessons with care and diligence he will have no trouble with the reading exercises which follow.

The student should first *memorise* the *Alphabet* and the select *Syllabic Signs.* These are fundamental and occur most frequently in all hieroglyphic texts. He should *read* chapter three with care, looking up each sign in the *Sign List* at the end of the book. Thus far the aim has been to acquaint the student with his signs. A careful *reading* of chapter four is all that is necessary. But the nouns, adjectives, pronouns, verbs, adverbs, prepositions, conjunctions, and other particles should be *committed to memory*, and the exercises on each lesson should be carefully read. Study the Syntax carefully, and do the exercises with diligence. The

Chrestomathy is sufficiently large to afford the student considerable practice in reading.

The author's object has been to make this book as brief and concise as possible. He warns students against thinking that they can acquire an adequate knowledge of Egyptian without much memory-work. If the above directions are followed, the author feels that the object for which the book has been prepared will be attained—namely, to add to the number of students interested in the study of Egyptian.

For a second academic year's work in Egyptian it is recommended that the student use KURT SETHE, *Ägyptische Lesestücke*, J. C. Hinrichs, Leipzig, 1924; ERMAN und GRAPOW, *Ägyptisches Handwörterbuch*, Reuther und Reichard, Berlin, 1921; together with the reading of some longer Egyptian text to be found in special publications. At the end of two years' work the student should be ready to do independent reading. He should then arm himself with ERMAN's *Ägyptische Grammatik*, Reuther und Reichard, Berlin (latest edition); GUNN's *Studies in Egyptian Syntax,* Geuthner, Paris, 1924; and (as soon as it is finished) with ERMAN and GRAPOW, *Wörterbuch der ägyptischen Sprache*, J. C. Hinrichs, Leipzig, 1925 ff. For further literature on all phases of the Egyptian language, see "Literatur" in ERMAN's *Ägyptische Grammatik.*

I cannot close this preface without expressing my indebtedness to the authors of the above mentioned books, for they have all been continually at my service during this work of compilation.

It remains only to thank Dr. JOHN A. MAYNARD, the Editor of this Series, who in reading this book in manuscript offered many valuable suggestions, and A. S. ARNOLD, Esq., Ph.D., of New York and Metuchen, New Jersey, who not only read the manuscript and made several valuable suggestions, but also, by his generous and intelligent backing made the publication of this book possible.

SAMUEL A. B. MERCER

Trinity College,
University of Toronto

May 10, 1926.

CONTENTS

GRAMMAR

SYNTAX

CHRESTOMATHY

GRAMMAR

Introduction

§ 1. The Egyptian language is related to the Semitic languages, as well as to certain African languages, such as Berber and the East African Hamitic languages.

The language of ancient Egypt experienced various changes throughout its long history. Accordingly, the language of the Old Kingdom is called *Ancient Egyptian*; that of the Middle Kingdom is called *Classical Egyptian*; the daily language of the New Kingdom is called *New Egyptian*; and the language of Christian Egypt is called *Coptic*.

§ 2. Various scripts were used by the ancient Egyptians. The *Hieroglyphic* is the oldest. It was used in the famous "Pyramid Texts," it was carved in stone and wood and sometimes painted in colours. It remained in constant use in all periods of Egyptian history, but was used chiefly for monumental purposes. The hieroglyphic is a picture script, and was written from right to left, or from left to right, and sometimes in perpendicular columns. The *Hieratic* began to be used extensively during the Middle Kingdom, and was written on papyrus. This script is really an abbreviated and cursive form of the hieroglyphic. It was usually written from right to left. The *Demotic* began to be used about 650 B.C., and was much used in official documents as late as the Roman period. The script is an abbreviated form of the hieratic. It was usually written from right to left. The *Coptic* is written in Greek letters, with some extra characters to express sounds not found in the Greek language.

§ 3. This little Egyptian grammar introduces the student to *Classical Egyptian.* Other forms of the Egyptian language are best taken up only after Classical Egyptian has been thoroughly mastered.

§ 4. *Samples of ancient Egyptian scripts.*

a. *Hieroglyphic:*

Perpendicular, from right to left

Perpendicular, from left to right

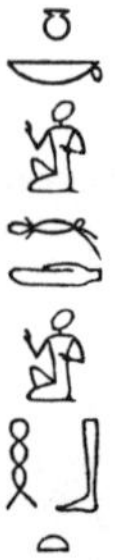

Horizontal, from right to left

Horizontal, from left to right

b. *Hieratic:*

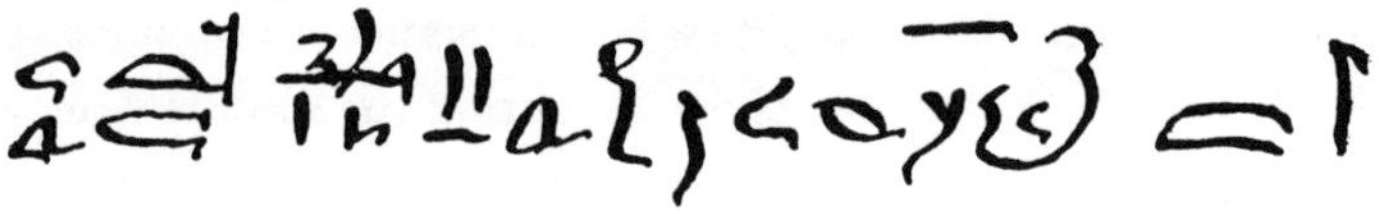

c. *Demotic:*

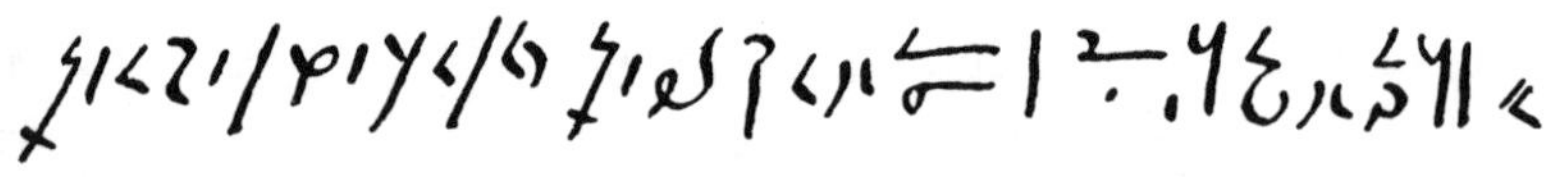

d. *Coptic:*

ϩⲛ̄ ⲧⲉϩⲟⲩⲉⲓⲧⲉ ⲛⲉϥϣⲟⲟⲡ ⲛ̄ϭⲓⲡϣⲁϫⲉ.

CHAPTER I

The Script

§ 5. The hieroglyphic is a picture script. At first only visible objects could be expressed in writing. Thus, was written for "man," or for "hand." But the picture of a man with his hand to his mouth, , was in time written to represent "to speak" or "to eat," and the sign for "eye," , was in time used also to represent "to see." The first great step in the evolution of the hieroglyphic script was made when the early Egyptians used their picture signs to express those abstract words, which happened to be pronounced in the same way as the words represented by the picture signs. Thus, the sign for "star," ★, was pronounced *dwꜣ*. But the word "to adore" was also pronounced *dwꜣ*. Therefore, in order to express the abstract idea "to adore," the concrete sign ★ was used.

§ 6. As very little account was taken of the expression of vowels, there being no separate vowel signs in Egyptian, some of the signs came to represent only one consonant. Such consonants were used as an alphabet. They were also used with another hieroglyph to make up a syllable or a word. Thus, the second great step was taken, namely, in the development of an alphabetic and of a phonetic script. Consequently, in the hieroglyphic script, we have *ideograms*, or pictures for whole words; *alphabetic* signs, or pictures for individual letters; and *phonograms*, or pictures for syllables.

§ 7. *Alphabetic signs:*

Hiero-glyphic	Approximate Sound	Semitic Equivalent	Approximate Name	Hieratic	Demotic
𓄿	*ꜣ*, *a*, *e*	א	eagle		
𓇋	*y*, *i*	י	leaf		
𓂝	*ʿ*, *gh*, *o*	ע	arm		
𓅱	*w*, *u*	ו	chick		
𓃀	*b*	ב	leg		
𓊪	*p*	פּ	box		
𓆑	*f*	פ	snail		
𓅓	*m*	מ	owl		
𓈖	*n*	נ	water		
𓂋	*r*	ר	mouth		
𓉔	*h*	ה, ه	court yard		
𓎛	*ḥ*	ח, ح	coil		
𓐍	*ḫ*	ח, خ	disk		
𓄡	*ẖ*	ח, ح, خ	club		
𓊃	*s*	ז	bolt		
𓋴	*ś*	שׂ	tape		
𓈙	*š*	שׁ	pond		
𓈎	*ḳ*, *q*	ק	triangle		
𓎡	*k*	כ	basket		
𓎼	*g*	ג, غ	stand		
𓏏	*t*	ת	loaf		
𓍿	*ṯ*	ס, ז	tongs		
𓂧	*d*	ט, ד	hand		
𓆓	*ḏ*	צ, ז	snake		

§ 8. Groups of consonants, e.g. *śḏm*, *ḥtp*, *ntr* are made pronounceable by the insertion of a short *ĕ* between the letters. Thus, we read these words *śeḏem*, *ḥetep*, *neter*. But the *ĕ*, it must be remembered, is quite conventional. It is not at all represented in the hieroglyphs.

§ 9. There are no written vowels in Egyptian. The letters , , , are really weak consonants. is often omitted: *ḏfꜣ* "food" for ; it is sometimes interchangeable with : "suffering" for . The letter is often omitted; it sometimes corresponds to ; and it sometimes changes to . The letter never changes. But is often omitted, and sometimes becomes .

§ 10. There is no separate sign for *l*. In order to represent a foreign *l*, Egyptians used or . Final was sometimes slurred to , and sometimes disappeared, but it often appeared as .

§ 11. The aspirates were sharply distinguished, as in "him," more energetic, as in the Scotch "loch," but was scarcely distinguishable from and partly interchangeable with it.

§ 12. The sibilants and were interchangeable.

§ 13. The dental often became , and became .

§ 14. At a later time in the history of the language, certain consonants in some words were transposed: *ḳmꜣ* "to create" became at a later date *ḳꜣm*.

§ 15. With the passage of time certain substitute letters were used. They were: for , for , for , for . And at a very early date was written for , and or was written for .

§ 16. The Egyptians wrote words as much as possible in square groups for the sake of symmetry. Thus they wrote instead of *ꜣšr·t*. Occasionally the spelling was sacrificed to symmetry. Thus, instead of *rmṯ*, and *ẖtf* instead of *ẖft*. For the same reason many signs were written either vertically or horizontally, e.g. or ; and some were placed one inside the other, e.g. instead of .

§ 17. The student should accustom himself to writing the hieroglyphs in a simpler form. Thus, the alphabet might be written somewhat as follows:

§ 18. Read and write:

CHAPTER II

Syllabic Signs or Phonograms

§ 19. A syllabic sign represents two or more consonantal sounds, e.g. *pr*, *nfr*, *mn*. Syllabic signs originated as ideograms or pictures for whole words. Afterwards these syllabic signs were used to represent only those letters in any word of which they were formed. Thus, *ḥr* is a syllable. It was originally the word for face, and was later often used in that sense. But it was often used as a syllable in a word where the combined sounds of *ḥ* and *r* were required, as in *ḥryt* "terror."

§ 20. Egyptian words were as a rule written partly with alphabetic and partly with syllabic signs, e.g. *śmꜣ* "to slay," which is composed of and the syllabic sign . Sometimes the Egyptians made use of a syllabic sign in addition to spelling out the syllable with alphabetic signs, e.g. *ḥntꜣśw* "lizard," which is composed of the alphabetic signs , , , , and the syllabic signs , and .

§ 21. Syllabic signs are very numerous and can be acquired only by practice. However, the following oft-recurring signs should be committed to memory as soon as possible:

ꜣw	*ym*	*ʿꜣ*	*wr*
ꜣb	*yn*	*wꜣ*	*wḏ*
yw	*ys*	*wp*	*bꜣ* / *bk*
ym	*yś*	*wn*	*bḥ* / *ḥw*

pꜣ	*nm*	*ẖꜣ*	*kp*
pr	*nś*	*ẖn*	*gm*
mꜣ	*nḏ*	*sꜣ*	*tꜣ*
mn	*rw*	*śꜣ*	*ty*
mr	*ḥꜣ*	*św*	*tyw*
my	*ḥp*	*śn*	*tm*
mḥ	*ḥn*	*śk*	*ṯꜣ*
mś	*ḥr*	*šꜣ*	*ḏꜣ*
nw	*ḥs*	*šw*	*ḏr*
nw	*ḫꜣ*	*kꜣ*	
nb	*ḫt*	*ḳd*	

§ 22. In many words, written with syllabic signs, the last letter of the syllable is written out. This letter is called the *phonetic complement.* It is not to be pronounced separately, but it is used in order that the reader may know how the syllable should end. Thus, in the word *km* "black," the sign reads *km* and means "black." The is merely a repetition of the *m* in . The phonetic complement is of real use, when a sign has more than one phonetic value. Thus, the sign may be *śḫm*, *ḫrp*, or *ʿbꜣ*; but the phonetic complement shows which value is to be used. Thus, is *śḫm*, is *ḫrp*, and is *ʿbꜣ*. These last two words illustrate another use: in *ḫrp* two of the letters are written out, for the sake of symmetry; and *ʿbꜣ* illustrates the fact that the phonetic complement is not always the *last* letter in a word, but the most characteristic, in *ʿbꜣ* it is the first letter and in *mrḥw* "unguent" it is the second letter, for is *mr*.

§ 23. Transcribe:

Study the following words with phonetic complements:

mrr, *tm*, *nfr*, *nḥḥ*, *śtꜣ*, *ḫpr*, *mśḏr*, *ḥꜣy*, *šnʿr*, *śn*.

CHAPTER III

Word Signs or Ideograms

§ 24. The picture of an object used as the word for that object is called a *word sign*, e.g. the picture of an eagle means "eagle," ⊙ the picture of the sun means "sun." But the *word sign* may also represent an *idea*, e.g. the picture of a falling wall represents the *idea* of "falling." Such *word signs* are called *ideograms.*

§ 25. It is sometimes difficult to distinguish between a word sign and a syllable or a determinative (§ 28). As a rule, however, the Egyptians designated a single sign which represented a whole word by means of an upright stroke |.

§ 26. A list of word signs or ideograms, arranged in order, makes an Egyptian glossary or dictionary. These word signs are very numerous. At this point the *Sign List* at the end of the book, immediately following the Chrestomathy, should be carefully studied. It cannot be learned all at once, but will come with practice.

§ 27. For practice in finding signs in the Sign List, the following words should be carefully read. In order to show the close relationship between Egyptian and Coptic, the Coptic equivalent of each Egyptian word is given.

	rn	name	ⲢⲀⲚ
	pt	heaven	ⲫⲉ
	nht	sycamore	ⲚⲞⲨϨⲈ
	ḫpr	to be	ϣⲱⲡⲓ

fꜣ	to carry	ϥⲁⲓ
rmṯ	man	ⲣⲱⲙⲓ
rꜣ	mouth	ⲣⲱ
rꜣ-pr	temple	ⲉⲣⲫⲉⲓ
bnr	date palm	ⲂⲈⲚⲚⲈ
ḥmt	copper	ϨⲞⲘⲦ
ytf	father	ⲈⲒⲰⲦ
nḥm	to deliver	ⲚⲰϨⲈⲘ
śry	to drink	ⲤⲰ
ꜣt	back	ⲰⲦ

§ 28. When words were spelled with alphabetic signs, and with syllabic values of picture signs which had no reference whatever to the original meaning of the signs, it was found necessary to invent some means whereby the meaning of words could be indicated. Such means was found in signs added to the words, which were pictures of the objects represented by the words. These signs are called *determinatives*. Thus, *ḥfꜣw* "snake" has the picture of a snake added to the word; *ps* "to cook" has a determinative which pictures fire.

Words which could not be expressed pictorially were followed by the picture of a roll of papyrus, which is the sign for abstract ideas, e.g. *rḫ* "to know."

§ 29. There are two groups of determinatives; one group consists of those which determine a single species, e.g. *tḫn* "obelisk," *ꜥꜣ* "donkey"; the second group consists of those which determine a whole class. This second group contains determinatives of a more general character, and which should be carefully studied. The following are very common. Note the way in which they are used:

	to call		*nyś*	to call
	to eat		*ym*	to eat
	a woman		*sꜣ·t*	daughter
	plant, flower		*ꜥnḫ*	flower
	foreign land	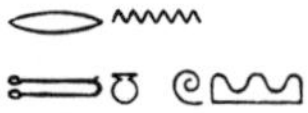	*rṯnnw*	Northern Syria
	house		*bḫnnw*	house
	to come		*śpr*	to come
	animal		*pnnw*	mouse
	bird		*ꜣpd*	duck
	fish		*nꜥrw*	the *nꜥrw* fish
	time		*rk*	time
	stone		*rd*	sandstone
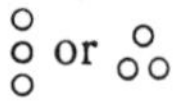 or	metal	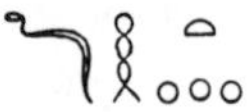	*ḏḥt*	lead
	wood	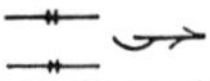	*ss*	bolt
	wind	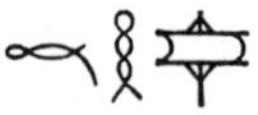	*mḥ*	air, wind
	liquid	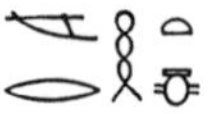	*mrḥ·t*	unguent
	abstract idea	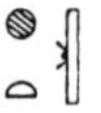	*ḫt*	thing

§ 30. Some words have no determinatives, e.g. *ḥnʿ* "with." Many words have more than one determinative, e.g. *šʿd* "to slay" has the determinatives "something which is cut to pieces," "a knife," and "strength." Many signs, of course, determine more than one word, e.g. is a determinative of all actions performed with the legs, thus, *ʿḥʿ* "to stand," *pḥ* "to arrive," *h3b* "to send," *ḫnd* "to step," *śpr* "to come."

§ 31. Words may be composed of only alphabetic signs, e.g. *śfnd* "knife," or of a mixture of alphabetic and syllabic signs, e.g. *ḥnkst* "hair."

§ 32. The upright stroke (§ 25) is a special kind of determinative. Besides indicating that the sign with which it is used represents the entire word, it is used with a picture determinative, e.g. *ś* "man."

§ 33. Oft-recurring formulae and titles occur mostly in abbreviated form. Thus, *ʿnḫ, wḏ3, śnb* "live, be happy, be well."

§ 34. Royal names are enclosed in an oblong, called a cartouche, e.g. *ȝ mn-ḥtp* Amenhotep.

§ 35. Signs for holy persons or things are placed *before* their accompanying signs, although they are pronounced after them, e.g. *ḥm-nṯr* "servant of god," "prophet"; *twt-ʿnḫ-ymn* Tutankhamen.

§ 36. Find the following signs in the Sign List and transliterate them:

Write alphabetically:

Add the phonetic complement to:

Add the determinative to:

ʿḳ "to enter,"  *pr* "to go out,"  *mrḥt* "oil,"  *šw* "dry,"  *ḥmt* "woman," *tꜣ* "land," 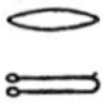 *rmṯ* "people."

Transliterate and translate:

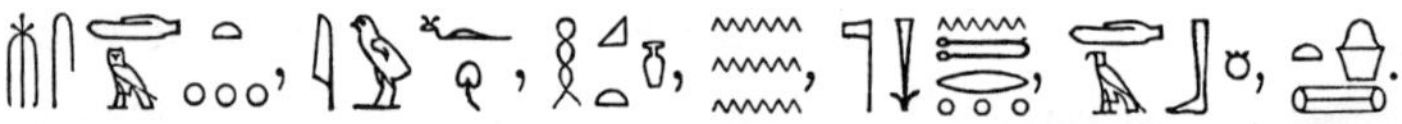

CHAPTER IV

Sentences *

§ 37. Generally speaking there are two kinds of sentences in Egyptian, *Verbal* sentences and *Nominal* sentences.

§ 38. *Verbal sentences* are so called because in them the verb is expressed, and usually occupies the chief position at the beginning of the sentence. The order of words in these sentences is as a rule essentially the same as in Semitic languages, namely: Verb, subject, object, further modifications.

§ 39. Verbal sentences may have a *transitive* verb, an *intransitive* verb, or the verb "to be" expressed.

Sentences with a transitive verb: *śḏm śḫ·ty ḫrw* "hears the peasant a voice"; *mr·n·f św* "loved he him"; *ḥmś·k ś3·k* "bend thou thy back"; *rdy ḥ3·ty-ʿ t3 n ḥḳr* "gives the count bread to the hungry"; *rdy·y n·k šfy·t·k m yb·w nw rmṯ* "I give to thee thy reputation in the hearts of men."

Sentences with an intransitive verb: *y3w h3w* "old age advances"; *ḥtp ytm m y3ḫ·t ymn·ty·t* "sets Atum in the horizon western."

Sentences with the verb "to be" expressed: *yw d3b ym·f* "there are figs in it."

---

* It has been thought advisable to introduce at this point a chapter on the sentence, in order that the student's exercises may not be confined for too long a period to the examination and parsing of *words*.

§ 40. *Nominal sentences* are so called because they are made up of nouns and adjectives, and have no verbs, except the verb "to be" understood. The usual order of words is: Subject, predicate.

Nominal sentences: *wy' nb ym3·t* "I (am) the lord of graciousness"; *rn·k nfr* "thy name (is) beautiful"; *ʿ3 by'·t·f ʿš3 b3ḳ·w·f* "its honey (is) enormous, its olive-trees (are) innumerable."

§ 41. Transliterate and translate:

CHAPTER V

The Noun

§ 42. A noun may have two or more consonants, e.g. *nb* "lord," *ḫprr* "beetle."

§ 43. Some nouns are formed by prefixing *m* to the root, e.g. *m·śḏm·t* "paint," from *śḏm* "to paint."

§ 44. Some abstract nouns are formed by the prefixes *nt*, *bw*, and *wn*, e.g. *nt-ḥśb** "accounting," *bw-nfr* "goodness," *wn-mꜣꜥ* "truth."

§ 45. Names of professions are formed by means of the prefix *yry*, e.g. *yry-ḥꜣ·t* "pilot."

§ 46. Compound nouns often have a special determinative, e.g. *rꜣ-pr* "temple."

§ 47. *Gender.*

Nouns may be masculine, feminine, or neuter.

Masculine nouns usually have no ending, e.g. *nb* "lord." They are occasionally distinguished by means of the ending *w*, e.g. *ynpw* Anubis, *šmśw* "servant."

Feminine nouns usually end in *t*, e.g. *ḥm·t* "woman." Besides nouns which are naturally feminine, such as *ḥm·t* "woman," various inanimate objects are considered feminine, e.g. *nś·t* "throne," and so are collectives, e.g. *ꜥšꜣ·t* "multitude," as

* A hyphen is used in compound words, while in all other words a dot is used to separate all additions from the root.

well as abstract conceptions, e.g. *nswy·t?* "kingdom," and names of foreign lands, e.g. *kꜣš ḫsy·t* "the wretched Cush (Nubia)."

Many feminine nouns take the stroke |, e.g. *n·t* "city."

Neuter nouns were in early times expressed by means of the feminine, e.g. *dyy·t p·t* "that which heaven gives," in more recent times it was expressed by the masculine, e.g. *yry·w* "that which is done."

§ 48. *Number.*

Nouns may be in the singular, dual, or plural.

Singular nouns in the masculine may or may not have a special ending. When they have such an ending it is *w* (§ 47), which may or may not be written. Singular feminine nouns end in *t* (§ 47).

Dual nouns in the masculine end in *wy*, and in the feminine in or *ty*.

The dual is written: 1. By repetition of the sign, e.g. *ʿ·wy* "both arms." 2. By repetition of the determinative, e.g. *rd·wy* "both feet." 3. By the addition of the dual-strokes \\, e.g. *śn·ty* "both sisters." Furthermore, the *suffix* of a noun in the dual can take the dual-strokes, e.g. *ynḥ·wy·f* "his eyebrows."

Plural nouns in the masculine end in *w*, in the feminine they end in *wt*.

The plural is written: 1. By writing the sign three times, e.g. *nṯr·w* "gods." 2. By writing the determinative three times, e.g. *ḥꜣ·tyw-ʿ* "chiefs." 3. By the addition of the plural-signs |||, , or ooo, e.g. *prw* "houses," *śrw* "princes."

The plural-signs often denote a singular word with a plural meaning. Such words are *collectives*, e.g. *yrp* "wine," or abstract nouns, e.g. *ḫʿw* "splendour." Even when written without the plural-signs, such words are often treated as if they were plurals, e.g. *yrṯ·ty ʿḳ·sn n·k* "my milk (streams) they enter thee."

In compound nouns, only the first of the compound takes the plural ending, e.g. or *ḥm·w-nṯr* "prophets."

In feminine plurals the plural-signs are written *after* the ⌓, but are pronounced before it, e.g. *nḥbw·t* "necks."

§ 49. *Case.*

The Egyptian noun has in itself no means of indicating the various cases.

Nouns in the *nominative* and *accusative* cases may be used: 1. *Absolutely*, e.g. *rʿ nb* "daily" ("each day"), *nfr ḥr* "beautiful in appearance" ("beautiful as to face"). 2. In *apposition*, e.g. *ynr ḥḏ ḳrś* "white stone, a sarchophagus" ("a sarchophagus of white stone"). 3. In *co-ordination*, e.g. *ḥmw·t ṯȝyw* "women and men."

The *dative* case is expressed by the preposition, e.g. *n nswt* (?)* "to the king."

The *genitive* case is expressed in one of two ways: 1. By direct proximity of the two words, e.g. *pr ymn* "house of Amon." 2. By means of the connecting word, which is declined to agree in gender and number with the preceding noun. Its declension is: Mas. sing. *n*, plu. or *nw*; Fem. sing. and plu. *n·t*, e.g. *ḥtp n šś·t* "an offering of alabaster," *s n wśr·t* "a man of strength," *ḥ·t-nṯr n·t wnnfr* "temple of Wnnfr."

* A question mark is placed here, because the reading, or, in this case, the order of letters in the reading, is at present uncertain. This particular word was formerly read *śtn*.

§ 50. *Vocabulary.*

yb "heart," *p·t* "heaven," *rdy* "to give," *tꜣ* "bread," *ʿ* "hand," *n* "of," "to," *ḥꜣ·ty-ʿ* "chief," *ḥḳr* "the hungry," *nṯr* "god," *rn* "name," *śḏm* "to hear," *tꜣ* "earth," "land," *wꜣḏ* "green," *rnp·t* "year," *šmʿy·t* "dancing-girl," *ḥ·t-nṯr* "temple," *ḥmw·t* "workshops," *rḫ* "to know."

§ 51. *Exercises.*

CHAPTER VI

The Adjective

§ 52. Adjectives and nouns are indistinguishable in form. Their genders and numbers are built in the same way.

The adjective follows its noun and agrees with it in gender and number, e.g. *ḥḳ·t nḏm·t* "sweet beer," *bḫnty wrty* "two great towers."

§ 53. *Notes.*

1. The adjective *ky* "another," fem. *kty*, is exceptional in that it precedes its substantive, e.g. *ky rmṯ* "another man."

2. The possessive suffix is sometimes repeated with the adjective, e.g. *s3·f wr·f* "his eldest son" ("his son, his great one").

3. The adjective *ḏś* "self" with suffixes is used in a special way, e.g. *nswt ḏś·f* "the king himself."

4. There are two compound expressions, meaning "all," "the whole," which are used with suffixes. They are: *r ḏr* "up to the border," *my ḳd* "commensurable with the circumference," e.g. *t3 r ḏr·f* "the whole land," *r3·w-pr my ḳd·śn* "the temples in their completeness."

5. An adjective preceding a noun indicates an attribute, e.g. *w3ḥ nswy·t* "fortunate in royalty."

§ 54. *Degrees of Comparison.*

1. The *comparative* is expressed by means of the preposition r placed after the adjective, e.g. *wr n·f yrp r mw* "he has more wine than water" ("great to him wine than water").

2. The *superlative* is expressed: 1. By an ordinary adjective following its noun, e.g. *s3·f wr·f* "his eldest son" ("his son, his great one"). 2. By *wᶜ* "one" before an adjective, e.g. *wᶜ yḳr* "most excellent" ("the one excellent"). 3. By an adjective in the dual, e.g. or *nfrwy* "most beautiful" ("twice beautiful").

§ 55. *The Gentilic.*

The Gentilic is a noun formed from an adjective by means of the suffix or *y*; it is also formed in the same way from prepositions. Sometimes the *y* is not written, especially in feminines.

1. Gentilics formed from feminine nouns have the following endings: Sing. mas. *tỷ*, Sing. fem. or *ty·t*; Plu. mas. *tyw*, Plu. fem. *tyw·t*, e.g. *ḥm·ty*, "artist" from *ḥm·t* "art," *nw·tyw* "municipal" from *nw·t* "town," *mḥ·ty* "northern" from *mḥ·t* "north."

2. Gentilics formed from prepositions, simple or compound, govern a following noun or suffix, like a preposition, but are declinable like other adjectives. Such gentilics are: *ym·y* "he who is in or on something," from "in"; *yr·y* "he who is at," from "at"; *ḥr·y* "he who is upon," from "upon"; *ẖr·y* "he who is under," from "under"; *myt·y* "he who is like," from *my* "like"; e.g. *ym·y-yb n nṯr nfr* "darling (he who is in the heart) of the king," *ḥr·y-yb 3bḏw* "inhabitant of Abydos."

§ 56. *Cardinal Numerals.*

1. The symbols used are:

𓏺	units	𓂭	tens of thousands
𓎆	tens	𓆐	hundreds of thousands
𓍢	hundreds	𓁨	millions
𓆼	thousands		

2. The Cardinals:

1	𓏺	*wʿ*	6	𓏿	*św*	100	𓍢	*šʒ·t*
2	𓏻	*śn·wy*	7	𓐀	*śfḫ*	1000	𓆼	*ḫʒ*
3	𓏼	*ḫmt*	8	𓐁	*ḫmn*	10,000	𓂭	*ḏbʿ*
4	𓏽	*fdw*	9	𓐂	*pśḏ*	100,000	𓆐	*ḥfn*
5	𓏾	*dwʒ*	10	𓎆	*mḏ*	1,000,000	𓁨	*ḥḥ*

3. The Egyptian numerals are used like Roman numerals. The greater number precedes the less as in English, e.g. [hieroglyphs] 12,425.

4. Numerals may be used either as nouns or as adjectives. The feminine and plural endings are rarely written.

5. The noun usually precedes the number and is usually in the plural, except in the case of the numeral 2 which takes the noun in the singular, e.g. [hieroglyphs] *wyʒ śn·wy* "two ships," and in accounts and in specifications of time and measure where the noun is also in the singular, e.g. [hieroglyphs] *rnp·t 110* "110 years."

6. [hieroglyphs] *wʿ* "one" is treated as an adjective and agrees with its noun in gender, e.g. [hieroglyphs] *rnp·t wʿ·t* "one year."

§ 57. *Ordinal Numerals.*

1. The suffix *nw* converts a cardinal numeral into an ordinal, e.g. *ḫmt·nw* "third." An exception to this rule is *tpy* "the first."

2. Ordinals may precede or follow the noun, except in the case of *tpy* "first," which always follows its noun.

§ 58. *Fractions.*

The prefix *r* indicates a fraction, e.g. *r-fdw* "a quarter." An exception to this rule is *ǵs* "a half."

§ 59. *Time.*

1. The chief divisions of time are:

ḥ3·t	"second"	*śd*	"30 years"
3t	"minute"	*ḥn*	"60 years"
wnw·t	"hour"	*ḥnty*	"120 years"
hrw	"day"	*ḥḥ*	"1,000,000 years"
3bd	"month"	*ḏ·t*	"eternity"
rnp·t	"year"		

2. The usual date formula is: "year, month, season, day, during (*ḫr*) the sovereignty of king N."

3. The seasons are:

3ḫ·t	"inundation"
pr·t	"spring"
šmw	"summer"

4. The months are:

Inundation (winter)	*Spring*	*Summer*
1. Thoth	1. Tybi	1. Pachons
2. Paophi	2. Mechir	2. Payni
3. Hathor	3. Phamenoth	3. Epiphi
4. Choiak	4. Pharmuthi	4. Mesorê

The sign "month 1" is often replaced by *tpy* "first."

5. After the twelfth month the five intercalary days are inserted: *ḥry·w rnp·t* "those above (beyond) the year."

§ 60. *Vocabulary*.

pẖr·t "remedy," *ḫ·t* "thing," *nb* "each," *šʿy* "sand," *nfr* "good," *wʿb* "clean," *ʿš3* "numerous," *wḏb* "shore," *yw* "island," *ḥm-nṯr* "prophet," "priest," *rnp·t* "year," *ḥm* "majesty," *twt* "image," *m3ʿ-ḫrw* "to justify," "blessed."

§ 61. *Exercises*.

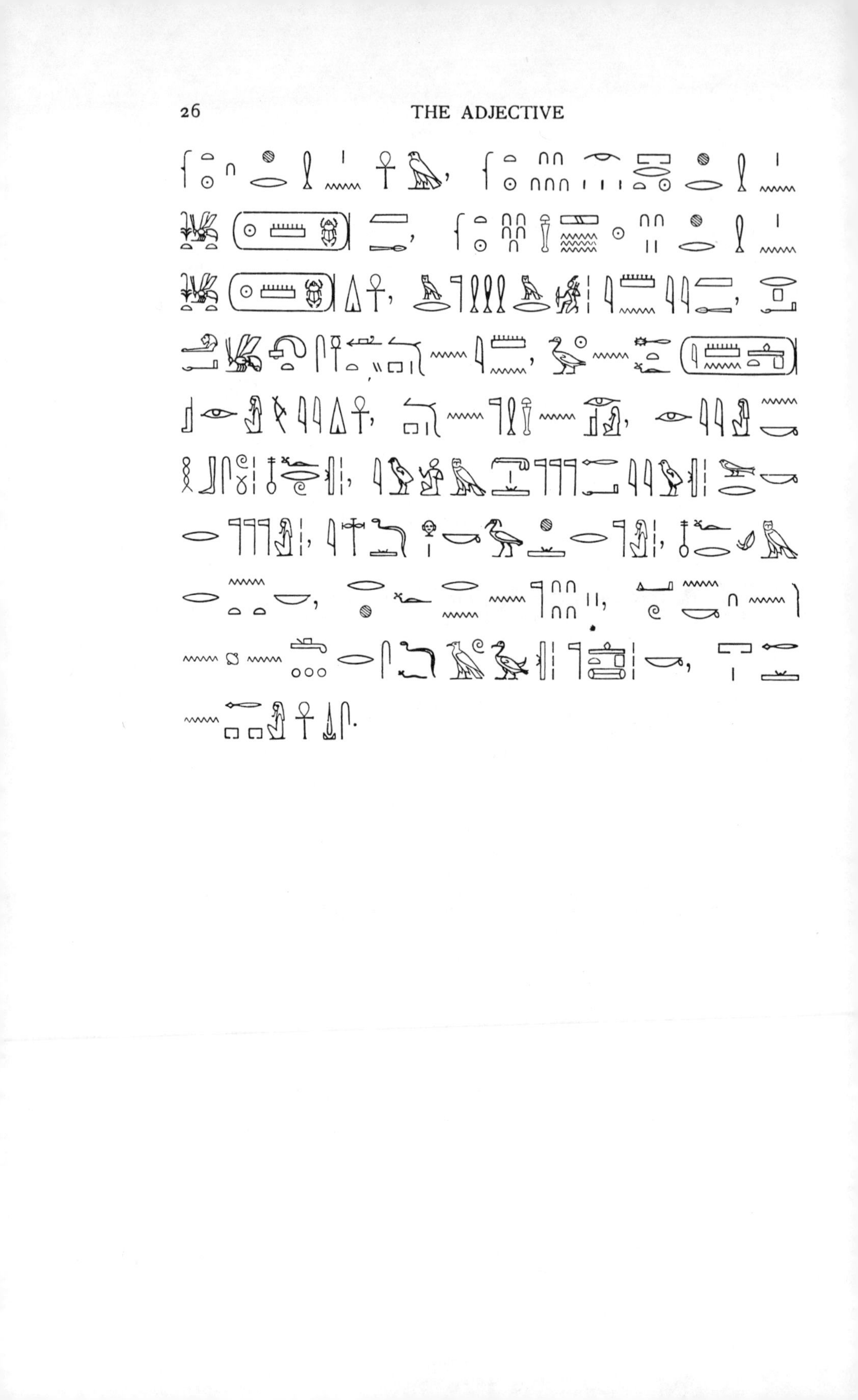

CHAPTER VII

The Pronoun

§ 62. *Personal Pronouns.*

1. Older forms:

Sing.		*Plu.*	
wy	" I "	*n*	" we "
ṯw	" thou "	*ṯn*	" you "
ṯn	" thou " (fem.)	*śn*	" they "
św	" he "		
śy	" she "		
śt	" it "		

2. Later forms:

ynk	" I "	*ynn*	" we "
ntk	" thou "	*ntṯn*	" you "
ntṯ	" thou " (fem.)	*ntśn*	" they "
ntf	" he "		
nts	" she "		

3. Suffixes:

Sing.		Plu.	
y	"my"	*n*	"our"
k	"thy"	*ṯn*	"your"
ṯ	"thy" (fem.)	*śn*	"their"
f	"his"		
ś	"hers"		

§ 63. The letters and , and and were interchangeable. The suffix *y* "my" was often omitted, or there could be substituted for it , , , or , according as the speaker was represented as god, king, man, or woman. In like manner, or could represent *wy* "I."

§ 64. The above forms are used as nominative, accusative, possessive, with nouns or verbs, and as dative with a preposition (usually). The neuter suffix is usually represented by *ś*. Examples: *ynk byk·k* "I am thy servant," *sꜣ·y n ẖ·t·y* "my son of my body," *ś·nḫn·y ṯw* "I bring thee up," *ḥsy wy ḥm·f ḥr·ś* "his majesty praises me on account of it"; *gm·n·f wy* "he found me," *rdy·k św* "thou givest him (or it)," *ḏd n·f nswt* "the king speaks to him."

§ 65. *Order of words:*

Verb, pronoun (or preposition with suffix), subject, object. Where there are two pronouns dependent upon the verb, the dative precedes the accusative, e.g. *dy·n·y n·k rnp·wt ḥr* "I gave to thee the years of Horus," *ḥsy·n wy nb·y* "my lord praised me," *wšb·n·y n·f ś·t* "I answered to him it (I answered him concerning it)."

§ 66. *Demonstrative Pronouns.*

1. The demonstrative "this," "these":

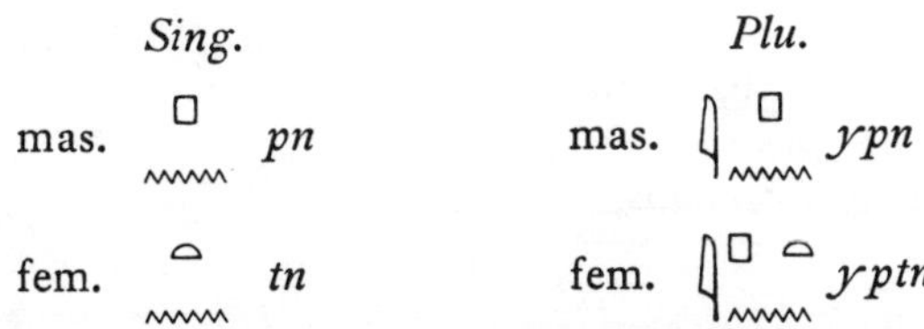

	Sing.		*Plu.*
mas.	*pn*	mas.	*ypn*
fem.	*tn*	fem.	*yptn*

2. The demonstrative "the ... here," "this":

mas.	*pw*	mas.	*ypw*
fem.	*tw*	fem.	*yptw*

3. The demonstrative "that," "those":

mas.	*pf3*	mas. and fem.	*nf3*
fem.	*tf3*		

4. A late demonstrative "this," "these," "the":

mas.	*p3*	mas. and fem.	*n3*, *nn*, *nn n*,
fem.	*t3*		*nw*, *p3w*

§ 67. As a rule, these demonstratives *follow* their nouns, e.g. *pr pn* "this house," *ḥ·t tn* "this temple." However, the late demonstratives precede their nouns, e.g. *p3 nswt* "this king," *nn n ḫ3ś·tyw* "these barbarians."

§ 68. Uses of *pw*:

1. In short sentences it is used for emphasis, e.g. *ynk pw* "I am it."

2. In nominal sentences, it is used instead of the verb "to be," e.g. *rꜥ pw* "it is Rꜥ," *rn·y pw ḫnt nṯrw* "my name is at the head of the gods," *tꜣ pw nfr* "it is a beautiful land."

§ 69. *Relative Pronouns.*

	Sing.		*Plu.*
mas.	*nty* "who"	mas. and fem.	*nty·w* "who"
fem.	*nty·t* "who"		

Relative pronouns often introduce relative sentences, e.g. *s nty tp tꜣ* "a man who is on the earth." Relatives are often used substantively, *pꜣ nty ḥm·f ym* "the place in which his majesty is."

§ 70. *Reflexive Pronouns.*

		Sing.	*Plu.*
1st pers.	mas.	*ḏś·y* "myself"	*ḏś·n* "ourselves"
	fem.	*ḏś·y* "myself"	
2nd pers.	mas.	*ḏś·k* "thyself"	*ḏś·ṯn* "yourselves"
	fem.	*ḏś·ṯ* "thyself"	
3rd pers.	mas.	*ḏś·f* "himself"	*ḏś·śn* "themselves"
	fem.	*ḏś·ś* "herself"	

These reflexive pronouns are mostly late. The earlier language used the personal pronouns to express the reflexive idea, e.g. *ś·š3y·n·y wy* "I satiated myself." An example of the later form is: *ynk nṯr ˁ3 ḫpr ḏś·f* "I (am) the great god who creates (creating) himself."

§ 71. From the demonstrative pronoun "this" *p3*, *t3*, *n3*, there was developed in the vernacular a *definite article*. In like manner the *indefinite article* "a," "an," was developed from the numeral *wˁ* "one." Examples: *p3 nṯr* "the god," *t3 ś·t* "the throne," *n3 ḫr·w* "the wretched ones," *wˁ·t ssm·t* "a mare." Very often the indefinite article is followed by the preposition , e.g. *wˁ n bḫnnw* "a house."

§ 72. The vernacular also developed a new means of expressing the idea of possession. Possession in the classical speech was expressed by means of the pronominal suffix (§ 64). The vernacular developed a form composed of the article and the suffix. The formula is: Sing. mas. , fem. , plu. mas. and fem. with the suffixes (§ 62, 3), e.g. (or) *py·f* "his," *ty·f* "hers," *ny·f* "ours"; *py·f śn* "his brother," *ḥ3ty·śn* "their heart."

§ 73. *Vocabulary.*

mḥ "to fill," *šdy* "to suckle," *yrṯ·t* "milk," *3ḫw* "splendour," *3wy* "to be wide," with *yb* "to make glad," *ˁḳ* "to come to," *w3ś* "good fortune," *nb* "gold," *śḫ·ty* "peasant," *ym* "in," "there," *mw·t* "mother," or *m* "in," "with," *wpw* (*ypw*) "messenger," *sš* "book," *ḏd* "to speak," *nṯr·t* "goddess," *rꜣ* "mouth."

§ 74. *Exercises.*

CHAPTER VIII

Synopsis of the Strong Verb

§ 75. Verbs may be classified thus:

1. *Strong Verbs*—verbs which have two, three, four, or more strong consonants. The most numerous are those with three consonants. Strong verbs include *Duplicating Verbs* which have three or more consonants, of which the last two are alike.

2. *Weak Verbs*—verbs which have three or more consonants, of which the last is a weak one (*y* or *w*).

3. *Irregular Verbs*—the most important of which are: 1. *yry* "to do," written also *yrr*. 2. *rdy* "to give," written also , , . The same word appears later as , , and *dy* "to give." The duplicating forms of *dy* are written , , and *dyy*. 3. *yy* (?), *yy* (*yꜣy*?), and *ywt*, *yw* "to come." The older form was *ywt*.

4. *Auxiliary Verbs*—verbs which are used to strengthen the usual verb forms.

§ 76. *The Simple Stem.*

ACTIVE

INDICATIVE

Present Tense

śdm·f "he hears"

śdm·kꜣ·f "thus he hears"

Past Tense

śdm·n·f "he heard"

śdm·yn·f "then he heard"

Future Tense

śḏm·ḫr·f "he will hear"

EMPHATIC

śḏm·f "he certainly hears"

PREDICATIVE

tm śḏm "he does not hear"

IMPERATIVE

Sing. *śḏm* "hear" : Plu. *śḏm·y* "hear ye"

INFINITIVE

śḏm "to hear"

PARTICIPLES

Perf. *śḏm* "having heard" : Imperf. *śḏm·w* "hearing"

RELATIVES

Pres. mas. *śḏm·w.f* "him whom he hears"

" fem. *śḏm·t·f* "her whom he hears" ("that which he hears")

Past mas. *śḏm·w·n·f* "him whom he has heard"

" fem. *śḏm·t·n·f* "her whom he has heard" ("that which he has heard")

Prospective mas. *śḏm·y·f* "him whom he will hear"

Prospective fem. *śḏm·ty·f* "her whom he will hear"

VERBAL ADJECTIVE

Sing. mas. *tyfy* Plu. mas. *tywśn*

" fem. *tyśy* " fem. *tywśt*

PASSIVE

Indicative

Present Tense

śḏm·w·f, *śḏm·tw·f* "he is heard"

śḏm·k3·tw·f "thus he is heard"

Past Tense

śḏm·w·f, *śḏm·n·tw·f* "he was heard"

śḏm·yn·tw·f "then he was heard"

Future Tense

śḏm·ḫr·tw·f "he will be heard"

Participles

Perf. *śḏm·y* "heard" : Imperf. *śḏm·w* "being heard"

§ 77. *The Conditional Stem (Qualitative or Pseudo-Participle).*

Sing.

(also , ,) *śḏm·kwy* "I am hearing, or heard"

(also) *śḏm·ty* "thou (mas. and fem.) art hearing, or heard"

(also ,) *śḏm·w* "he is hearing, or heard"

(also) *śḏm·ty* "she is hearing, or heard"

Dual.

śḏm·wy "they two are hearing, or heard"

śḏm·tyw "they two (fem.) are hearing, or heard"

Plu.

(also) *śd̲m·wyn* "we are hearing, or heard"

(also) *śd̲m·tywny* "ye (mas. and fem.) are hearing, or heard"

(also) *śd̲m·w* "they are hearing, or heard"

(also) *śd̲m·ty* "they (fem.) are hearing, or heard"

§ 78. *The Causative Stem.*

ś·śd̲m·f "he causes to hear"

§ 79. *Remarks on the above synopsis of the Strong Verb.*

1. Almost all tenses, in both active and passive, can be used impersonally, e.g. *śd̲m·f* "one hears."

2. The "present" or *śd̲m·f* tense may be translated also by the past tense. In fact its "time" must be judged by the context. It occurs in dependent as well as in independent sentences. It is used in assertions, questions, and requests, and especially after verbs of causing, seeing, finding, &c., to express a condition, purpose, or result, e.g. *śd̲m·f* "he hears," or "he heard," *dy·y mꜣ·śn ḥm·k* "I cause that they see thy majesty," *dy·śn pr·t-r-ḫrw* "may they (one) give a funerary offering."

3. The *śd̲m·kꜣ·f*, which is a form of the "present" tense, usually appears in the apodosis of conditional sentences, e.g. *nḥm·kꜣ·tw śṯpt* "then the oblation is taken away."

4. The "past" or *śd̲m·n·f* tense denotes a completed action, and is generally used in narratives. It also corresponds to a pluperfect, when it is preceded by *m-ḫt*, e.g. *m-ḫt śd̲m·n·f śt* "after he had heard it."

5. The *śḏm·yn·f* is a form of the "past" tense, and is used in a similar way to *śḏm·n·f*. It was originally ceremonial, and is especially used when the subject is a person to whom respect is due; e.g. [hieroglyphs] *rdy·yn ḥm·f* "his majesty gave."

6. The future or *śḏm·ḫr·f* tense is a rare form, occasionally used in descriptions, and sometimes to express a mild command, e.g. [hieroglyphs] *ḏd·ḫr·k r·ś* "say thou to her." The future is also expressed by means of the auxiliary [hieroglyphs] followed by [hieroglyph] and the infinitive, e.g. [hieroglyphs] *yw·f r śḏm* "he will hear."

7. The emphatic mood appears in the weak and duplicating verbs, in that they duplicate the second consonant of the root to lay special stress on the idea expressed by the verb. Thus [hieroglyphs] *mrr·f* "he certainly loves," or "may he love," instead of [hieroglyphs] *mry·f* "he loves." It is used in sentences of wish, condition, question, consequence, &c., and sometimes introduced by a conjunction. It is frequent only in the active *śḏm·f*, but is also found in the passive, *śḏm·tw·f*, e.g. [hieroglyphs] *n-ʿꜣ·t-n mrr·y św* "because I certainly love him." The emphatic mood occurs in the regular strong verbs also, although it cannot be satisfactorily seen on account of the absence of vowels. In the synopsis I have, therefore, given the form [hieroglyphs] which is possible, and more symmetrical, as the model verb *śḏm* is used throughout. Other forms could easily have been used, which would have shown the duplicating in a graphical manner, e.g. [hieroglyphs] *mśḏḏ·f* "he certainly hates," [hieroglyphs] *dd·f* "he certainly gives," [hieroglyphs] *yrr·f* "he certainly makes."

8. The predicative is an old and rare form, which has the ending *w*. This ending, however, is usually not written. The predicative does not take a suffix, and is followed either by a substantive or an independent pronoun. In it the duplicating verbs show the doubling, and the weak verbs usually omit the last weak

consonant. It is used only in negative sentences after the verbs *tm* and *ymy* "not to be," and usually has an active meaning, e.g. NN *r3 n tm wnm N* "charm for the not-to-be-eaten of N" ("charm that N be not eaten").

9. The imperative has no means of showing difference in gender, although as Coptic shows there was a difference in vocalization. The duplicating verbs show their doubling in the imperative. (See § 87.)

10. The infinitive may be used as a verb or as a noun. In strong verbs its form is that of the simple root (e.g. *śḏm*), and in duplicating verbs it doubles the last consonant, e.g. *m33* "to see." (See § 88.)

11. In all participles the root of the duplicating verbs shows the doubling, e.g. *mrr·w* "loving." Participles are used like both adjectives and nouns. (See § 89.)

12. The relatives are forms derived from the *śḏm·f* and *śḏm·n·f* and used like nouns. The prospective relative form has recently been demonstrated by Gunn, *Studies in Egyptian Syntax*. The duplicating verbs have the doubling of the last consonant. (See § 90.)

13. Most passives are distinguished by the ending *tw* before the suffix. The passive with *w* in the singular (e.g. *śḏm·w·f* "he is heard") has *y* in the plural. But *w* and *y* in this passive are rarely written, and it is difficult to distinguish it from the active, e.g. ||| *mś n·k ẖrd·w ḫmt* "three children are born to thee." Duplicating verbs show the doubling.

14. The conditional stem, or the pseudo-participle is the old inflection of the verb. Its place has been taken by the *śḏm·f*. Its transitive-active use is not extant, except in the case of the verb *rḫ* "to know." The pseudo-participle is, therefore, always intransitive and passive, e.g. *yw*ᶜ*·kwy m nb* "I was rewarded with gold." (See § 94.)

§ 80. *Vocabulary.*

ḫrw "voice," *wȝḏ* "to be green," *šsp* "to take," "receive," *sʿḥ* "freedom," *wḏ* "to command," *ḫft* "to," "before," *nḥm* "to take away," *ḥtp* "to rest," "to set free," "to satisfy," *ḫr-ḥȝ·t* "before," *dbȝ* "to pay," *yȝw·t* "office," *mky* (*mʿky*) "to protect."

§ 81. *Exercises.*

* In old texts when the subject of verb in the simple stem is a noun or absolute pronoun, the stem may take the ending .

CHAPTER IX

The Conjugation of the Strong Verb

The Simple Stem

§ 82. *Simple Stem–Active–Indicative.*

Present Tense

śḏm·f

śḏm·y	"I hear"
śḏm·k	"thou hearest"
śḏm·ṯ	
śḏm·f	"he hears"
śḏm-ś	"she hears"
śḏm·n	"we hear"
śḏm·ṯn	"you hear"
śḏm·śn	"they hear"

śḏm·kꜣ·f

śḏm·kꜣ·y	"thus I hear"
śḏm·kꜣ·k	"thus thou hearest"
śḏm·kꜣ·ṯ	

śḏm·k3·f "thus he hears"

śḏm·k3·ś "thus she hears"

śḏm·k3·n "thus we hear"

śḏm·k3·ṯn "thus you hear"

śḏm·k3·śn "thus they hear"

Past Tense

śḏm·n·f

śḏm·n·y "I heard"

śḏm·n·k "thou heardst"

&c.

śḏm·yn·f

śḏm·yn·y "then I heard"

śḏm·yn·k "then thou heardst"

&c.

Future Tense

śḏm·ḫr·f

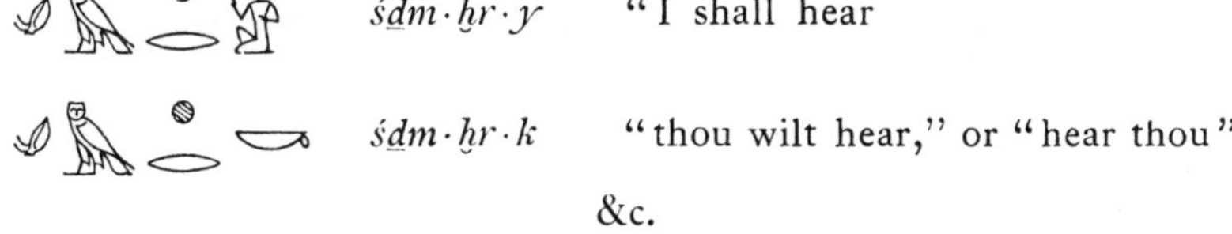

śḏm·ḫr·y "I shall hear

śḏm·ḫr·k "thou wilt hear," or "hear thou"

&c.

§ 83. *Simple Stem–Passive–Indicative.*

Present Tense

śḏm·w·f or *śḏm·tw·f*

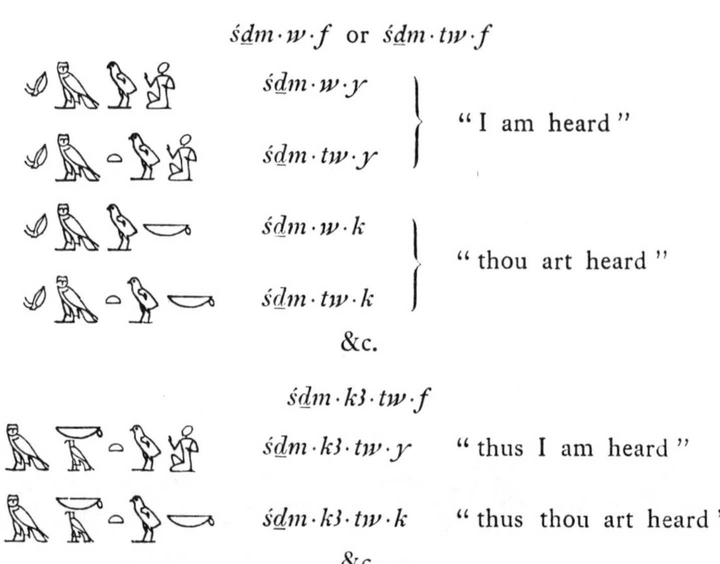

śḏm·w·y, *śḏm·tw·y* — "I am heard"

śḏm·w·k, *śḏm·tw·k* — "thou art heard"

&c.

śḏm·kꜣ·tw·f

śḏm·kꜣ·tw·y "thus I am heard"

śḏm·kꜣ·tw·k "thus thou art heard"

&c.

Past Tense

śḏm·w·f or *śḏm·n·tw·f*

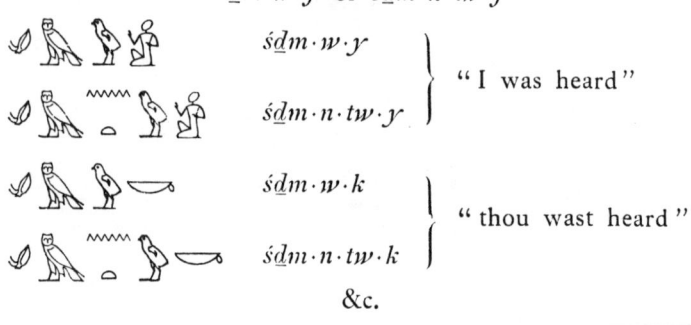

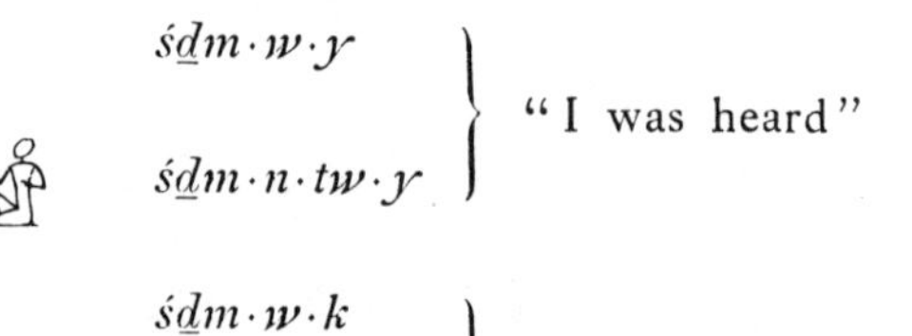

śḏm·w·y, *śḏm·n·tw·y* — "I was heard"

śḏm·w·k, *śḏm·n·tw·k* — "thou wast heard"

&c.

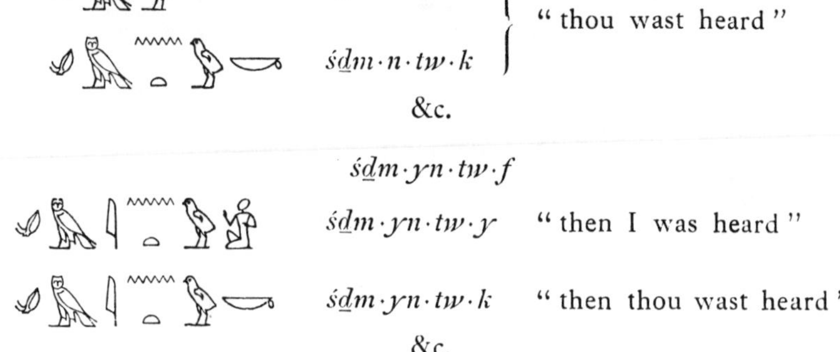

śḏm·yn·tw·f

śḏm·yn·tw·y "then I was heard"

śḏm·yn·tw·k "then thou wast heard"

&c.

Future Tense

ś͟dm·ḫr·tw·f

ś͟dm·ḫr·tw·y	"I shall be heard"
ś͟dm·ḫr·tw·k	"thou wilt be heard"
&c.	

§ 84. *Simple Stem—Active—Emphatic.*

Present Tense

ś͟dm·f

ḳbb·y	"I am cool"
ḳbb·k	"thou art cool"
&c.	

ś͟dm·k3·f

ḳbb·k3·y	"thus I am cool"
ḳbb·k3·k	"thus thou art cool"
&c.	

Past Tense

ś͟dm·n·f

ḳbb·n·y	"I was cool"
ḳbb·n·k	"thou wast cool"
&c.	

ś͟dm·yn·f

ḳbb·yn·y	"then I was cool"
ḳbb·yn·k	"then thou wast cool"
&c.	

Future Tense

śḏm·ḫr·f

ḳbb·ḫr·y "I shall be cool"

ḳbb·ḫr·k "thou wilt be cool," or "be thou cool"

&c.

§ 85. *Simple Stem–Passive–Emphatic.*

Present Tense

śḏm·tw·f

mꜣꜣ·tw·y "I am seen"

mꜣꜣ·tw·k "thou art seen"

&c.

śḏm·kꜣ·tw·f

mꜣꜣ·kꜣ·tw·y "thus I am seen"

mꜣꜣ·kꜣ·tw·k "thus thou art seen"

&c.

Past Tense

śḏm·n·tw·f

mꜣꜣ·n·tw·y "I was seen"

mꜣꜣ·n·tw·k "thou wast seen"

&c.

śḏm·yn·tw·f

mꜣꜣ·yn·tw·y "then I was seen"

mꜣꜣ·yn·tw·k "then thou wast seen"

&c.

Future Tense

śḏm·ḫr·tw·f

[hieroglyphs]	*m33·ḫr·tw·y*	"I shall be seen"
[hieroglyphs]	*m33·ḫr·tw·k*	"thou wilt be seen"

&c.

§ 86. *Predicative.* For this form see § 79, 8.

§ 87. *Imperative.*

Strong Verb

[hieroglyphs]	*śḏm*	"hear thou"
[hieroglyphs]	*śḏm·f*	"let him hear"
[hieroglyphs]	*śḏm·ś*	"let her hear"
[hieroglyphs]	*śḏm·y*	"hear ye"
[hieroglyphs]	*śḏm·śn*	"let them hear"

Duplicating Verb

[hieroglyphs]	*ḳbb*	"be thou cool"
[hieroglyphs]	*ḳbb·y*	"be ye cool"

1. The imperative is strengthened either by an independent pronoun, by the particle [hieroglyphs], [hieroglyphs] *yr*, or by the preposition [hieroglyph], e.g. [hieroglyphs] *ʿḥʿ yr·k* "stand up, thou," [hieroglyphs] *šsp n·k ḥtp-nṯr* "take to thyself the divine offering."

2. The negative of the imperative is [hieroglyphs] *ymy* "be not" with a following predicative, e.g. [hieroglyphs] *ymy śnḏ* "fear not."

§ 88. *Infinitive.*

Strong Verb *Duplicating Verb*

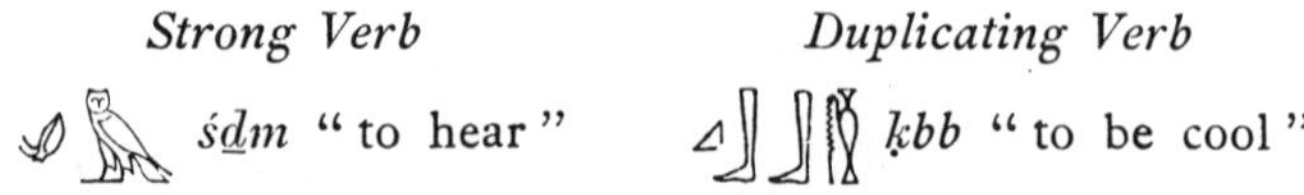
śḏm "to hear" *ḳbb* "to be cool"

1. Weak verbs (see §§ 99 ff.) and the causative of verbs of two consonants take the feminine ending, e.g. *mśy·t* "to give birth to," *śmn·t* "to establish."

2. Uses of the infinitive:

a) As a noun, e.g. *nḥt·y pw yr·t n·f śt* "my wish it is to do it for him."

b) After verbs of commanding, willing, &c., e.g. *wḏ·n·f db3 śt* "he commanded to pay it."

c) After verbs of kindred meaning, as a complementary infinitive, to strengthen the idea expressed by the verb, e.g. *ẖnn·śn ẖn·t* "they rowed well" ("they rowed a rowing").

d) Governed by an adjective, e.g. *nfr mdw* "excellent (in) speaking" ("excellent to speak").

e) Used after prepositions, e.g. with to denote time, *m yy·t* "when they came"; with to express purpose, *r śẖr·t ḫftyw·f* "to overthrow his enemies"; with to express simultaneousness, *gm·n·f św ḥr pr·t* "he found him as he was going out"; with and to express cause, *mᶜ yr·t m3ᶜ·t* "because (I) wrought truth"; with *ḥnᶜ* and a preceding verb, *yw·f ḥr wnm ḥnᶜ śwry* "he eats and drinks."

f) Used in an explanatory clause, e.g. "she made it as her monument for her father Amon, *yr·t n·f tḫn·wy* making for him two obelisks."

g) There is a circumstantial form *śḏm·t·f* which has the appearance of a feminine infinitive, e.g. *pḥ·t·śn* "they arrived at" ("their arriving at"). It is used in a dependent clause, when the subject is different from the preceding clause, e.g. "I was astonished, *m yy·t·śn* when they came."

h) The logical subject introduced by or follows the infinitive, e.g. *dw3 Wśyr yn rpʿ·ty* "worship of Osiris by the count."

i) If the object of an infinitive is a noun it follows immediately after the infinitive, but if it is a pronoun it is added to the infinitive as a suffix, e.g. *ḥr dw3·f* "to adore him."

j) An infinitive may occur in successive sentences where we should expect a verb, e.g. *yr·t n·f śb3 m ynr* "and he made a door of stone for him."

§ 89. *Participle.*

The following forms apply to the perfect or imperfect, active or passive:

	Strong Verb		*Duplicating Verb*
	Sing.		*Sing.*
mas.	*śḏm*	mas.	*m3*
fem.	*śḏm·t*	fem.	*m3·t*
	Plu.		*Plu.*
mas.	*śḏmy·w*	mas.	*m33·w*
fem.	*śḏmy·wt*	fem.	*m3·t*

1. The logical subject of passive participles is introduced either directly or by means of , e.g. *mry rʿ* "beloved of Rʿ," *mś n ḏḥwty* "created by Thot."

2. The rare participle *śḏm·n* "audible" indicates possibility.

§ 90. *Relatives.*

Strong Verb

śḏm·t·y "that which I hear"

śḏm·t·k "that which thou hearest"

&c.

Duplicating Verb

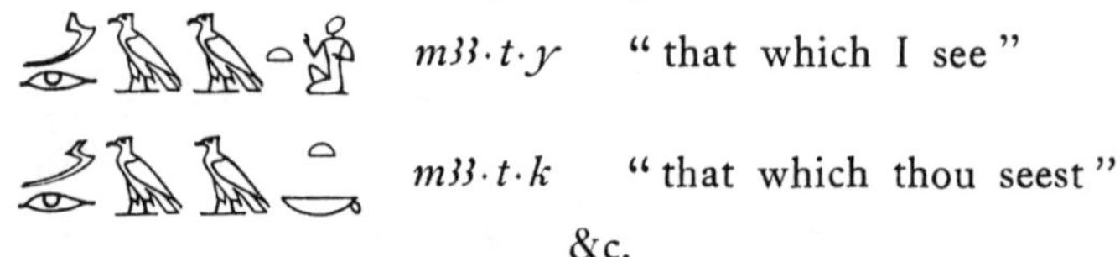

mꜣꜣ·t·y "that which I see"

mꜣꜣ·t·k "that which thou seest"

&c.

The relative forms usually introduce a relative sentence, e.g. *nfr yrr·t·y n·k* "that which I do to thee is good."

§ 91. *Verbal Adjectives.*

Verbal adjectives are really participles with a future meaning. The form is *śḏm·tyfy* "he who will hear." The root of a duplicating verb shows the doubling. Example, *m yꜣḫ·t n śḏm·tyfy* "as a splendid thing for him who will hear it."

§ 92. *Vocabulary.*

šmśy "to serve," "to follow," *ʿš* "to call," *ymy* "give," "put," *nṯr nfr* "good god" = "the king," *wr* "great," "to be great," *ḳny* "to be strong," *ẖrd* "child," *ḏw·t* "evil," *ḫnty* "to journey southward," *yny* "to bring," *wꜣ·t* "way," "road," *rd* "leg," "foot," *ynb* "wall," *ẖr* "under," "with," *ḥrw* "to be content."

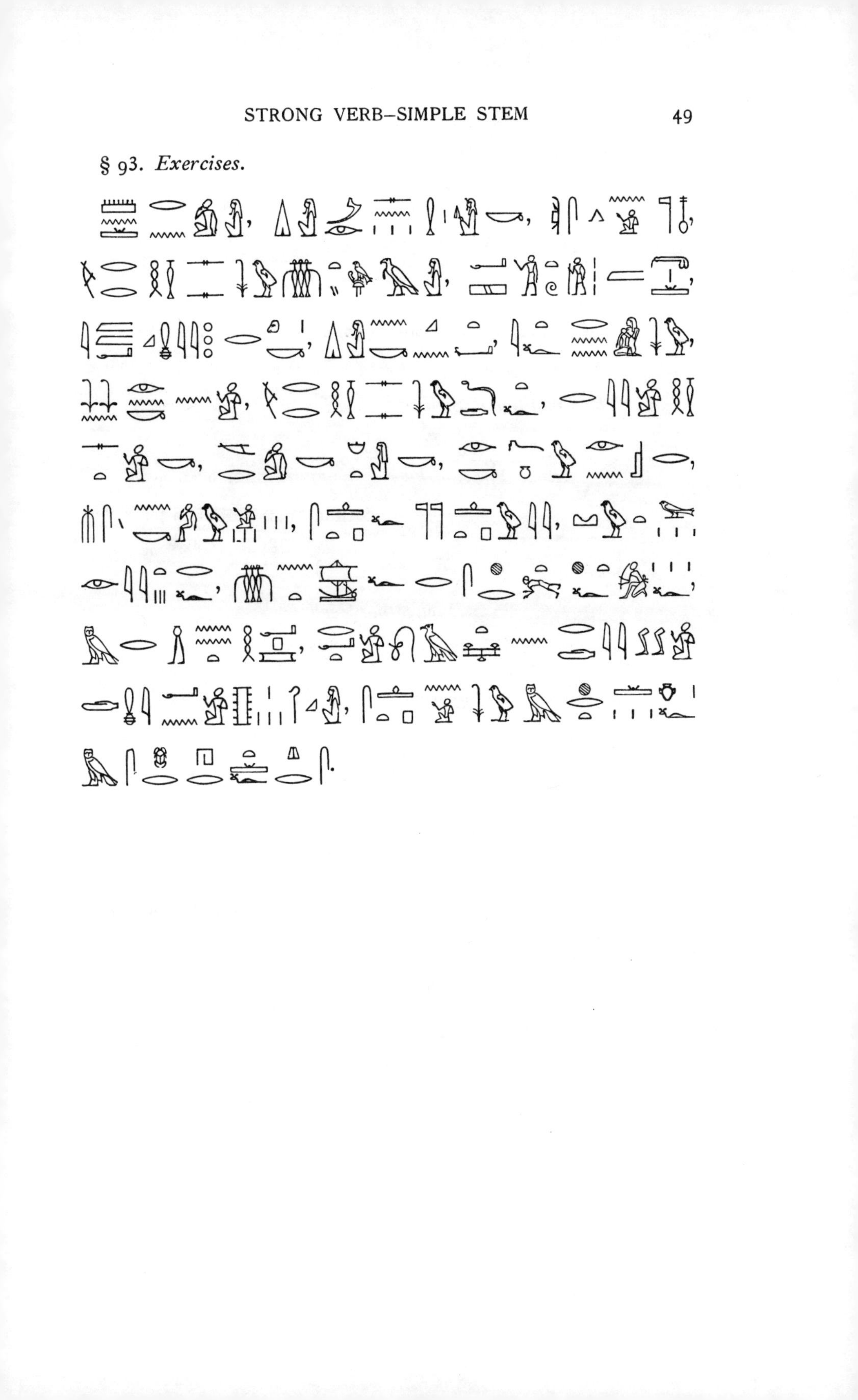

§ 93. *Exercises.*

CHAPTER X

The Conjugation of the Strong Verb (*Continued*)

The Conditional, Causative, and other Stems

§ 94. *The Conditional Stem (Qualitative or Pseudo-Participle).*

Strong Verb

śḏm·kwy "I am hearing, or heard"

śḏm·ty "thou (mas. and fem.) art hearing, or heard"

&c. (See § 77.)

Duplicating Verb

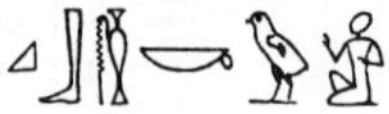

ḳb·kwy "I am cool"

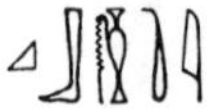

ḳb·ty "thou art cool"

&c.

1. The conditional stem or pseudo-participle is used:

a) In dependence upon another verb, like a participle, e.g. *wꜣḥ·f wy wḏꜣ·kwy* "he laid me down when I was healed."

b) With the verb *ẖpr* "to become" in all its meanings, e.g.  *tny ẖpr·w* "old age comes to pass."

2. See above § 79, 14.

§ 95. *The Causative Stem.*

Strong Verb

ś·śḏm·y "I cause to hear"

ś·śḏm·k "thou causest to hear"

&c.

Duplicating Verb

ś·ḳbb·y "I cause to be cool"

ś·ḳbb·k "thou causest to be cool"

&c.

1. Causatives are used more often with intransitive than with transitive verbs, e.g. *ś·nfr* "to make beautiful," *ś·ẖr* "to cause to fall."

2. Causatives of three consonants are treated like four-consonant verbs, and are quite regular, but two-consonant causatives take a feminine infinitive, e.g. *ś·mn·t* "to establish."

§ 96. *Other Stems.*

1. There are isolated forms which look like the Semitic Niphal, e.g. *n·ḏdḏd* "to endure" from *ḏd.*

2. There are also forms which repeat the final consonant, e.g. *śpdd* "to prepare"; and others which repeat two of the consonants, e.g. *śẖśẖ* "to hasten," *śd3d3* "to tremble."

§ 97. *Vocabulary.*

ḥʿy "to rejoice," *y3wy* "old age," *k3* "soul," "Ka," *h3y* "to advance," *wʿb* "to be clean," *ymy*(?) "make," "give," *r3-pr* "temple," *r3* "mouth," "entrance," *ytḥ* "to drag," *mnw* "monument," *ʿ3y* "to be great," *my* "like," "as," *ḏw* "mountain," *ymnty* "west," "right," *śmḥy* "east," "left," *r3-yt* "door," *bn·t* "harp," *mʿḥʿ·t* "tomb."

§ 98. *Exercises.*

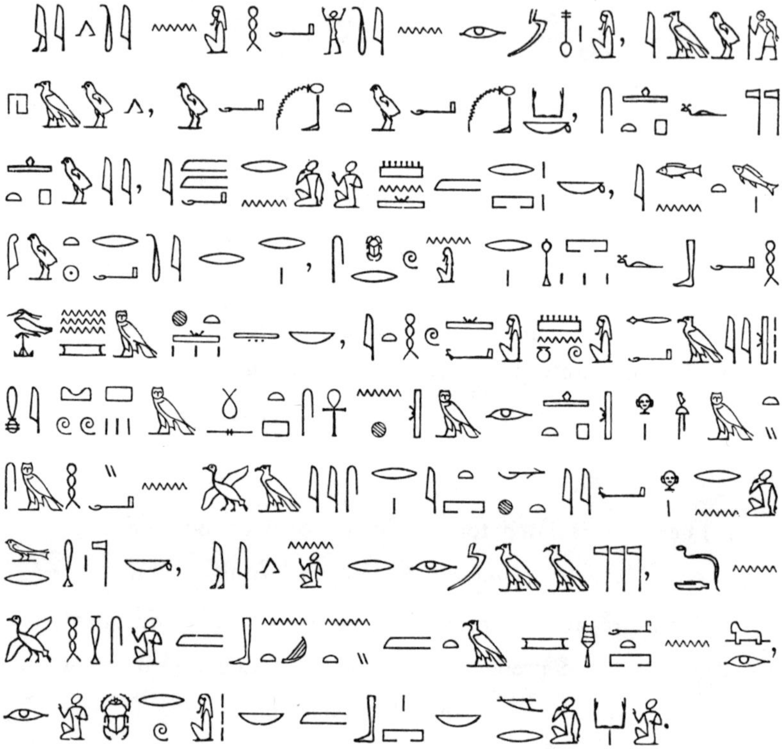

CHAPTER XI

Weak Verbs

§ 99. *Weak Verb—Active—Indicative.*

Present Tense

śḏm·f

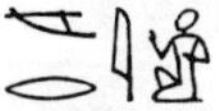

	mry·y	"I love"
	*mr·k*	"thou lovest"

&c.

śḏm·kꜣ·f

	mr·kꜣ·y	"thus I love"
	*mr·kꜣ·k*	"thus thou lovest"

&c.

Past Tense

śḏm·n·f

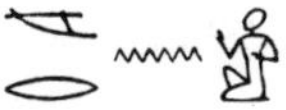

	mr·n·y	"I loved"
	*mr·n·k*	"thou lovedst"

&c.

śḏm·yn·f

	mr·yn·y	"then I loved"
	*mr·yn·k*	"then thou lovedst"

&c.

Future Tense

śḏm·ḫr·f

mr·ḫr·y "I shall love"

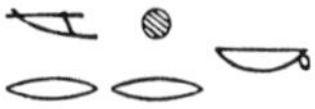

mr·ḫr·k "thou wilt love," or "love thou"

&c.

§ 100. *Weak Verb–Passive–Indicative.**

Present Tense

śḏm·tw·f

mr·tw·y "I am loved"

mr·tw·k "thou art loved"

&c.

Past Tense

śḏm·n·tw·f

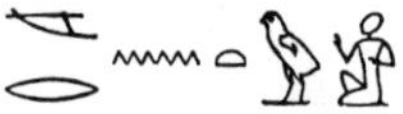

mr·n·tw·y "I was loved"

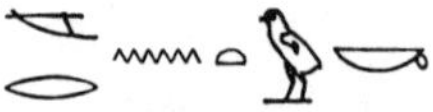

mr·n·tw·k "thou wast loved"

&c.

§ 101. *Weak Verb–Emphatic.***

Present Tense

śḏm·f

mrr·y "I love"

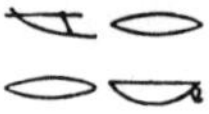

mrr·k "thou lovest"

&c.

§ 102. *Imperative.*

mr "love thou"  *mr·w* "love ye"

---

* The other parts of the *passive* can easily be constructed on the model of the forms in § 83.

** The other forms of the *emphatic* can easily be constructed on the model of the forms in §§ 84 ff.

§ 103. *Infinitive.*

	mr·t	"to love"

§ 104. *Participles.*

	mr	"having loved"
	mrr·w	"loving"
	mry	"loved"
	mrr·w	"being loved"

§ 105. *Relatives.*

	mrr·t·y	"that which I love"
	mrr·t·k	"that which thou lovest"

&c.

§ 106. *Conditional Stem (Qualitative or Pseudo-Participle).*

	mr·kwy	"I am loving, or loved"
	mr·ty	"thou (mas. and fem.) art loving, or loved"
	mr·w	"he is loving, or loved"
	mr·ty	"she is loving, or loved"
	mr·wyn	"we are loving, or loved"
	mr·tywny	"ye (mas. and fem.) are loving, or loved"
	mr·w	"they are loving, or loved"
	mr·ty	"they (fem.) are loving, or loved"

§ 107. *Causative Stem.*

ś·mr·t "to cause to love"

§ 108. *Remarks on the Weak Verb.*

1. The weak consonant (*y* or *w*) is usually not written.
2. Weak verbs as well as causatives of two-consonant verbs take the feminine ending ⌓ in the infinitive.
3. In weak verbs doubling often appears in the *śḏm·f*.
4. In the conditional or pseudo-participle, the final weak consonant (*y* or *w*) of the root is not written.
5. Passives of weak verbs usually omit the last weak consonant.
6. In the predicative the weak verbs do not have the last weak consonant *y* before the predicative ending *w*.
7. The plural ending *y* (later also *w*) of the imperative merges into the last weak consonant of weak verbs.
8. Weak verbs show the doubling in imperfect participles.
9. In relative forms, weak verbs double the last strong consonant.

§ 109. *Vocabulary.*

msḏy "to hate," *drp* "to offer sacrifice," *šsp* "to take," *n-ˁ3·t-n* "because," *m-mˁ* "with," *y* "Oh!" *nṯr* "god," or *nṯry* "divine," *ḥtp* "offering," *ḫpy·t* "death," *ḳm3* "to create," *rnn* "to rear," "bring up," *ḥḳ3* "to rule over," *ḏ·t* "for ever," *mky* "to protect," *km·t* "Egypt," *ḫ3ś·t* "foreign country," *śr* "high official," or *św3y* "to pass by," *yny* "to bring," *ḥˁpy* "Nile."

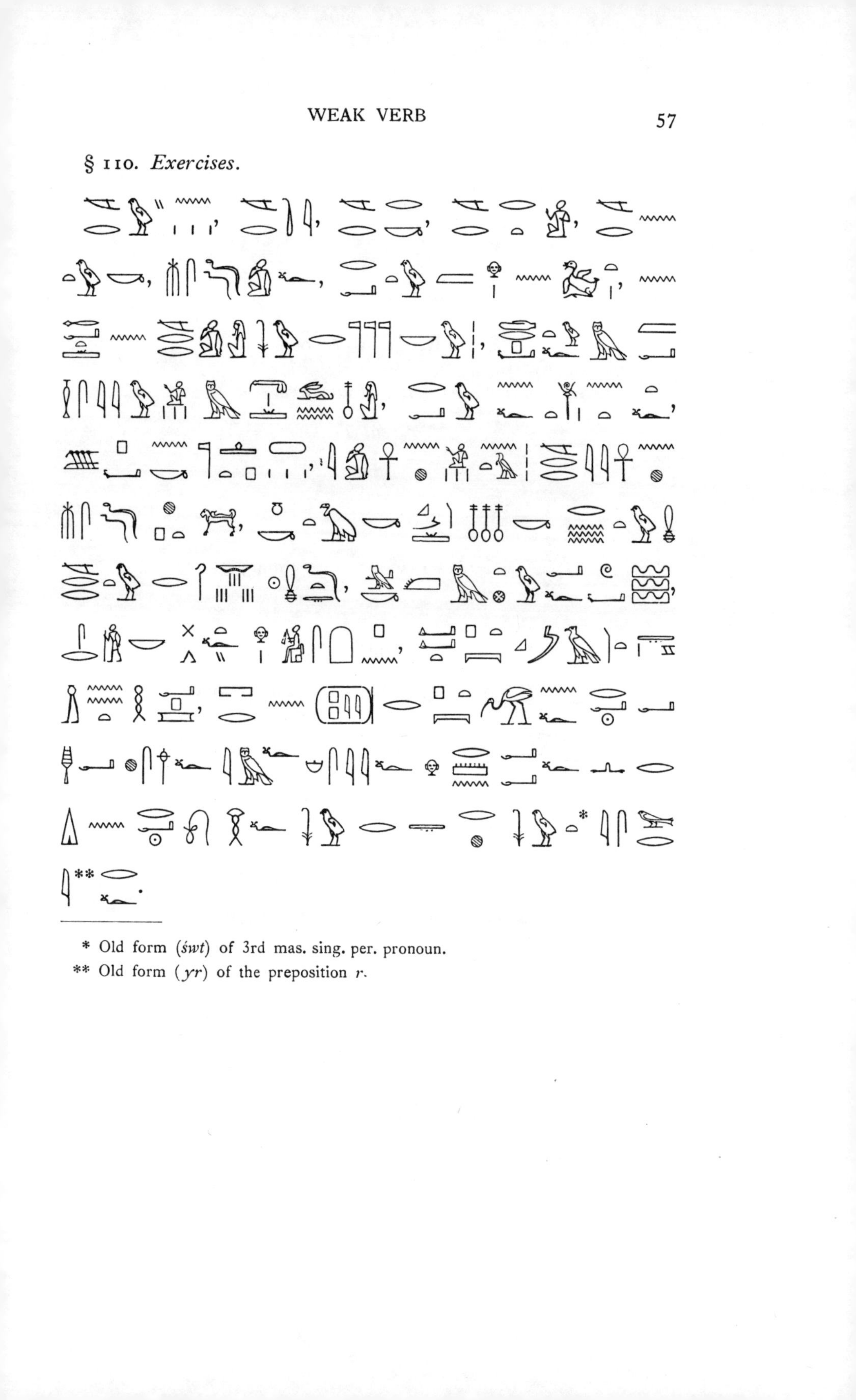

§ 110. *Exercises.*

* Old form (*śwt*) of 3rd mas. sing. per. pronoun.

** Old form (*yr*) of the preposition *r*.

CHAPTER XII

Irregular Verbs

§ 111. *Irregular Verb—Active—Indicative.*

Present Tense

śḏm·f

dy·y	"I give"
dy·k	"thou givest"

&c.

śḏm·kꜣ·f

dy·kꜣ·y	"thus I give"
dy·kꜣ·k	"thus thou givest"

&c.

Past Tense

śḏm·n·f

rdy·n·y	"I gave"
rdy·n·k	"thou gavest"

&c.

śḏm·yn·f

rdy·yn·y	"then I gave"
rdy·yn·k	"then thou gavest"

&c.

Future Tense

śḏm·ḫr·f

rdy·ḫr·y "I shall give"

rdy·ḫr·k "thou wilt give," or "give thou"

§ 112. *Irregular Verb–Passive–Indicative.**

Present Tense

śḏm·tw·f

dy·tw·y "I am given"

dy·tw·k "thou art given"

&c.

Past Tense

śḏm·n·tw·f

dy·n·tw·y "I was given"

dy·n·tw·k "thou wast given"

&c.

§ 113. *Irregular Verb–Emphatic.***

Present Tense

śḏm·f

dydy·y "I give"

dydy·k "thou givest"

&c.

---

* The other parts of the *passive* can easily be constructed on the model of the forms in § 83.

** The other forms of the *emphatic* can easily be constructed on the model of the forms in §§ 84 ff.

§ 114. *Imperative.*

	ymy	"give thou"
	ymy·w	"give ye"

§ 115. *Infinitive.*

	rdy·t	"to give"

§ 116. *Participles.*

	rdy	"having given"
	dydy	"giving"
	rdy	"given"
	dydy·w	"being given"

§ 117. *Relatives.*

	dydy·t·y	"that which I give"
	dydy·t·k	"that which thou givest"

&c.

§ 118. *Conditional Stem (Qualitative or Pseudo-Participle).*

	dy·kwy	"I am giving, or given"
	dy·ty	"thou (mas. and fem.) art giving, or given"
	dy·w	"he is giving, or given"
	dy·ty	"she is giving, or given"
	dy·wyn	"we are giving, or given"
	dy·tywny	"ye (mas. and fem.) are giving, or given"
	dy·ty	"they are giving, or given"

§ 119. *Causative Stem.*

ś·rdy "to cause to give"

§ 120. *Vocabulary.*

wḏꜣ "to be glad," *wḏ* "to command," *gb* (*gbb*) the god Geb, *ḫtf* "according as," *nḫn* "to be young," *bw ḫr* "place at which," *wꜣ·t* "way," *m ḫd* "northward," *śnḏ* "fear," *ḥ·t* "fortress," "castle," *św* "the sun," "light," *hꜣy* "go away," "pour in," or , *yr*, *r*, used for emphasis "namely." It takes the pronominal suffixes. *šmśy* "to follow," *mꜥ* "because," *mꜣꜥ·t* "truth," *nb* "lord," *ḥtp dy nswt* "an offering which the king gives," *pr·t-r-ḫrw* "funeral offering."

§ 121. *Exercises.*

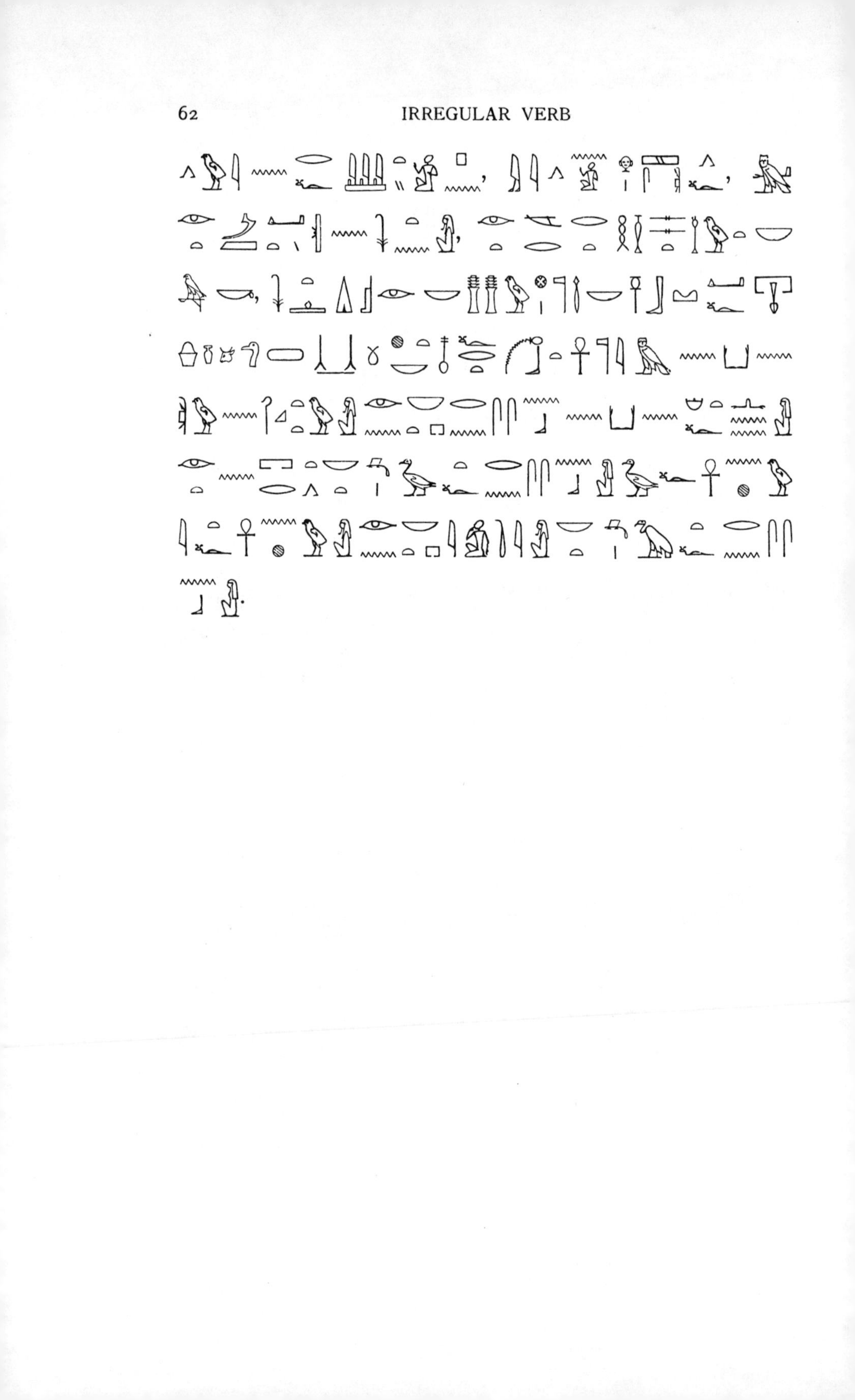

CHAPTER XIII

Auxiliary Verbs

§ 122. *The Auxiliaries* *yw* and * *wn* *wn·t* "to be."

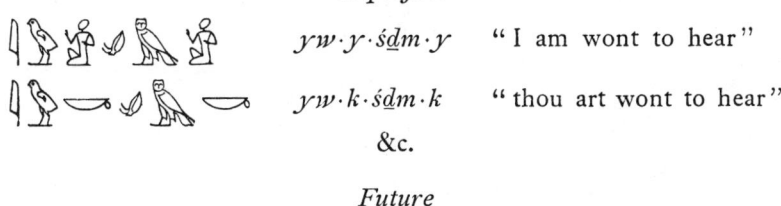

1. With strong verbs:

Present

yw·śḏm·y "I hear"

yw·śḏm·k "thou hearest"

&c.

Imperfect

yw·y·śḏm·y "I am wont to hear"

yw·k·śḏm·k "thou art wont to hear"

&c.

Future

yw·y·r·śḏm "I shall hear"

yw·k·r·śḏm "thou wilt hear"

&c.

2. With duplicating verbs:

Present

yw·ḳb·y "I am cool"

yw·ḳb·k "thou art cool"

&c.

---

* The auxiliary *wn* is used in the same way as .

Imperfect

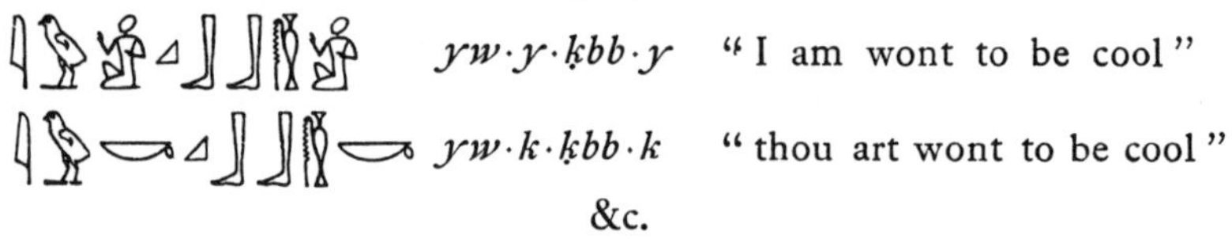

yw·y·ḳbb·y "I am wont to be cool"

yw·k·ḳbb·k "thou art wont to be cool"

&c.

Future

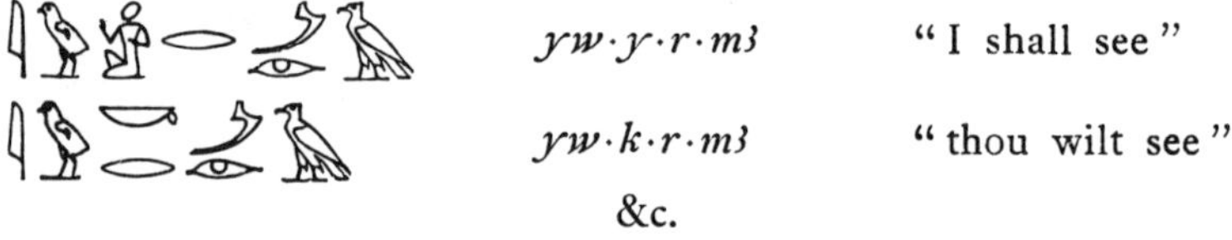

yw·y·r·mꜣ "I shall see"

yw·k·r·mꜣ "thou wilt see"

&c.

3. With weak verbs:

Present

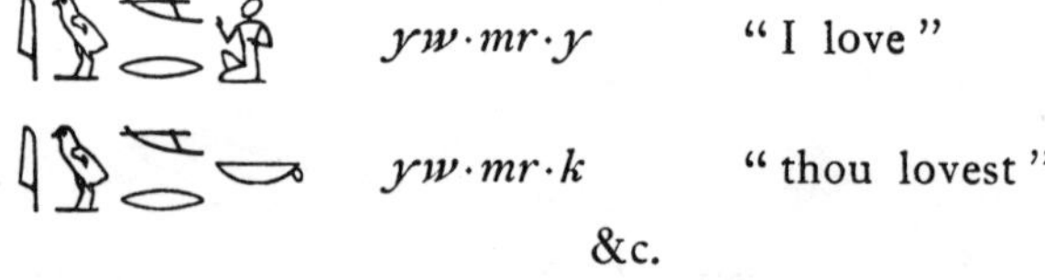

yw·mr·y "I love"

yw·mr·k "thou lovest"

&c.

Imperfect

yw·y·mr·y "I am wont to love"

yw·k·mr·k "thou art wont to love"

&c.

Future

yw·y·r·mr·t "I shall love"

yw·k·r·mr·t "thou wilt love"

&c.

4. With irregular verbs:

Present

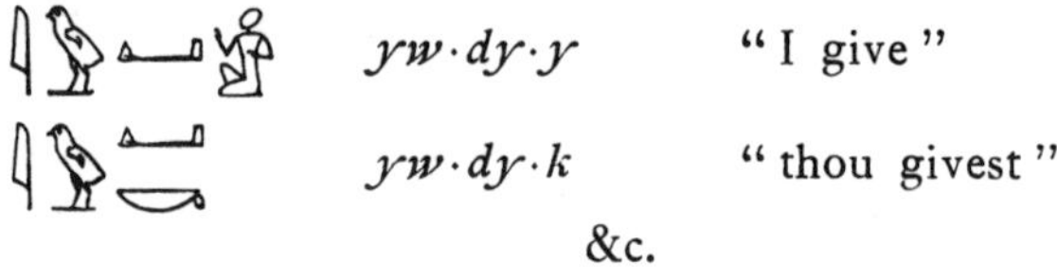

yw·dy·y "I give"

yw·dy·k "thou givest"

&c.

Imperfect

	yw·y·dy·y	"I am wont to give"
	yw·k·dy·k	"thou art wont to give"

&c.

Future

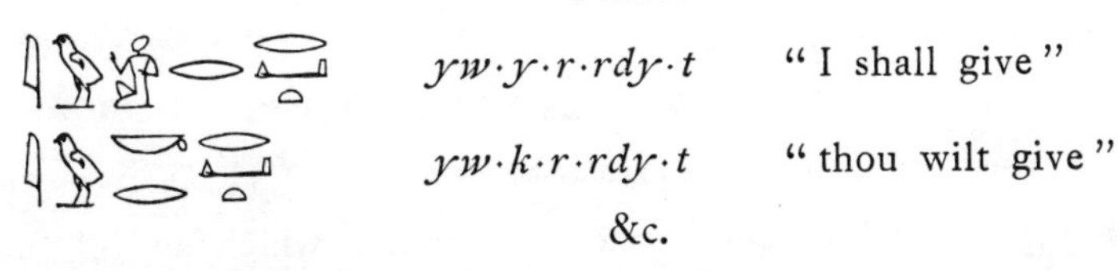

	yw·y·r·rdy·t	"I shall give"
	yw·k·r·rdy·t	"thou wilt give"

&c.

5. Remarks and examples:

a) These auxiliaries emphasize the idea in the verb, e.g. *yw ṯ3 mdw* "the chicken chirps."

b) They are used also in nominal sentences, e.g. *yw ˁb·wy·ś m ḏ3ḏ3·k* "her horns are on thy head."

c) They are used with *ḥr* and the infinitive, e.g. *yw bw-nb ḥr dw3 nfrw·f* "everyone praised his beauty."

d) They are used in nominal sentences with the conditional (pseudo-participle), e.g. *yw·f śḏm·w* "he is hearing"; also with *ḥr* and the infinitive, e.g. *yw·f ḥr śḏm* "he is hearing."

e) The *r* of the future tense is also used in verbal sentences with or without the auxiliary, e.g. *yb n ḥm·k r·ḳbb* "the heart of thy majesty will be cool."

§ 123. The auxiliary *ˁḥˁ* "to stand" precedes the verb. It is usually rendered by "then." Transitive verbs follow this auxiliary in the *śḏm·f* form; intransitives take the conditional (pseudo-participle), e.g. *ˁḥˁ·n ṯḥn·n ḥm·f ḫnˁ·śn* "then his majesty came into conflict with them," *ꜥḥꜥ·n rdy·kwy r yw* "then was I thrown on the island."

§ 124. The auxiliaries *yyn*, *prn*, and *yw* are used in the same way as *ꜥḥꜥ*.

§ 125. The auxiliary *yry* "to do" is used with a following infinitive, e.g. *yry·y šm·t* "I went" ("I did the going"). The past tense, *yry·n·f*, with *pw* and an infinitive, is used in historical narrative, e.g. *šm·t pw yry·n·f* "he went" ("to go was that which he did").

§ 126. The auxiliary *pꜣ* "to have been," "to have had," especially in negative sentences, is used with the infinitive to denote a past condition or action, e.g. *n sp pꜣ·tw yr·t myty·t* "never was done the like."

§ 127. *Vocabulary.*

drp "to make libation," *hꜣb* "to send out," "to go down," *ꜥḳ* "to enter," *dp·t* "ship," *yny* "to bring," *ynw* "gifts," "offerings," *pry* "to go out," *nḏm* "to be sweet, well," *ꜥ* "side," "place," *wꜣḥ* "put," "place," *d·t* (?), *ḏr·t* "hand," *mḥ* "to fill," "to be full," *ś·ḫpr* "to cause to exist," *šm* "to go," *tw* "one."

§ 128. *Exercises.*

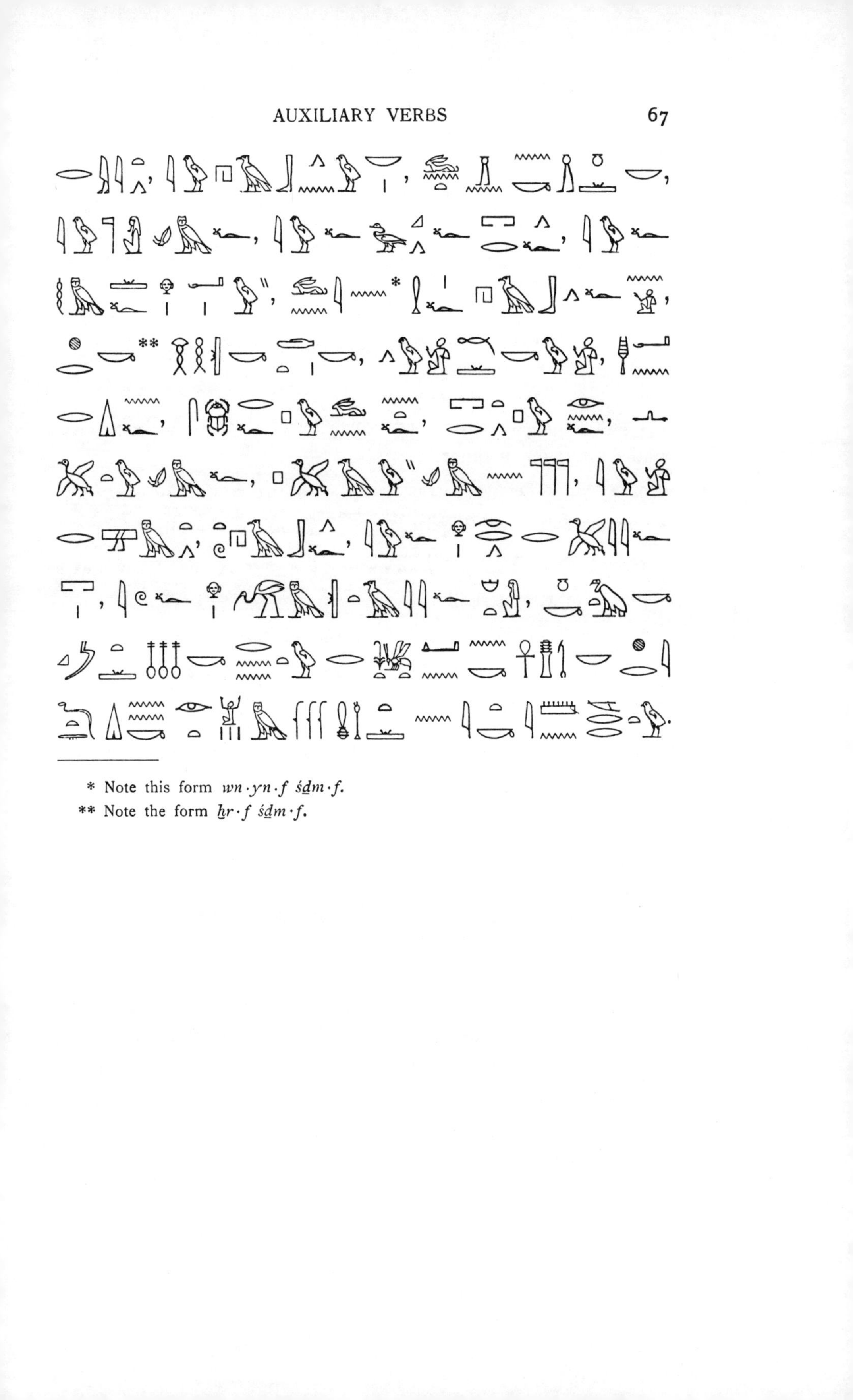

* Note this form *wn·yn·f śḏm·f.*

** Note the form *ḫr·f śḏm·f.*

CHAPTER XIV

Adverbs, Prepositions, and Conjunctions

§ 129. *Adverbs.*

There being no special adverbial form, adverbs are expressed in the following manner:

1. By an adjective, occasionally with the ending *w* or *t*, e.g. *wr·t* "very," "quite," *nfr·w* "well," *ḏ·t* "eternally"; *ꜣw yb·k my Rʿ ḏ·t* "thy heart is glad like Reʿ eternally."

2. By an adjective preceded by the preposition, e.g. *r mnḫ* "excellently," *r yḫ·t nb·t* "above all," *r ʿꜣ·t* "very."

3. By means of prepositional forms, e.g. *ym* "there," "yonder," "therein," "thereof," &c., *ḫnt*, *m-bꜣḥ*, *ḥr-ḥꜣ·t* "before," *ḫft* "in front," *ḏr-bꜣḥ* "formerly," *m-ḫt*, *m-sꜣ*, *ḥr-sꜣ*, *r-sꜣ*, *n-sꜣ* "afterward."

§ 130. *Prepositions.*

Prepositions may be divided into two classes, simple and compound. The following are examples of both classes; others will be found in the vocabulary. The following should be committed to memory.

1. *Simple prepositions:* When they are combined with suffixes they occasionally have a fuller writing, e.g. *ym·f* "in him," *yr·f* "to him."

	m	"in," "at," "from," "with," "into," "out of," "among," "to," "of," "as," "like," "according to," "into," "by means of," &c.
	r	"at," "by," "to," "into," "as far as," "toward," distributively of time, &c.
	n	"for," "to," "because of," "in (of time)," "of," &c.
	ḥr	"at," "in," "down," "upon," "with," "because of," "on account of," &c.
	ẖr	"under"
	ḫr	"with," "under" (during the reign of)
	yn	used with the passive, and to emphasize the subject; also with the infinitive
	mʿ	"in possession of," "from," "by," "because of"
	ḫft	"in front of," "according to," "corresponding to," "simultaneously with"
	my	"like," "as"
	ḥnʿ	"together with"
	ḫnt	"before," "at the head of"
	tp	"upon"
	ḏr	"when," "since"

2. *Compound prepositions:* They are generally simple prepositions combined with nouns. The following examples should be committed to memory.

, *m-b3ḥ* "before"

m-ḥ3·t "before," "at the head of"

m-ḥr	"in front of"
m-ḫt	"behind," "after"
m-dy	"together with"
n-mrw·t	"on account of," "in order that"
r-gś	"near," "at the side of"
ḥrw-r	"outside," "distant from"
r-śꜣ	"behind," "after"
ḥr-śꜣ	"behind," "after"
ḫft-ḥr	"in front of"
ẖr-ḥꜣ·t	"at the head of"

§ 131. *Conjunctions.*

Conjunctions may be divided into two classes, enclitics and absolute conjunctions.

1. *Enclitic conjunctions.*

yr, *yrf*, *rf*	"if," used for emphasis after the emphasized word
yś	"namely," "yes," "surely," introducing an explanatory addition
n-yś	"but not"
śwt, *ḥm*	"but," expressing the opposite to the preceding clause"
gr, *gr·t*	"but," "moreover," "also," "likewise"

2. *Absolute conjunctions.*

yśṯ, *śṯ* "since," "when," "behold," "however"

yśk "when"

ḫr "and," "but," "now," "since"

kꜣ used in directions, promises, threats, to strengthen what is stated

§ 132. *Vocabulary.*

wꜣśy "to be decayed," *hrw* "day," *mw* (*myw*) "water," *ḫʿy* "to shine," *śwꜣy* "to pass by," *šm* "to go," *wꜣḏ-wr* "sea," *mḥ* "ell," *ꜣw·t* "length," *yw* "island," *ḥfꜣw* "snake," *mry·t* "river-bank," *hꜣw* "near," *yꜣš*, *ʿš* "to call," *ḥknw* "praise," *nʿy* "to journey," "to sail," *ḫdy* "sail down stream," "northwards," *ẖnw* "residence."

§ 133. *Exercises.*

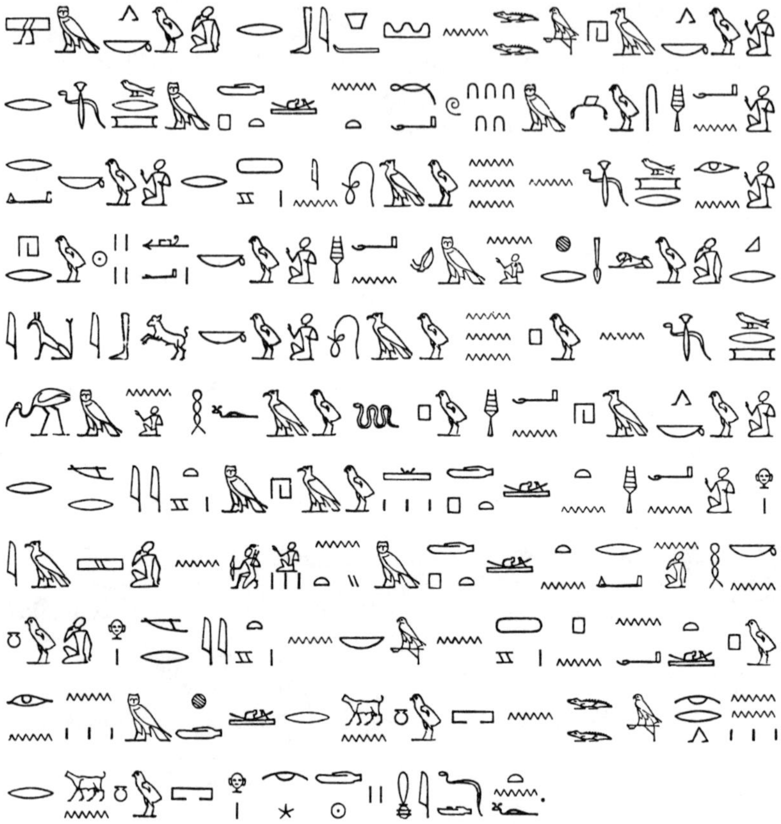

CHAPTER XV

Other Particles

§ 134. *Interjections.*

The two commonest interjections are *y* and *h3* "O!", "Ha!", e.g. *y ʿnḫ·w* "O ye living!" They often stand before a proper noun which is then usually followed by *pn* "this," e.g. *h3 Ppy pn* "O thou king Pepi!"

The article *p3* is often used in the nominative of address as an interjection, e.g. *p3 ytn ʿnḫ* "O thou living Aton!"

Certain interjections take a suffix, e.g. *ynd-ḥr·k wśyr nb ḥḥ* "Hail, thou, Osiris, lord of eternity!"

§ 135. *Particles of Negation.*

1. The negative *n* is used in nominal sentences, e.g. *n ntf pw m3ʿ·t* "it is not he in truth"; in verbal sentences, e.g. *n rḫ·y św* "I know him not"; and with *sp* "time," e.g. *n sp* "never."

2. The negative *nn* is used in verbal sentences with a future meaning, e.g. *nn psš·f* "he will not divide"; with an infinitive, e.g. *wdʿ nn rdy·t ḥr gś* "judging, not putting on one side"; and with a noun or pronoun, e.g. *nn mw ym nn wy ym* "no water is there, I am not there."

3. The emphatic negative is or *nfr n*, e.g. *nfr n yrtw mytt* "never was the like done."

4. The negative *ym* is used in optative and final sentences, e.g. *ym·k yr yḫ·t r·ś* "do not do anything against it."

5. The negative *tm* is used in conditional sentences, e.g. *tm-ḫr·ś ḫpr m ḥśb·t* "it does not become worms"; and in combination with *rdy*, meaning "to prevent," e.g. *kt nt tm rdy pr ḥfꜣw* "another (remedy) for preventing snakes from going forth."

6. The negative *m* is used in imperative and optative sentences, e.g. *m ꜥꜣ yb·k* "let not thy heart be proud."

7. The particle *nywty* is a negative relative, e.g. *nywty mw·t·f* "he who is without his mother."

8. Note the negative part of the phrase: *ntt nywtt* "that which is and that which is not."

§ 136. *The Relative Particle.*

The relative particle, *nty* "he who is," "that which is," is really a declinable pronoun (§ 69), and is used in relative clauses, e.g. *s nty mr* "a man who is ill."

§ 137. The particles *yr* and *my* (or *m*) are used in *Conditional* sentences, e.g. *yr gm·k ḏꜣyśw* "if thou findest a wise man"; *my ḏd·n·k* "if it is said to thee."

§ 138. *Interrogative Particles.*

1. The particle *mꜥ* or *m* is very common, and occurs at the end of a sentence, e.g. *yrtw nn my mꜥ* "like what is this done?"

2. At the beginning of a sentence is used with *yn*, e.g. *yn mꜥ ḏd św* "who says it?"

3. The particle *yn* or *ynyw* is used in rhetorical questions, e.g. *yn ꜥwꜣy·tw·y r·f m yꜣ·t·f* "shall I be robbed upon his place?"

4. The particle *ptry* or *pty* always stands at the beginning of a sentence, e.g. *pty ꜣḥ·t·f* "what is his field?"

5. The particle *trw* always follows the first word of the sentence, e.g. *yn yw trw śḫꜣ·n·k* "didst thou remember?"

6. Other interrogative particles:

	yššt	"who?" "what?"
	ysy	" "
	ysnw	"when?"
	tn	"where?"

§ 139. *Emphatic Particles.*

1. The particle , *yr* "but," "now," "namely," "verily," generally begins a sentence, e.g. *yr ntt nb·t m sš śḏm śt* "verily, all that is in writing, hear it."

2. The particle , *yr·f* takes second place in a sentence, e.g. *ḥḏ·n yr·f tꜣ* "when the earth became bright."

3. Both *yr* and *yr·f* are used for emphasis after the imperative, when they take a suffix, e.g. *ꜥḥꜥ yr·k* "stand up, thou"; and also in interrogative sentences. (§ 154.)

4. The particle *yn* emphasizes the subject of a sentence, but it is not translated, e.g. *yn ḥm·f rdy yr·t·f* "his majesty caused that it be made."

§ 140. *Other Particles.*

1. The adverbial particle *wy* "how," "pray," follows the first word of a sentence, e.g. *nḏm wy ymꜣ·t·k* "how beautiful is thy goodness."

2. The particle *mʿ*, later *mʿ·k* or *m·k* "behold," stands at the head of a sentence, and often immediately precedes the subject.

§ 141. *Vocabulary.*

pḥ "to reach," *ḏr* "since," *rk* "time," *pśš* "to divide," *yꜣ·t* "place," "holy place," *ꜣḫw* "the blessed ones," *mr* "overseer," *śḳdy* "to sail," *yry-ʿ·t* "officer," *kꜣ·t* "work," *kꜣwty* "workman," *ẖr·t* "necropolis," "grave," *sš* "book," "writing," *mr* "canal," *śmꜣ* "to kill," *ḥʿy* "to shine," *wbn* "to rise (sun)."

§ 142. *Exercises.*

, , ,

, , , ,

, ,

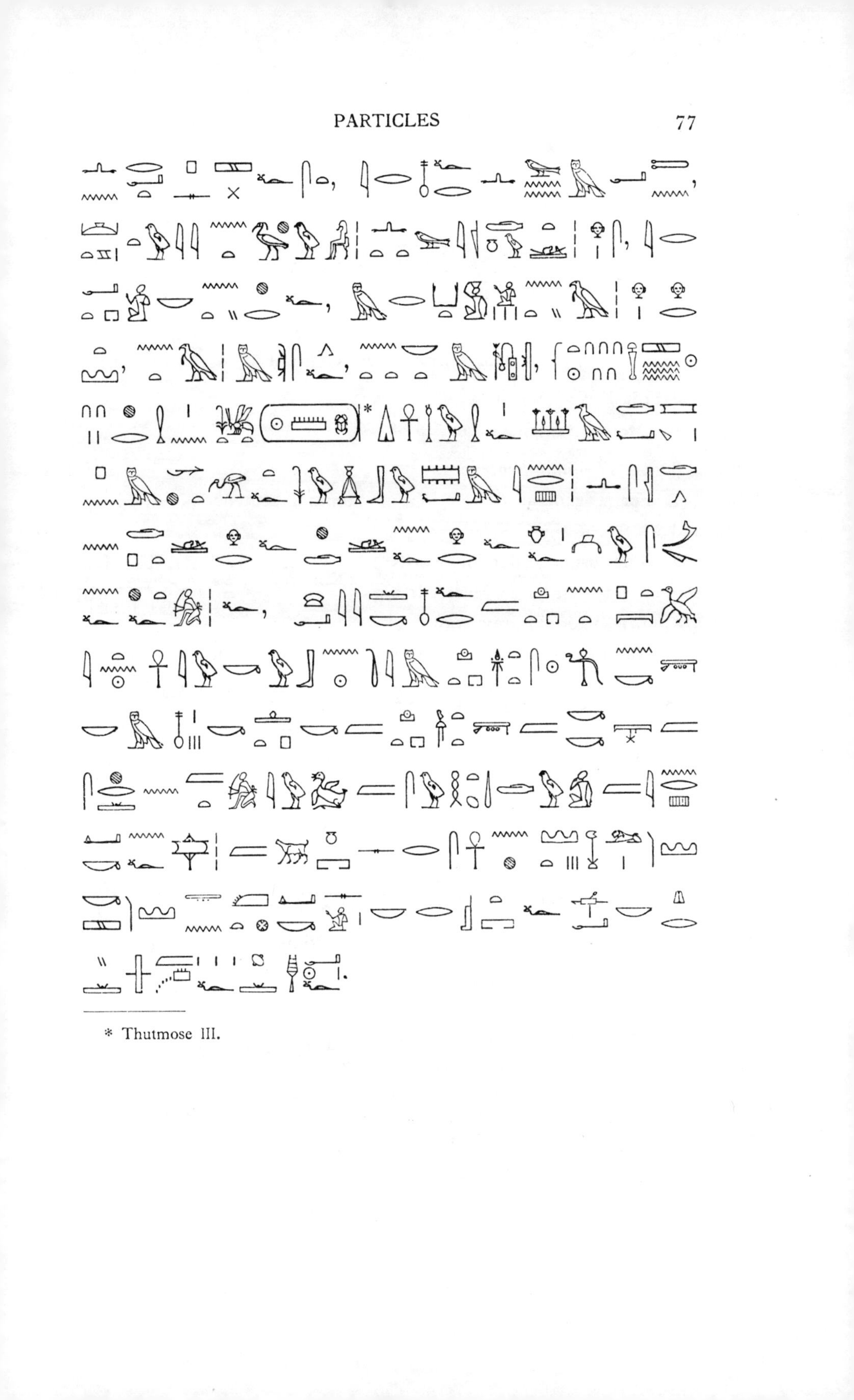

* Thutmose III.

SYNTAX

CHAPTER XVI

The Sentence in General

§ 143. *Verbal Sentences.*

For verbal sentences, see §§ 38–39.

§ 144. *Nominal Sentences.*

1. For a general description of nominal sentences, see §§ 37 and 40.

2. The usual order of words is: Subject, predicate, but for emphasis the order is reversed, e.g. *nfr mṯny* "good is my way."

3. Nominal sentences are used to express a simple act, e.g. *mʿk·wy m-b3ḥ·k* "behold, I am before thee"; to express circumstance, e.g. "thou ascendest *wr·t m ḫt·k* when a greater one is behind thee"; and to express a relative idea, e.g. *s śt·t m nḥb·t·f* "a man on whose neck are swellings."

4. Nominal sentences often have *pw*, e.g. *pḫr·t pw* "it was medicine"; and sometimes *m*, e.g. *yb·y m śnw·y* "my heart was my companion."

5. Nominal sentences are introduced by *yw* "to be," e.g. *yw w3t·f wʿ·t ḫr mw* "its one side was under water"; and by *wnn* "to be," e.g. *wn yn nfr śt ḥr yb·śn* "it was good for their heart."

§ 145. *Order of Words in Sentences.*

1. Note what has been said about the order of words in §§ 38 and 144, 2.

2. Furthermore: *a*) When the subject and both objects are nouns, the order is, Subject–Accusative–Dative, e.g. *rdy·n nswt nb n bꜣk·f* "the king gave gold to his servant"; *b*) When the subject and objects are partly pronouns, the pronouns precede the nouns, e.g. "the king gave me gold," "the king gave it to his servant," "he gave me gold"; *c*) When both objects are pronouns, the suffix precedes the absolute pronoun, e.g. "the king gave it to me," "he gave it to me."

§ 146. *Emphasis.*

Emphasis is expressed in the following manner:

1. By irregular word-order, e.g. *tꜣ·n pḥ·n św* "we have reached our land (our land, we have reached it)."

2. By means of the particle *yr*, e.g. *yr ntt nb·t m sš śḏm śt* "all which is in a book, hear it."

3. By means of the particle *yn*, which emphasizes the subject, e.g. *yn ḥm·f rdy·f* "his majesty it was who gave."

4. By means of *r*, *yr*, with a suffix, after the emphasized word, e.g. *rdy·k r·k ny* "give thou to me." In later times an unchangeable *r·f*, *yr·f*, was used, e.g. *pr·t·y r·f* "when I went out."

§ 147. *Ellipse.*

1. Very often omitted words must be understood. This is usual in poetry. It is also common in comparisons, e.g. *ś·3w·f yb n b3k·y ym my ḥḳ3 n ḫ3ś·t nb·t* "he makes glad the heart of my servant even as (the heart of) the prince of any country."

2. Almost any part of a sentence may be omitted, when the context makes it clear what it should be, e.g. *yr·n·s m mnw·s* "she made (this) as her monument."

3. Other examples of ellipses are: The omission of *dd* "to say," e.g. *yn Rᶜ* "Reᶜ says"; *yn·śn* "they say"; *nṯrw ḥr* "the gods say."

§ 148. *Vocabulary.*

ym3·t "graciousness," *ḥs·t* "praise," *rwyy* "to flee," *hd* "hero," *w3y* with "to be far from," *dw* "evil," *ᶜš* "to call," *wr* "prince," *mnḫ* "to be pleasant," *ṯsw* "to command," *ḥśḳ* "to cut off," *yty* "king," *tyw* "yes," *ymy* (?) "give," "allow," *y* "Oh!", *rmṯ* "mankind," *mk* "behold," *yry* "belonging to," "of such a nature," *mn·t* "anything," *m-myt·t* "likewise."

§ 149. *Exercises.*

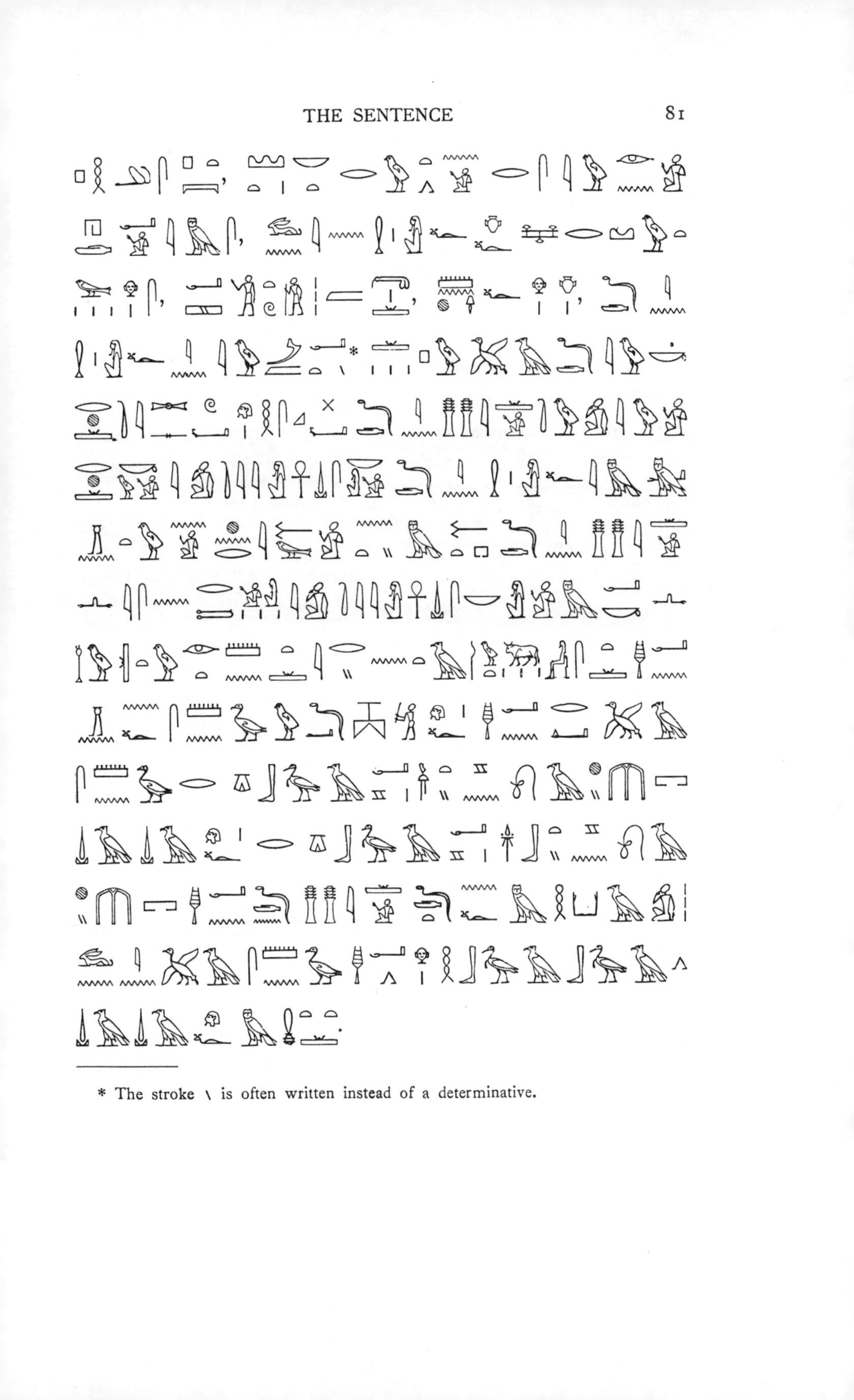

* The stroke \ is often written instead of a determinative.

CHAPTER XVII

Various Kinds of Sentences

§ 150. *Negative Sentences.*

1. Read again § 135.

2. Principal sentences are made negative by means of *n*, later *nn*. These particles always stand first in a sentence, e.g. *n rḫ·y św* "I know him not."

3. Dependent sentences are made negative by the auxiliary verbs *tm* and *ymy* "not to be," "not to have," e.g. *tm·f yry bw nfr* "he does nothing good"; N N *r3 n tm wnm N* "charm that N be not eaten."

4. Relative sentences are made negative by means of the particle *nyw·ty*, *nyw·tt* "who has not," "who is not." The particle agrees in gender and number with the noun, which it follows, e.g. *nyw·ty yh·t·f* "he who has not got his things." It can also be used as a substantive, e.g. "that which does not exist."

5. Commands are made negative by means of (later) *m*, e.g. *m yry* "do not."

§ 151. *Temporal Sentences.*

1. Dependent temporal sentences sometimes precede and sometimes follow the principal sentence, e.g. *ḥd·n t3 pḥ·n·y* "when the earth had become light, I arrived"; *dᶜ pr yw·n m w3d-wr* "a storm arose, (as) we were on the sea."

2. Dependent temporal sentences may or may not have a particle of dependence, e.g. *yw wp·n·f rꜣ·f r·y yw·y ḥr ẖ·t·y* "he opened his mouth against me (while) I was on my belly"; *ḫʿ·yn ḥm·f r śmꜣ m-ḫt śḏm ś·t* "his majesty appeared to do battle, after he had heard it."

§ 152. *Conditional Sentences.*

1. Most conditional sentences have no conditional particle, e.g. *ḥtp·k m yꜣḫ·t ymn·tt tꜣ m kwkw* "when thou settest in the western horizon, the earth is in darkness."

2. The conditional particle is *yr* "if," e.g. *yr gm·k ḏꜣyśw ḫꜣm ʿwy·k* "if thou findest a wise man, bend thy arm (salute)."

§ 153. *Final Sentences.*

1. Final sentences as a rule have no introductory particle, e.g. *ḏd·n·f ʿḥꜣ·f ḥnʿ·y ḥmt·n·f ḥwt·f wy* "he said, 'he would fight with me; he thought, he would smite me."

2. Final sentences often follow *rdy* "to cause," "to make" *rdy·t mꜣ·śn šw* "to make them see the sun."

§ 154. *Interrogative Sentences.*

1. Read again § 138.

2. Interrogative sentences are usually introduced by a particle (§ 138), often followed by the enclitic , *yr·f (r·f)*, e.g. *yn mʿ yr·f yn·f św* "who brings it?"

§ 155. *Relative Sentences.*

1. Read again *Relative Pronouns* (§ 69), *Relatives* (Verbal §§ 75 and 90), *The Relative Particle* (§ 136).

2. Relative sentences may be introduced without any particle, and may have no external sign of relationship, e.g. *p3 t3-ḥḏ ddw·ṯn n·y* "the white bread which thou givest to me."

3. Other relative sentences have a verb in the relative form (§ 90), e.g. *ḫ3ś·t nb·t rw·t·n·y r·ś* "each country to which I went."

4. Many relative sentences are introduced by relative pronouns (§ 69), e.g. *p3 t3 nty rdy·n·y n·ṯn św* "the bread which I have given to you."

5. Relative pronouns are used as nouns in relative sentences, e.g. *nty·t nb·t ym·f* "all which is in it."

6. For the negative of relative sentences, see § 150, 4.

§ 156. *Vocabulary.*

tp-ᶜ "before," *s3ḥ* "to reach," *śpr* "to arrive," "to come," *w3ḥ* "to last," "to be happy," *śwḏ* "to convince," *ẖrd* "child," *my* "when," *ḥsy* "to praise," *n·t* "city," *šdy* "to read," *ḫrp* "stela," "tombstone," *r-ḏd* introduces a final clause, *r-nty·t* introduces a final clause, *w3y* "to be inclined to," *bšṯ* "to revolt," *ᶜḥ3* "to fight," *yry* "belonging to," *rd* "foot," *sp* "time," indicates that what precedes is to be read twice, *ḫnd* "to tread," *pry* "a hero," *m3ᶜ·t* "truth," *bw* in *bw nb* "all men."

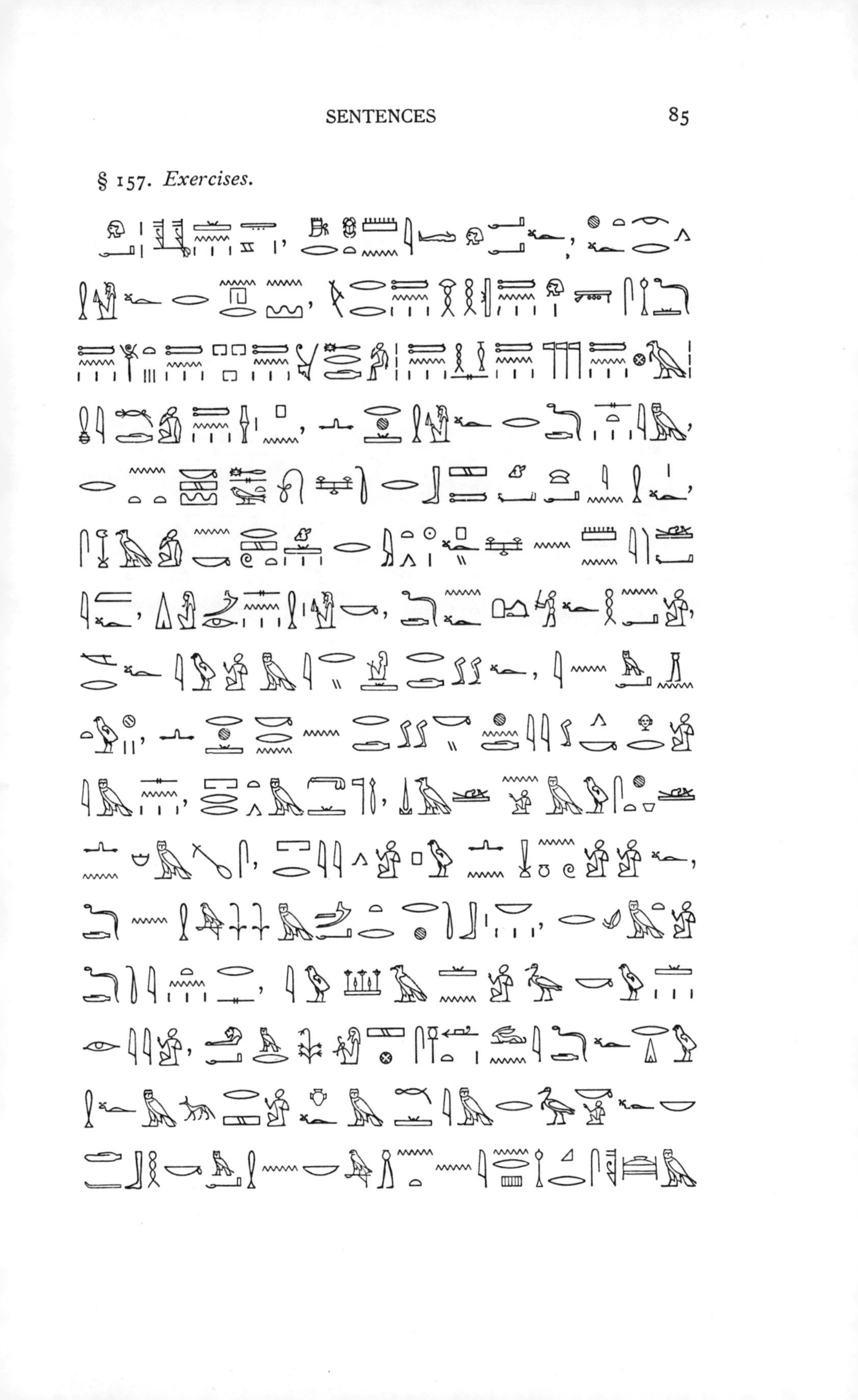

§ 157. *Exercises.*

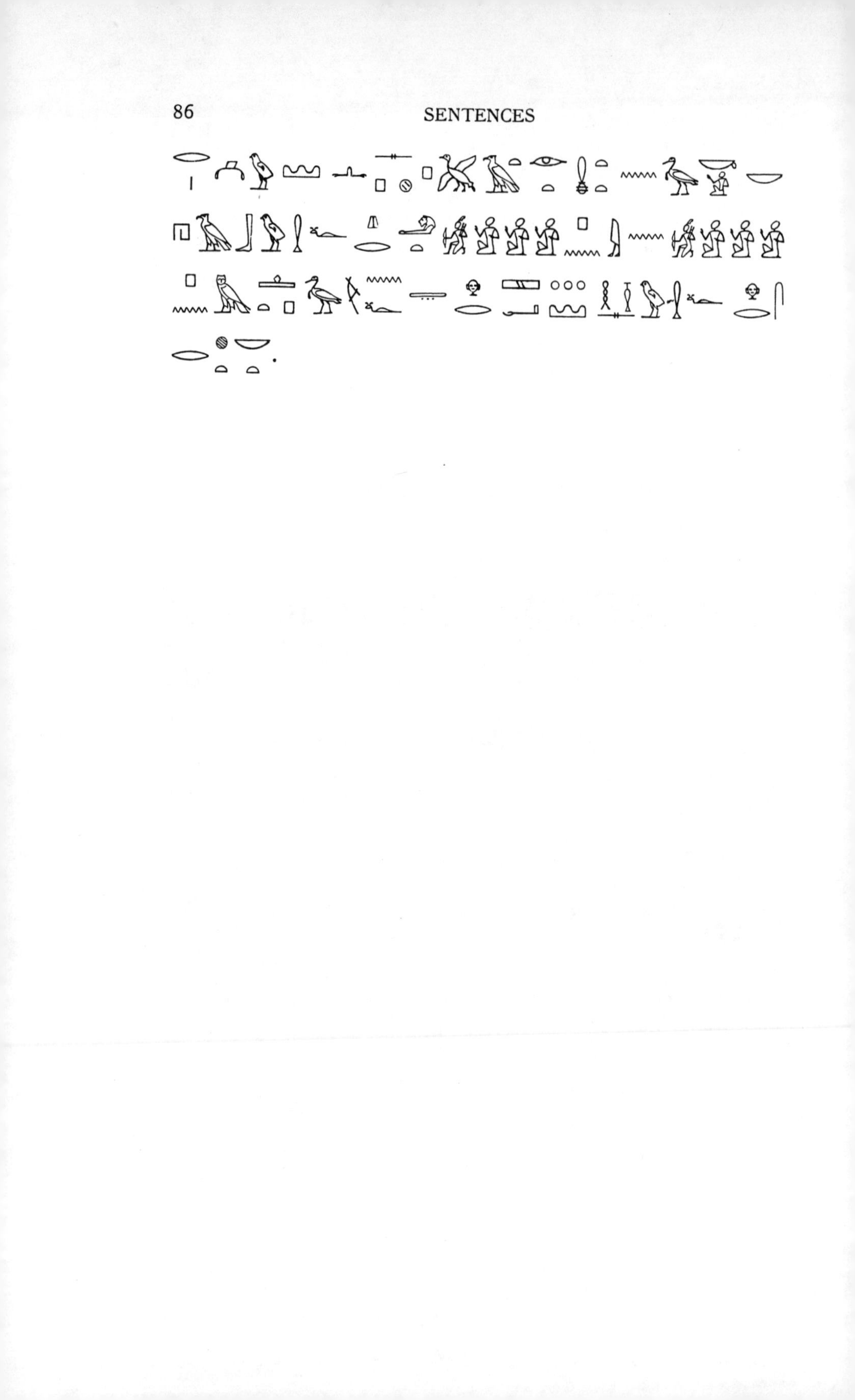

CHRESTOMATHY

I

Some Short Pieces from Various Sources

1. *Admiral Ahmose relates his deeds*

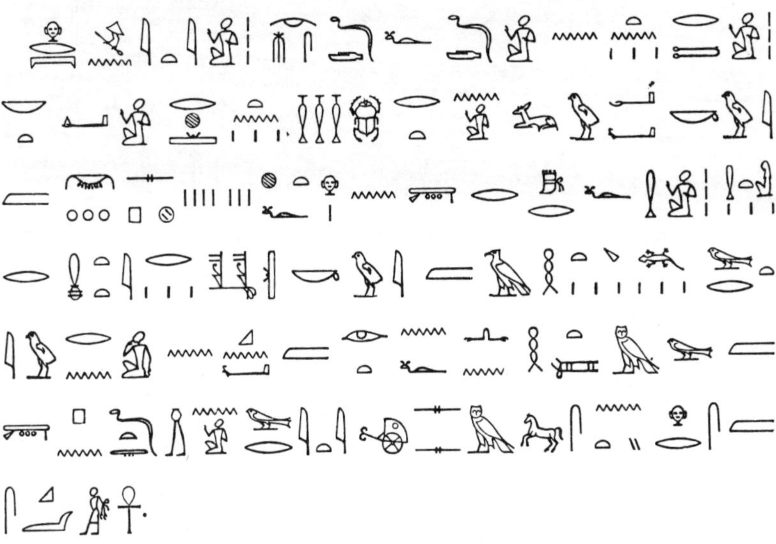

2. *Death of Thutmose III and accession of Amenophis II*

3. *Dedication of a Temple by Thutmose III*

4. *Victory of Thutmose III over Naharina*

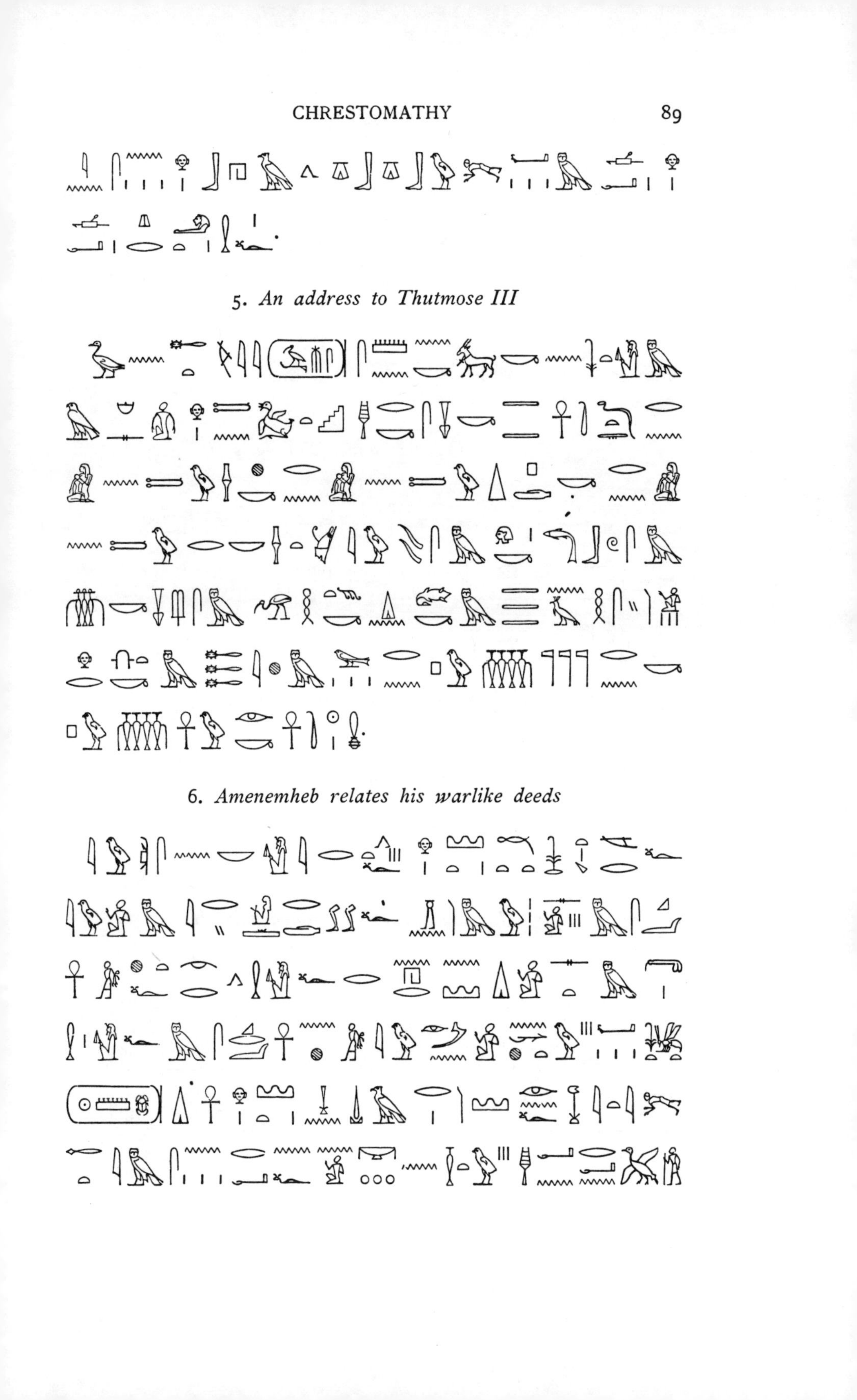

5. *An address to Thutmose III*

6. *Amenemheb relates his warlike deeds*

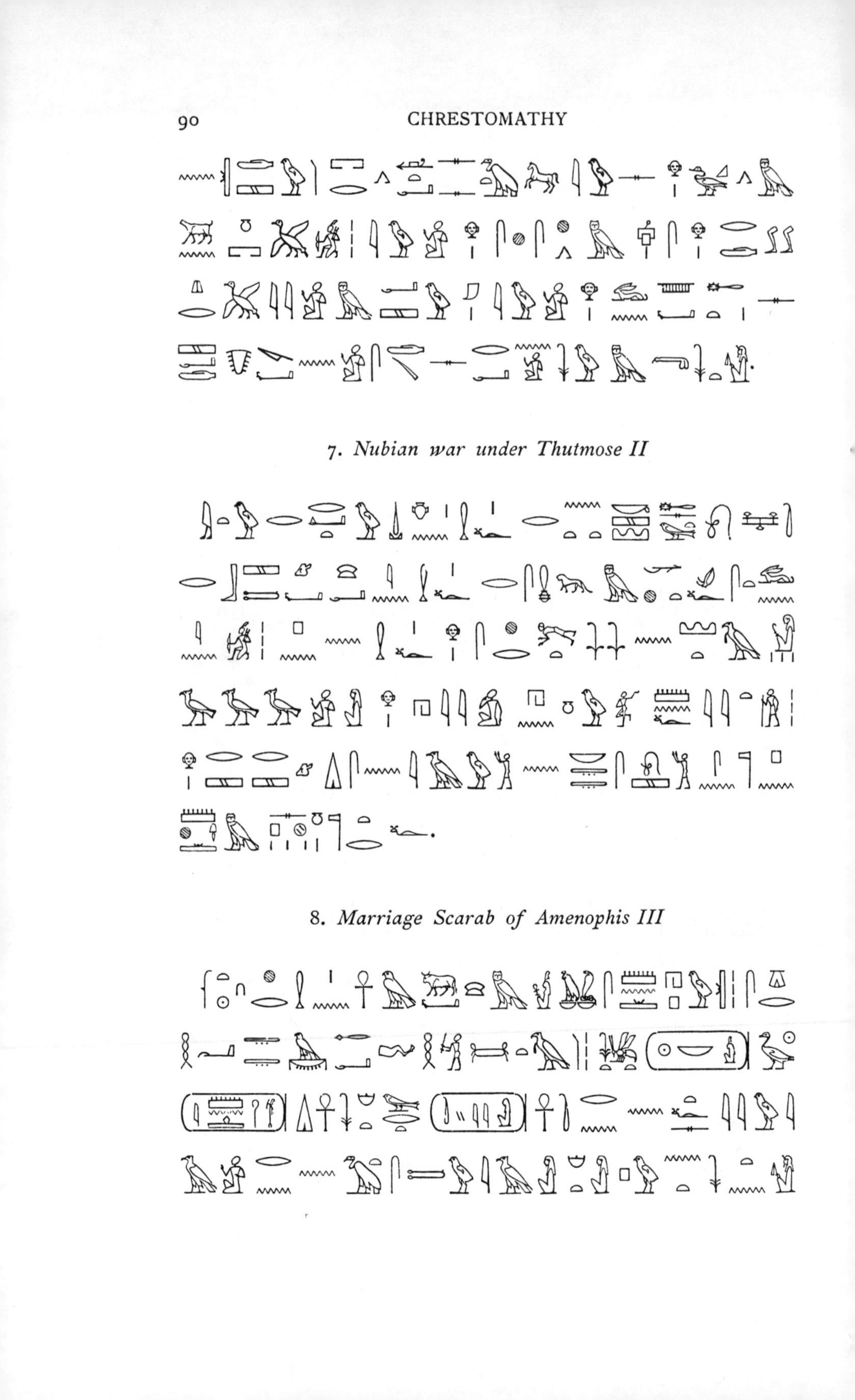

7. *Nubian war under Thutmose II*

8. *Marriage Scarab of Amenophis III*

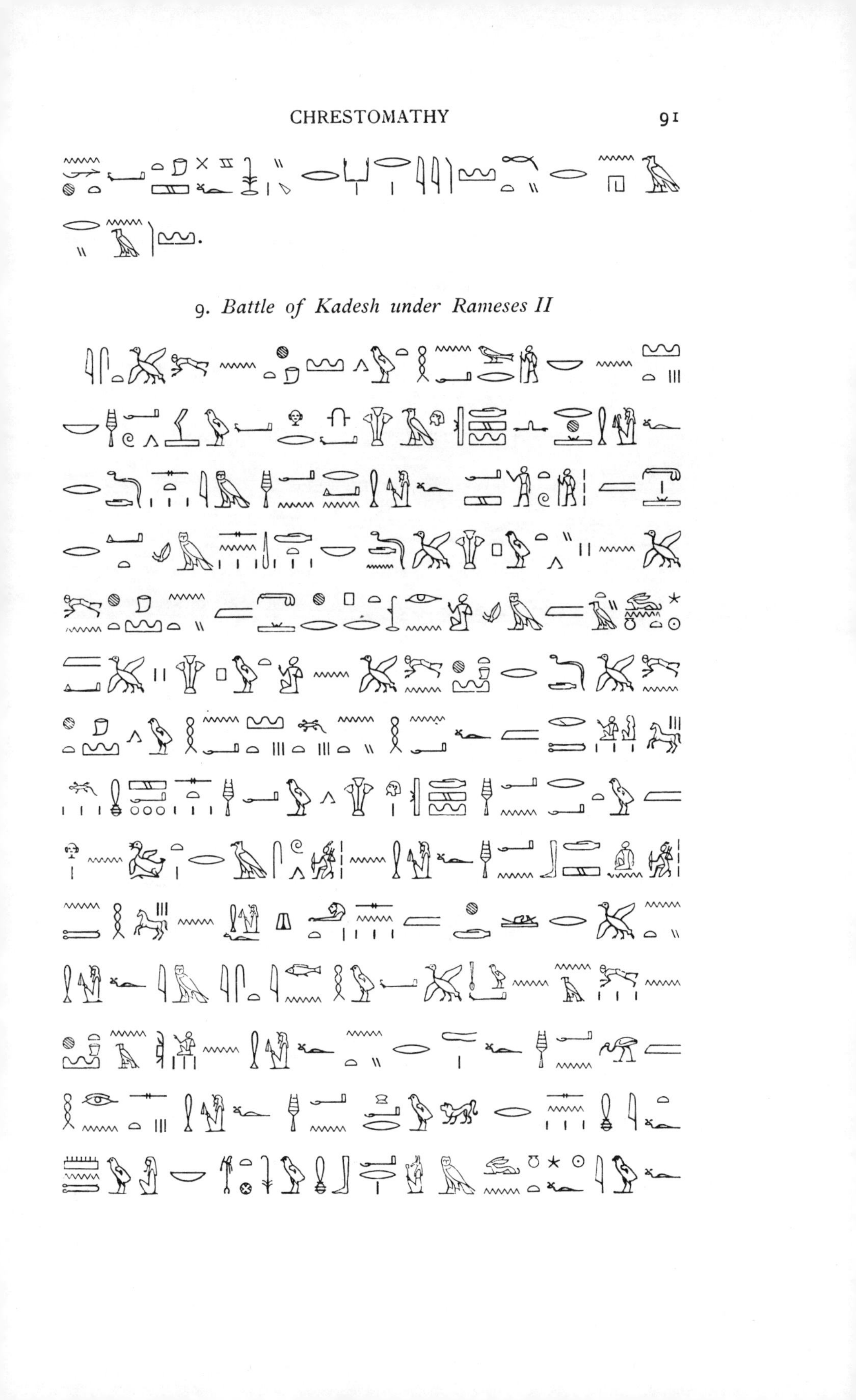

9. *Battle of Kadesh under Rameses II*

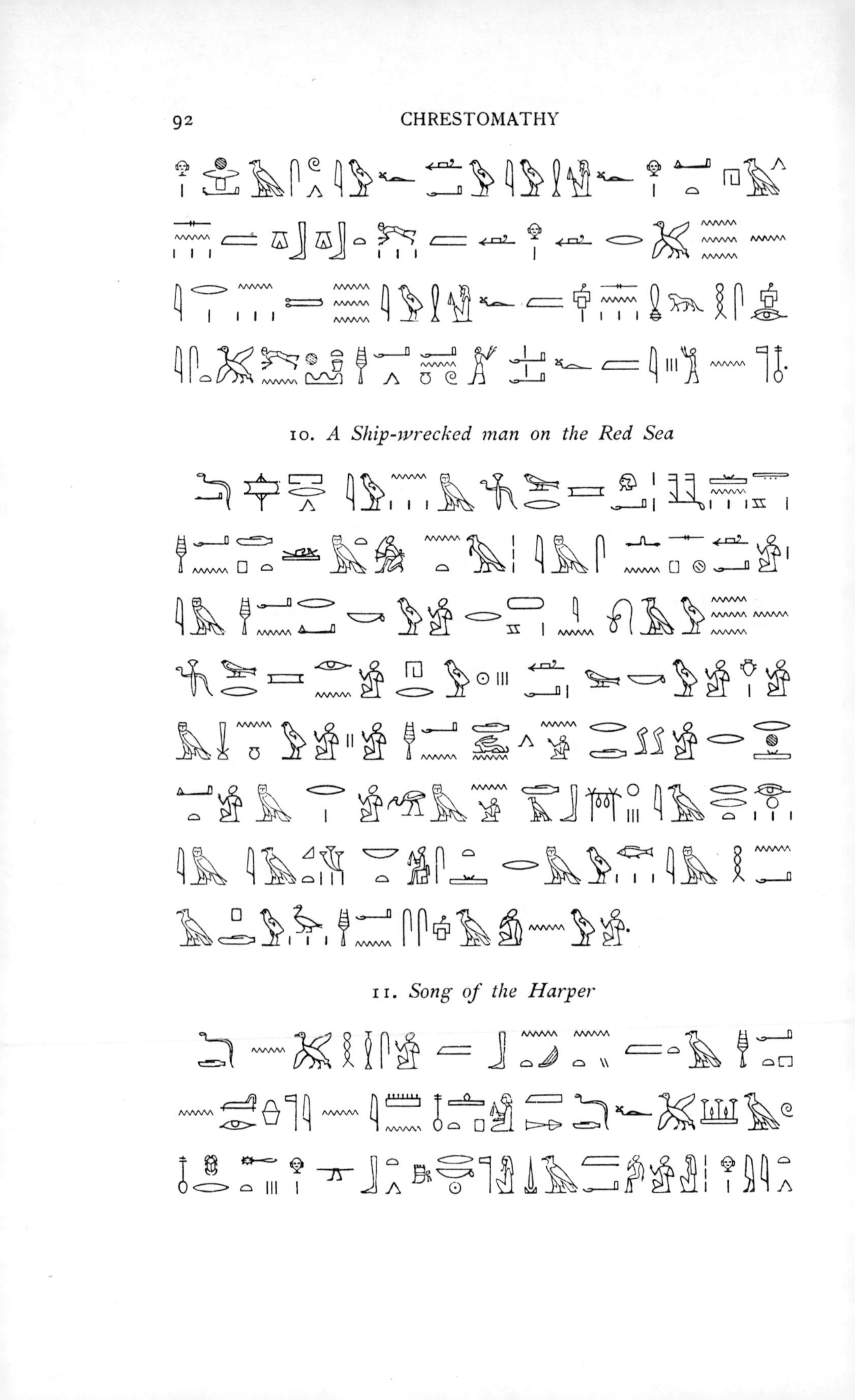

10. *A Ship-wrecked man on the Red Sea*

11. *Song of the Harper*

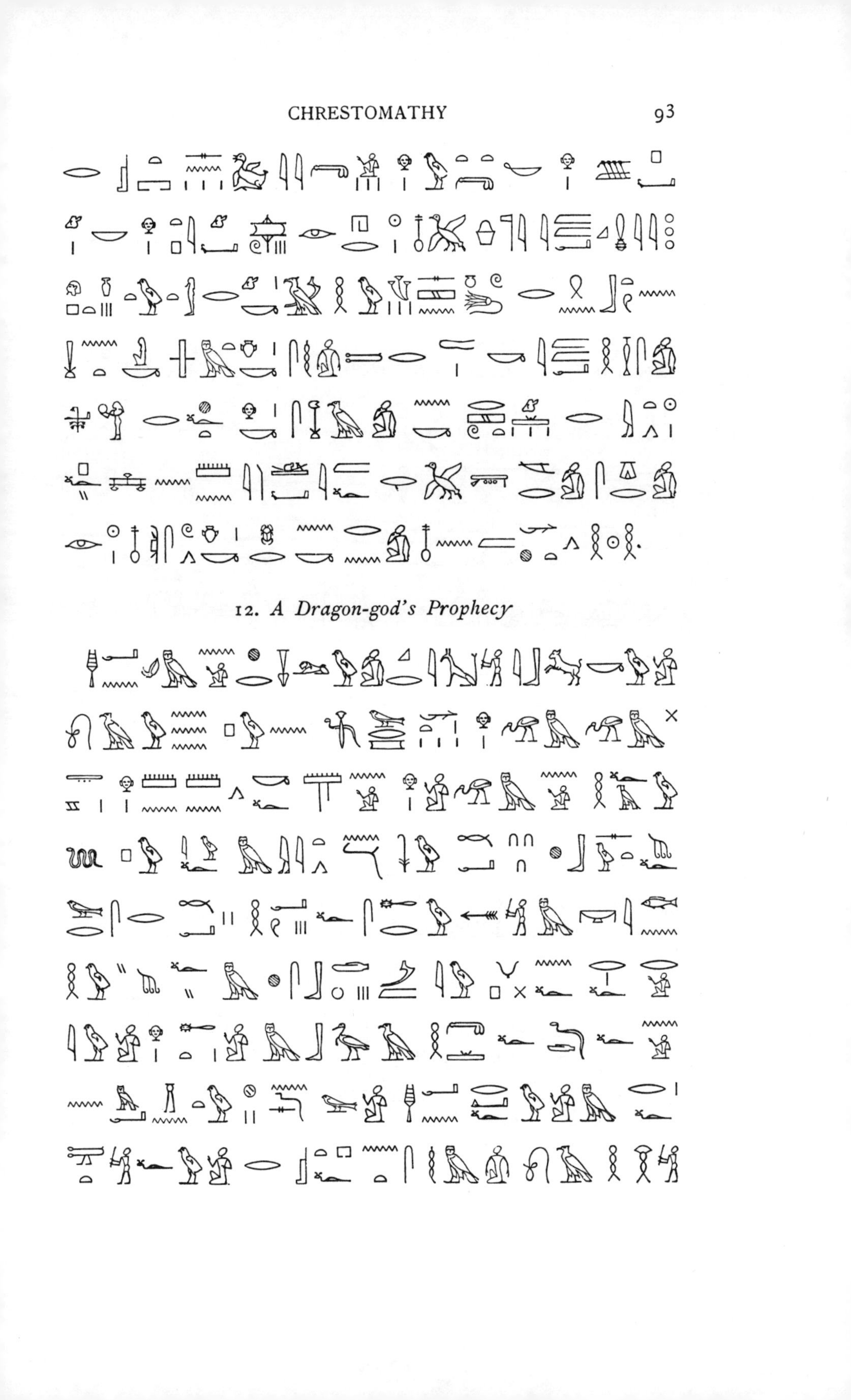

12. *A Dragon-god's Prophecy*

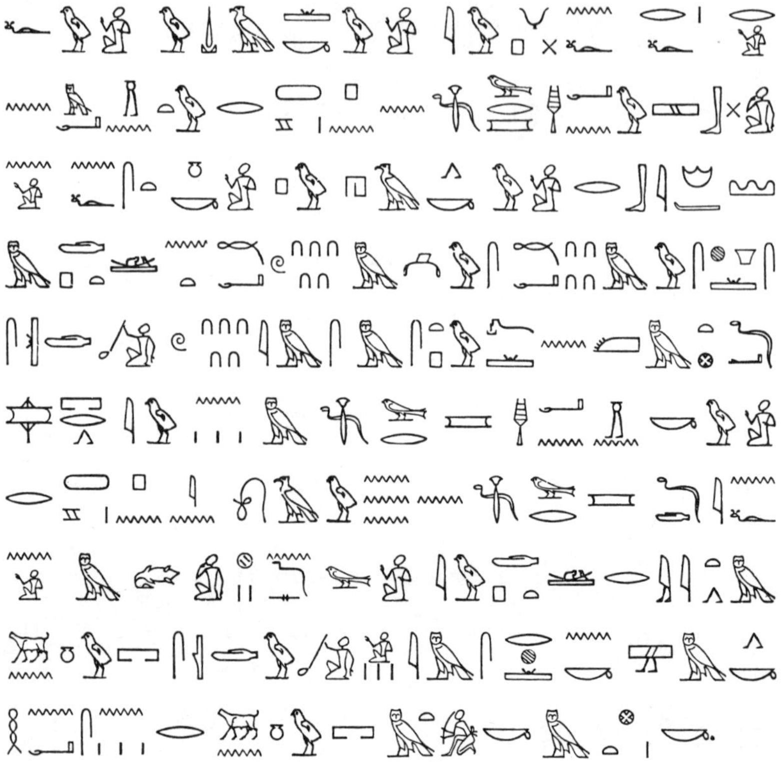

13. *Horus appointed World-ruler*

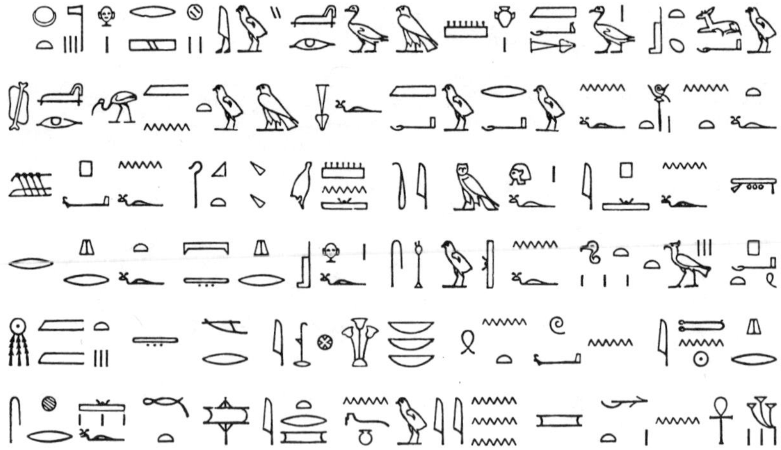

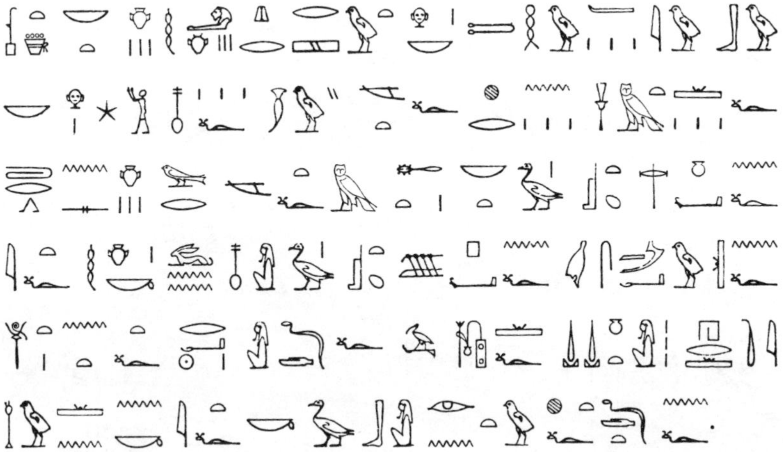

14. *A Hymn to Osiris*

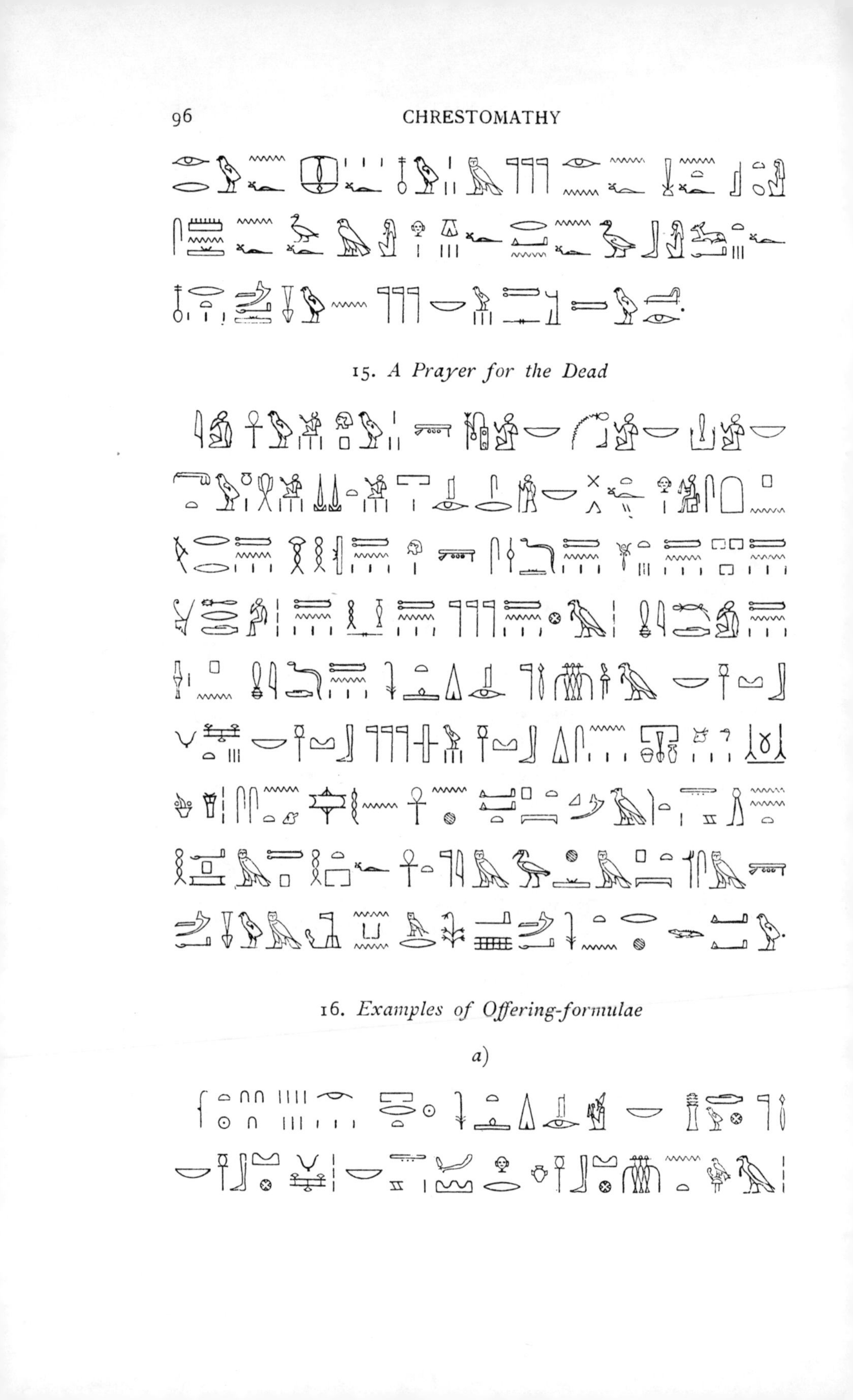

15. *A Prayer for the Dead*

16. *Examples of Offering-formulae*

a)

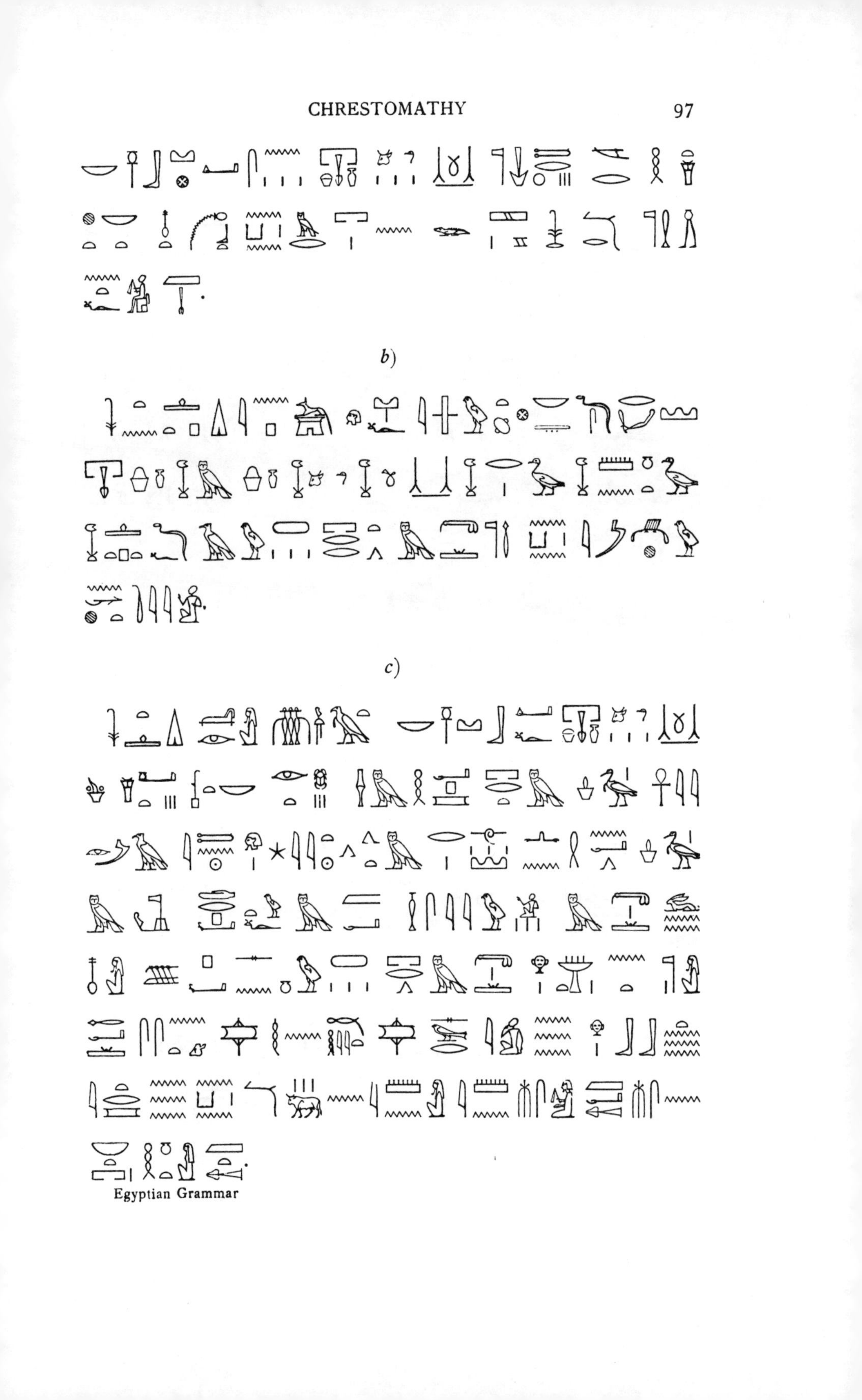

b)

c)

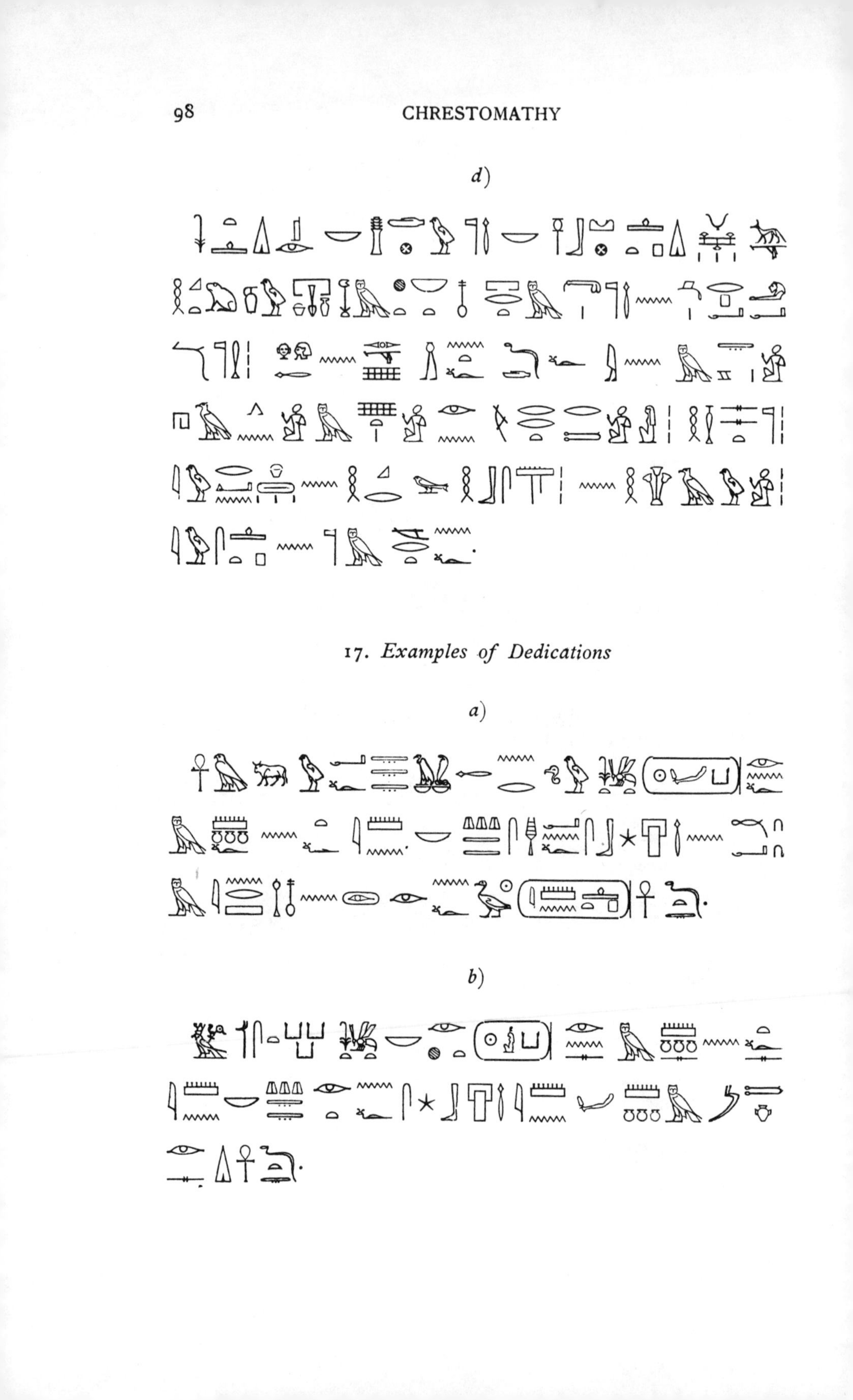

d)

17. *Examples of Dedications*

a)

b)

c)

d)

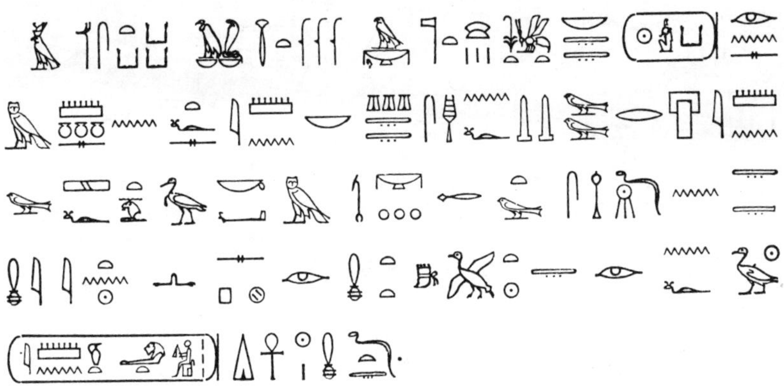

II

Extracts from the Pyramid Texts

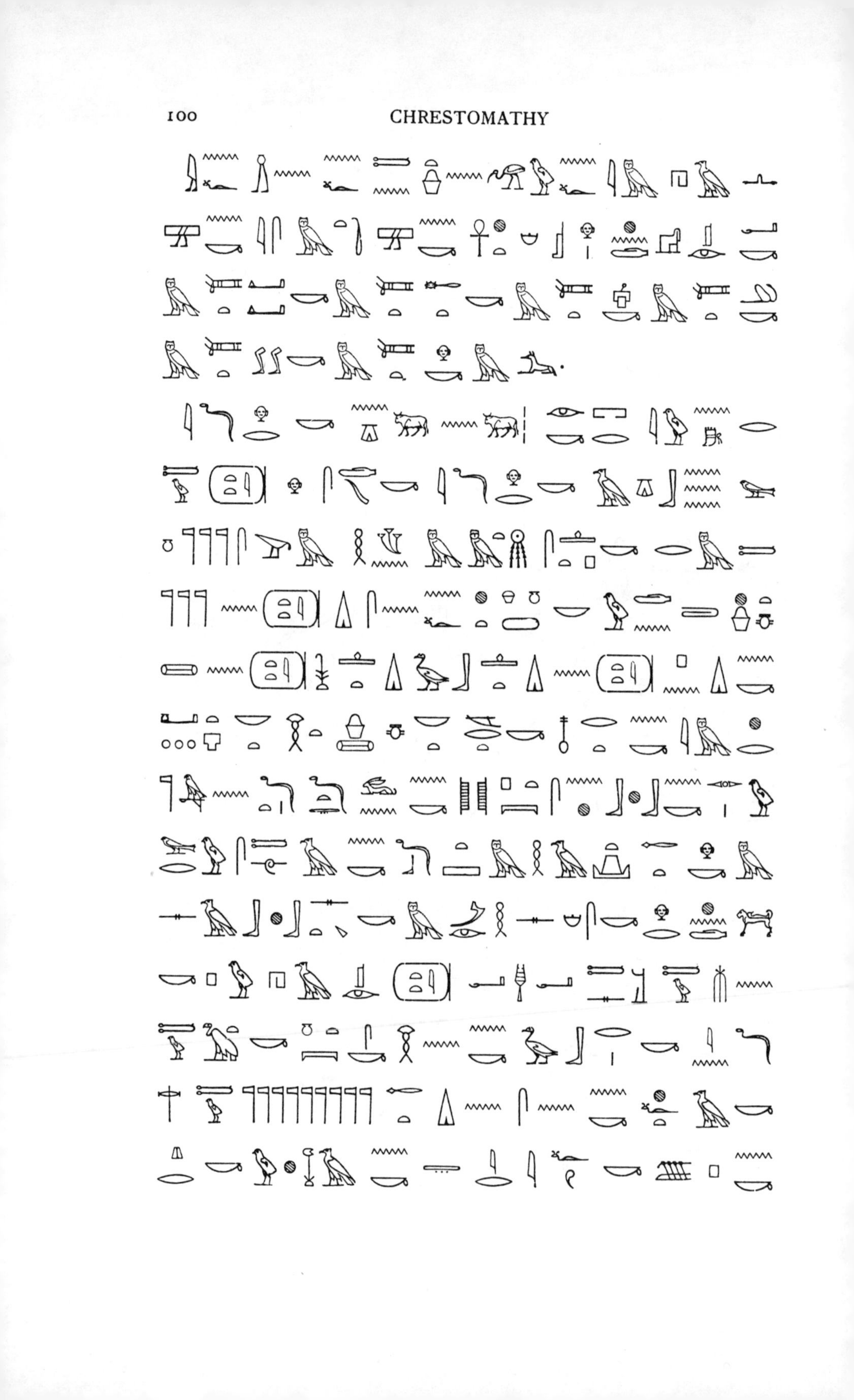

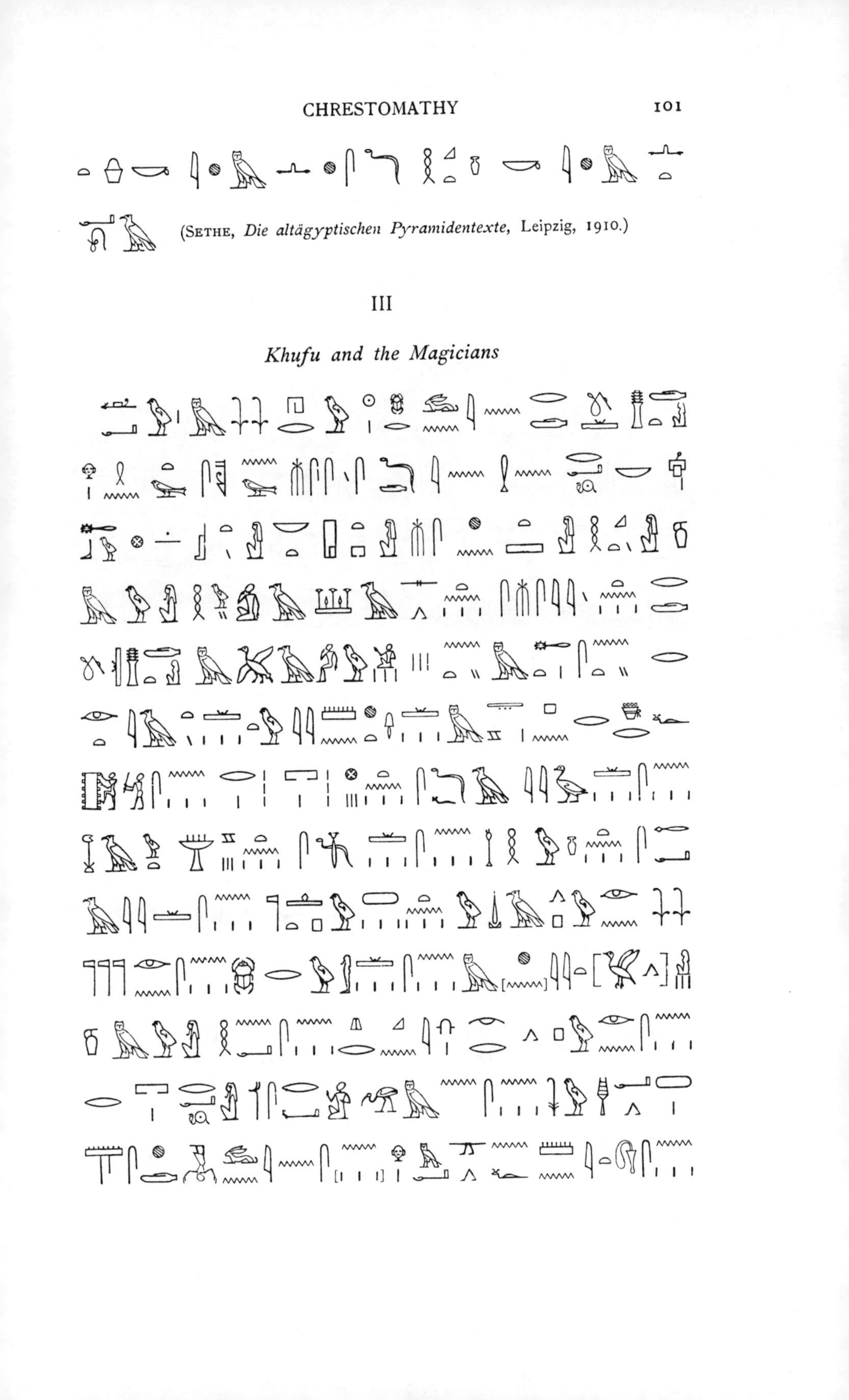

(SETHE, *Die altägyptischen Pyramidentexte*, Leipzig, 1910.)

III

Khufu and the Magicians

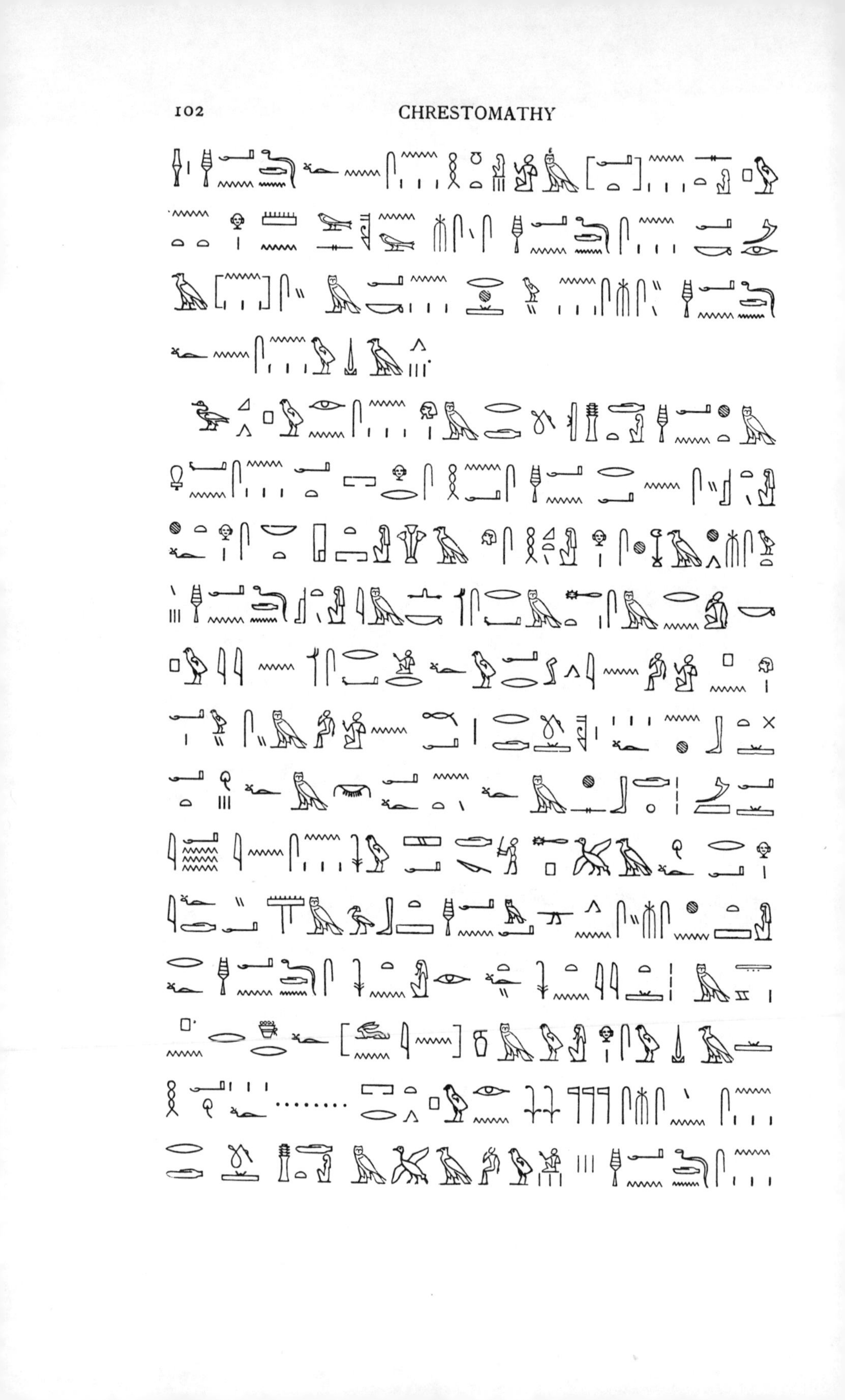

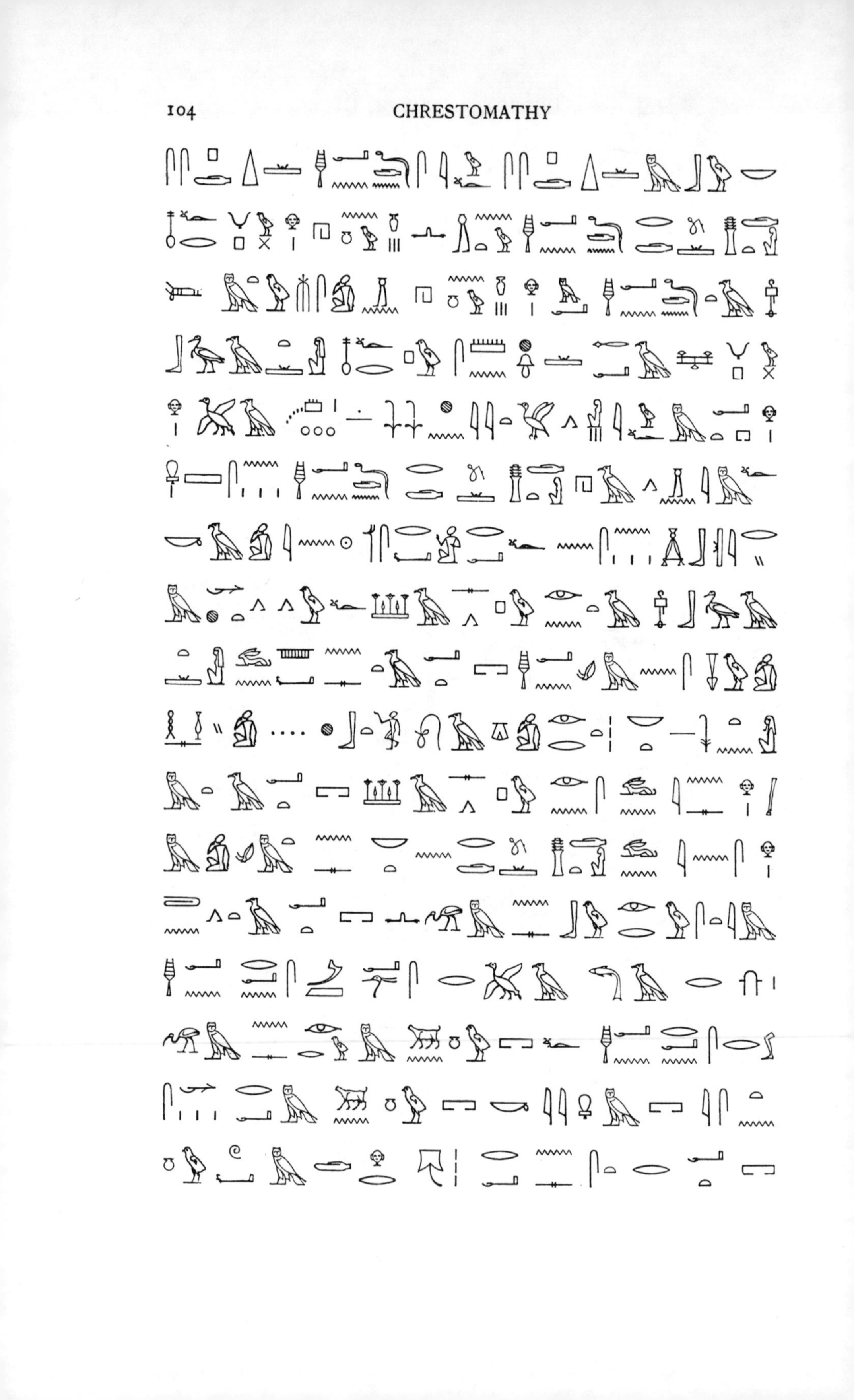

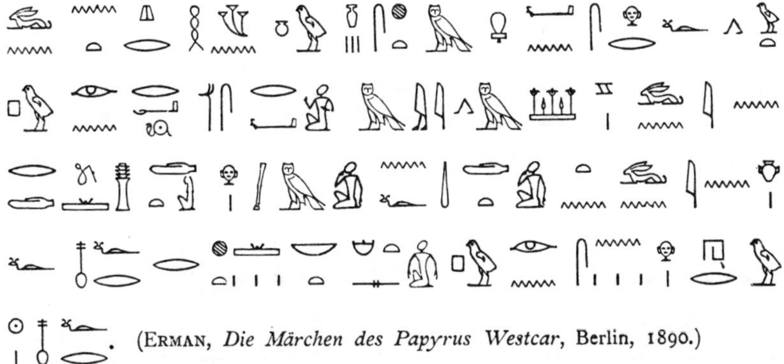

(Erman, *Die Märchen des Papyrus Westcar*, Berlin, 1890.)

IV

From the Precepts of Ptaḥ-Ḥotep

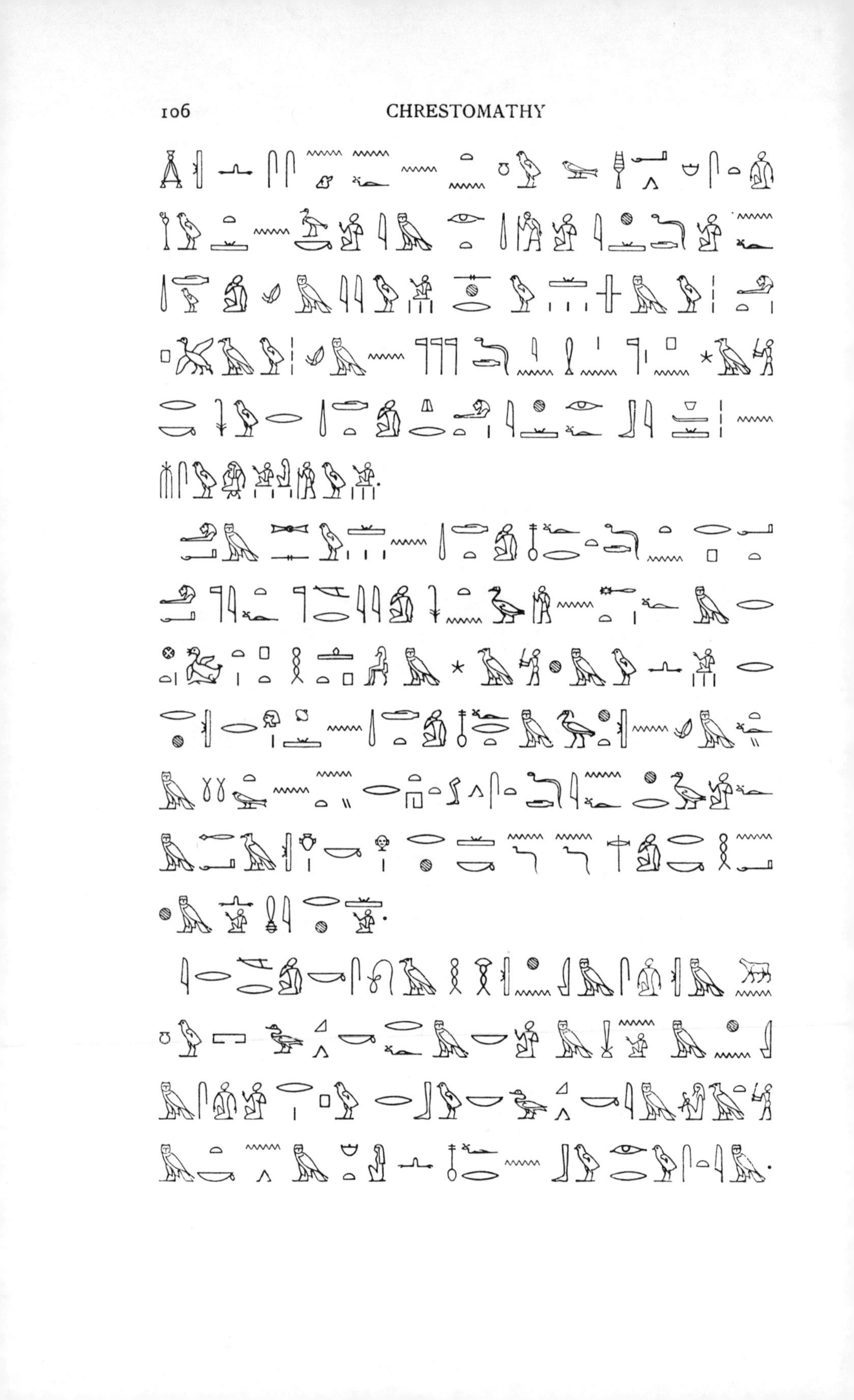

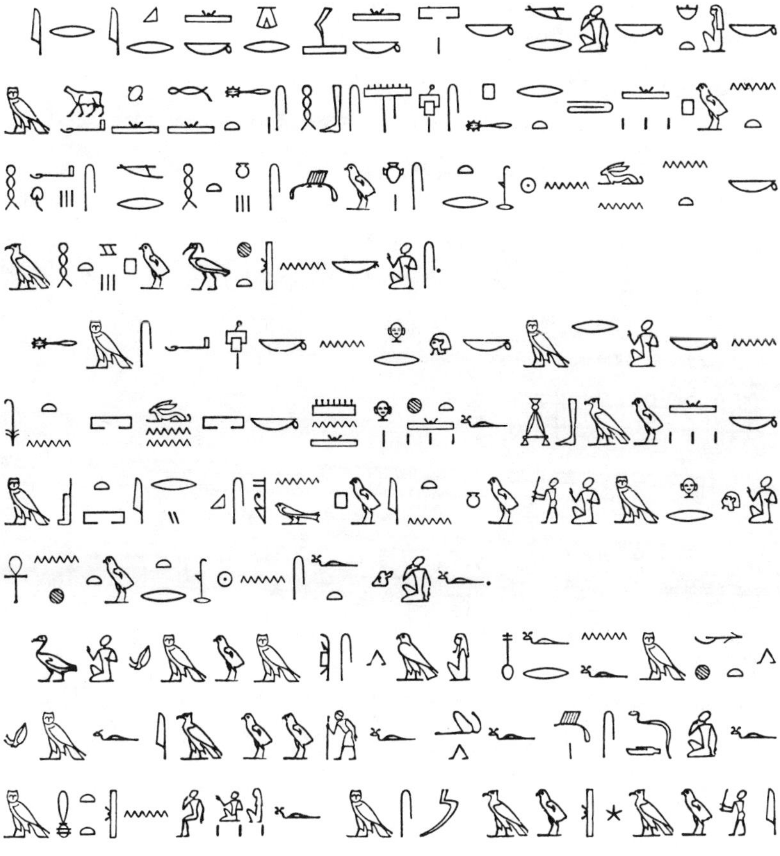

(Dévaud, *Les Maximes de Ptahhotep*, Fribourg, 1916.)

V

From the Eloquent Peasant

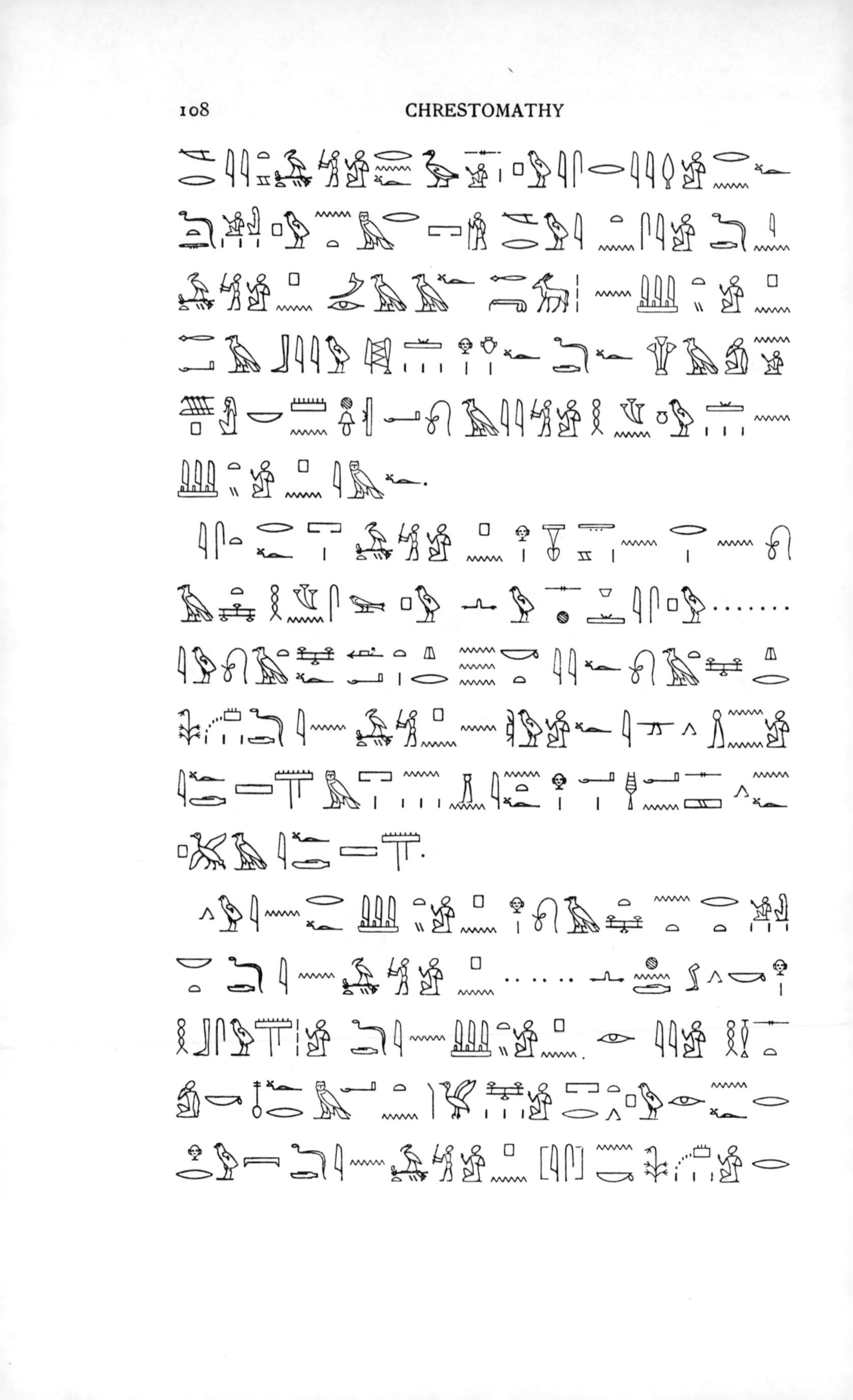

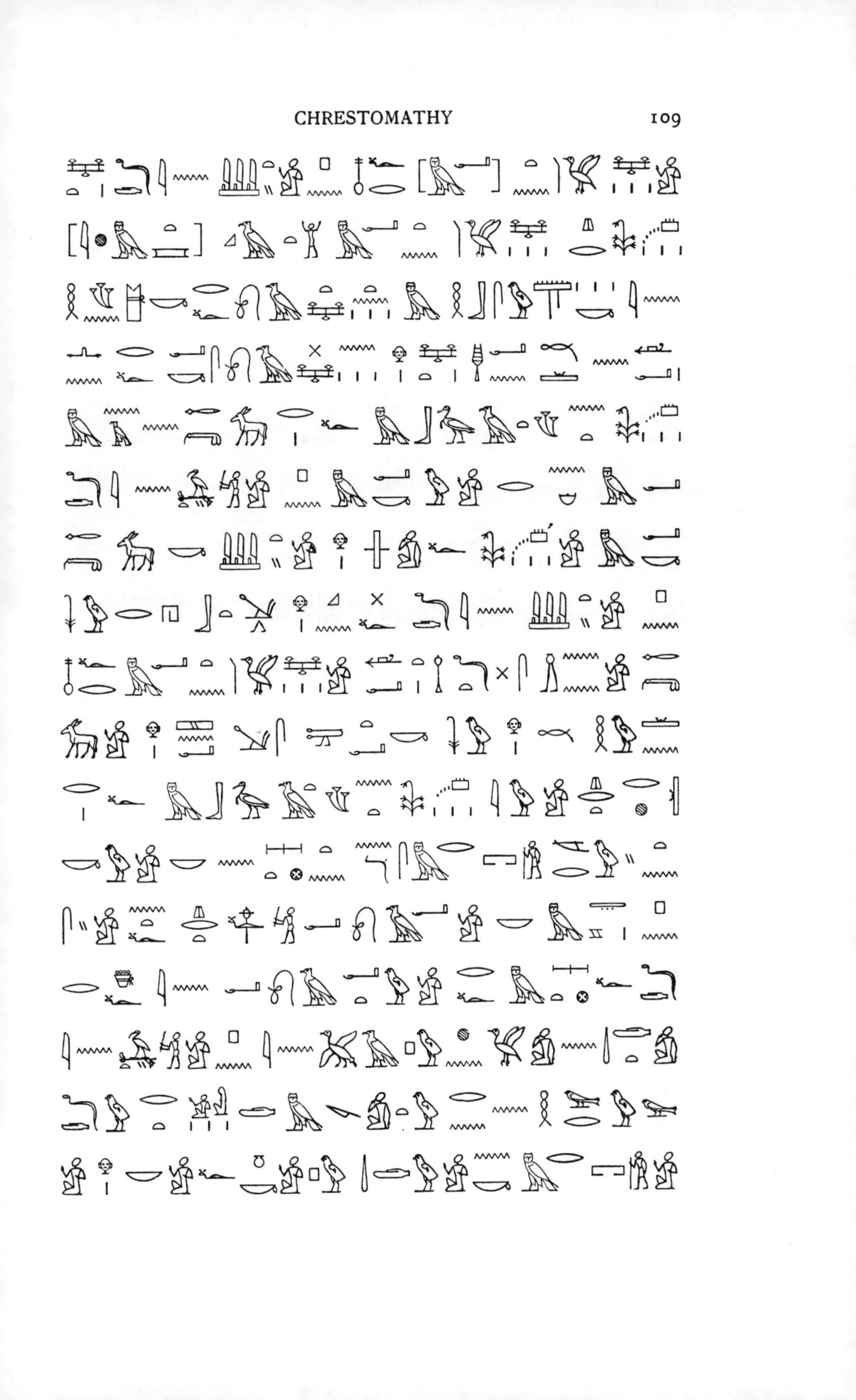

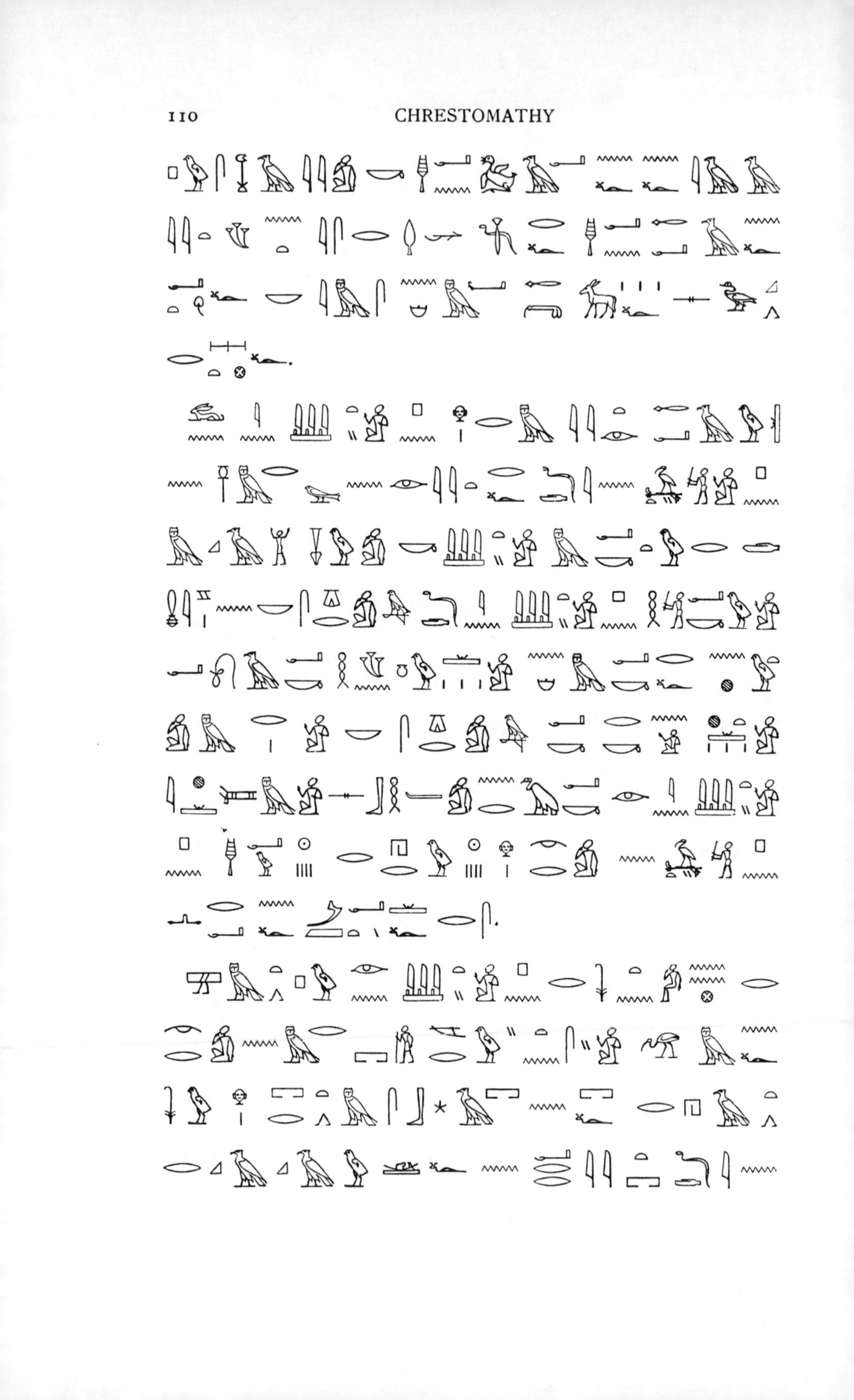

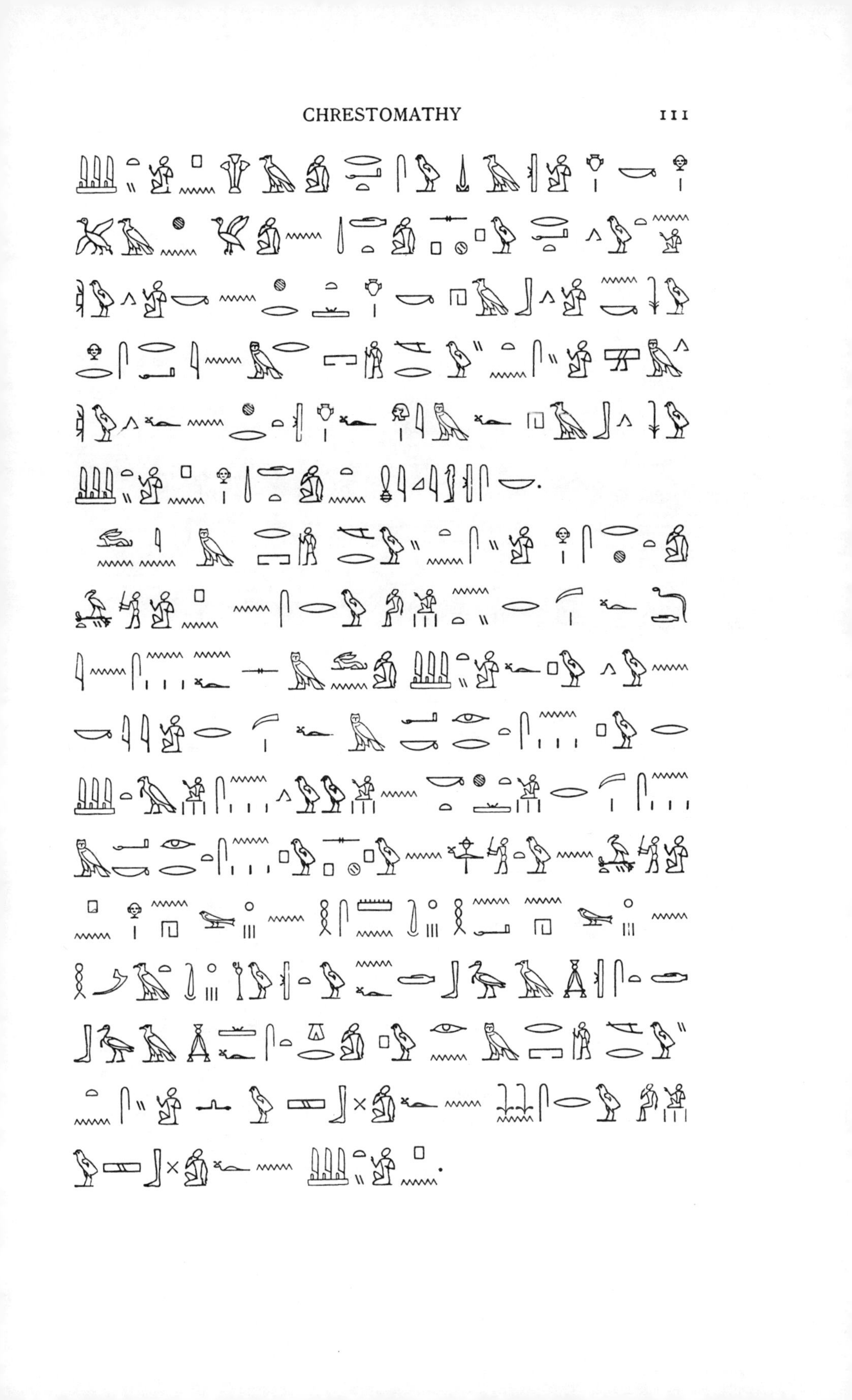

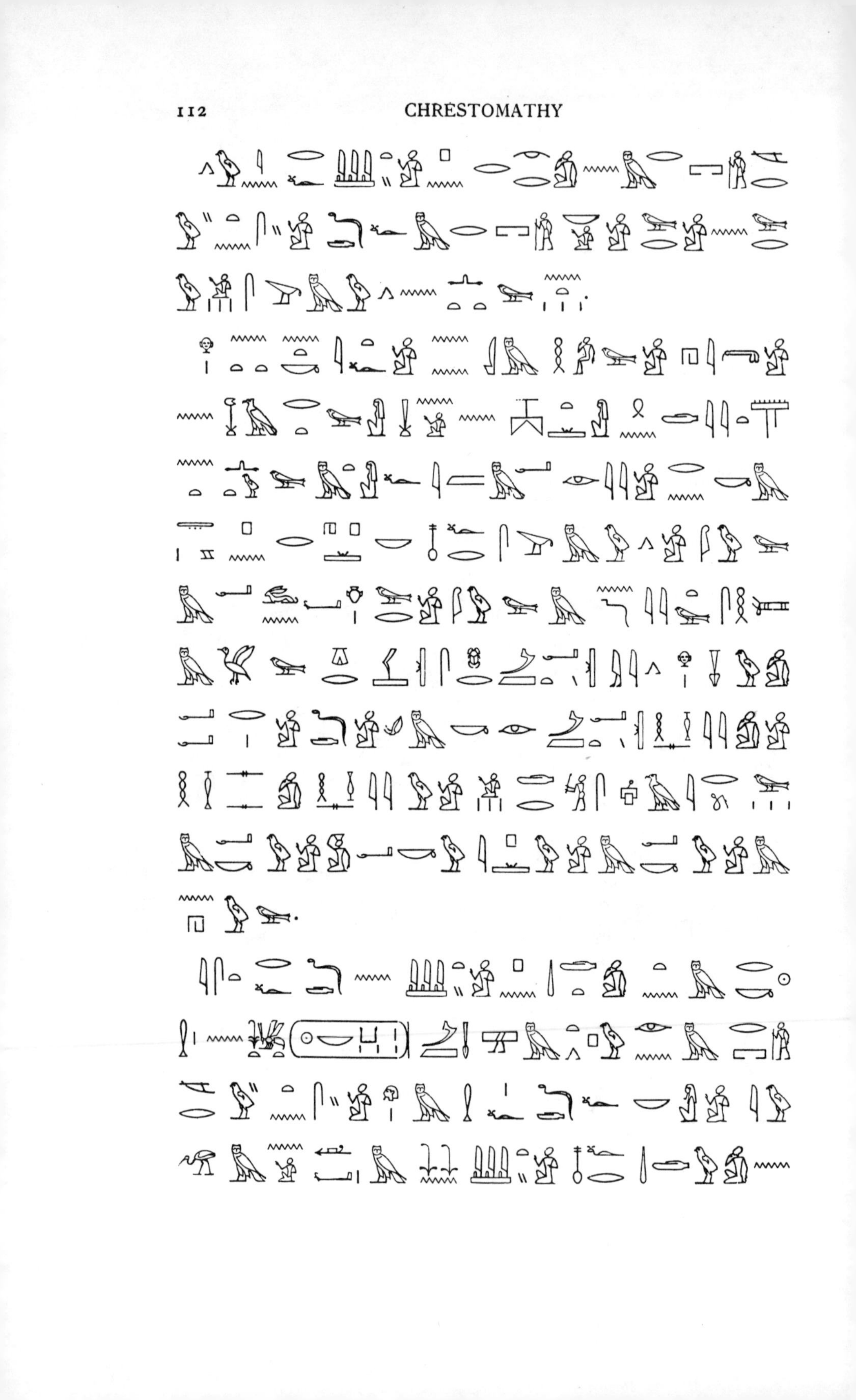

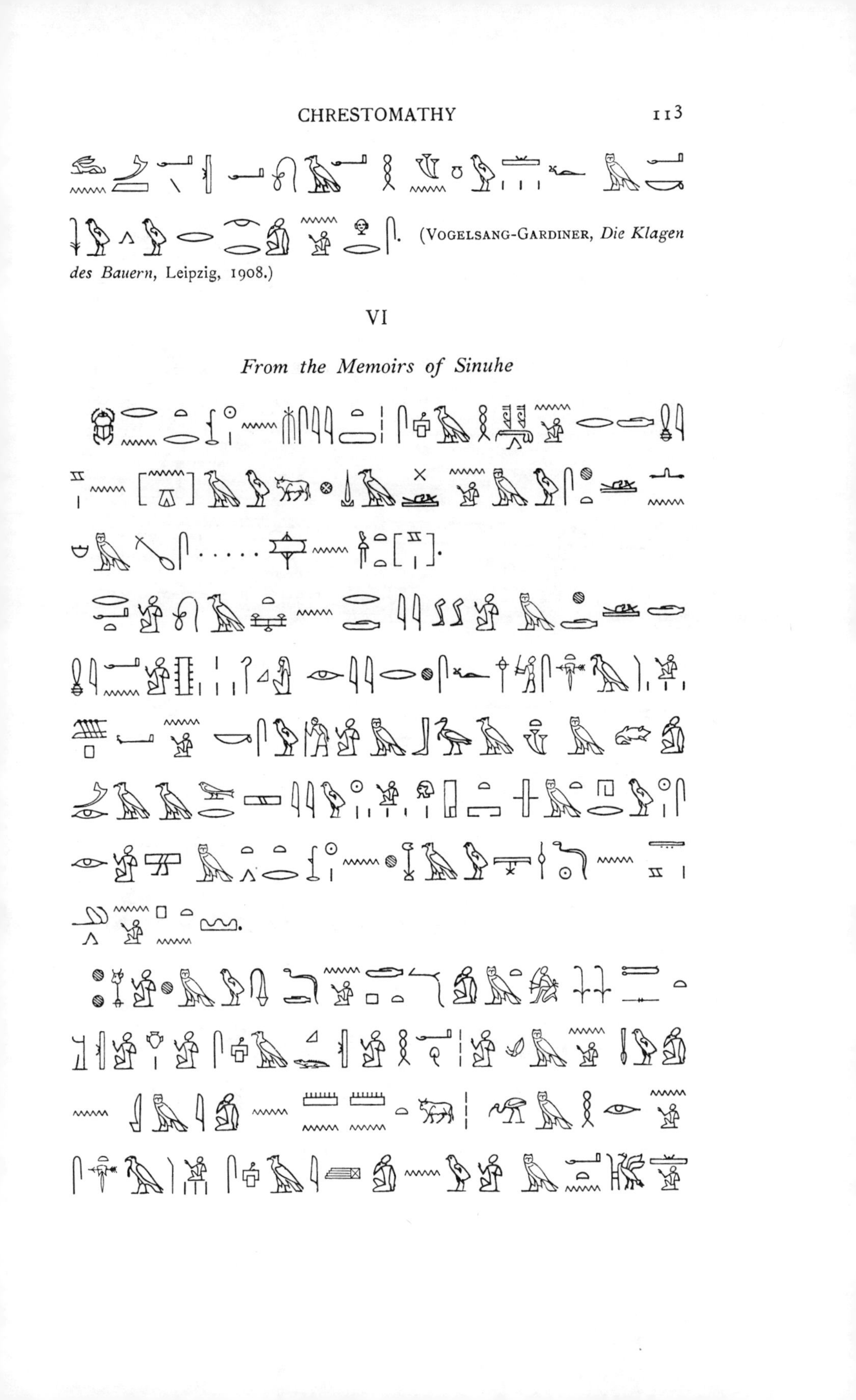

(VOGELSANG-GARDINER, *Die Klagen des Bauern*, Leipzig, 1908.)

VI

From the Memoirs of Sinuhe

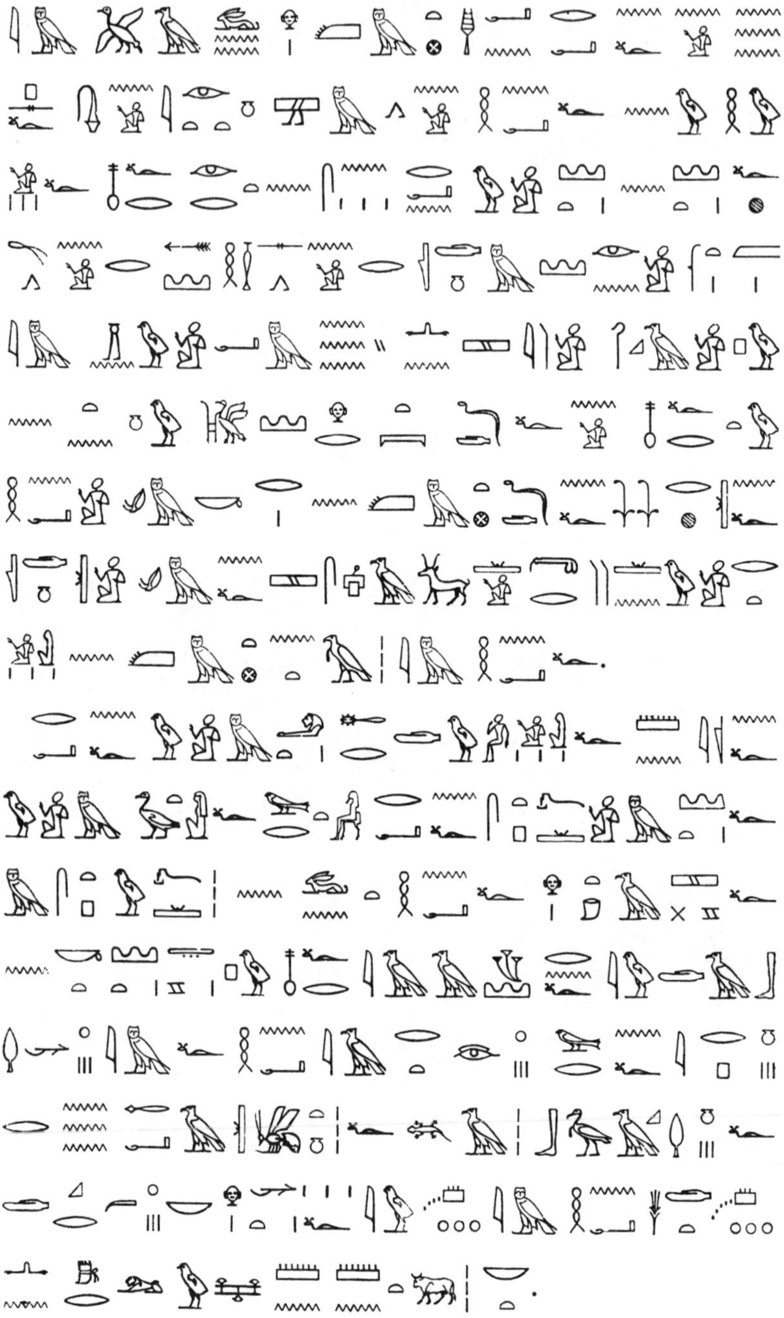

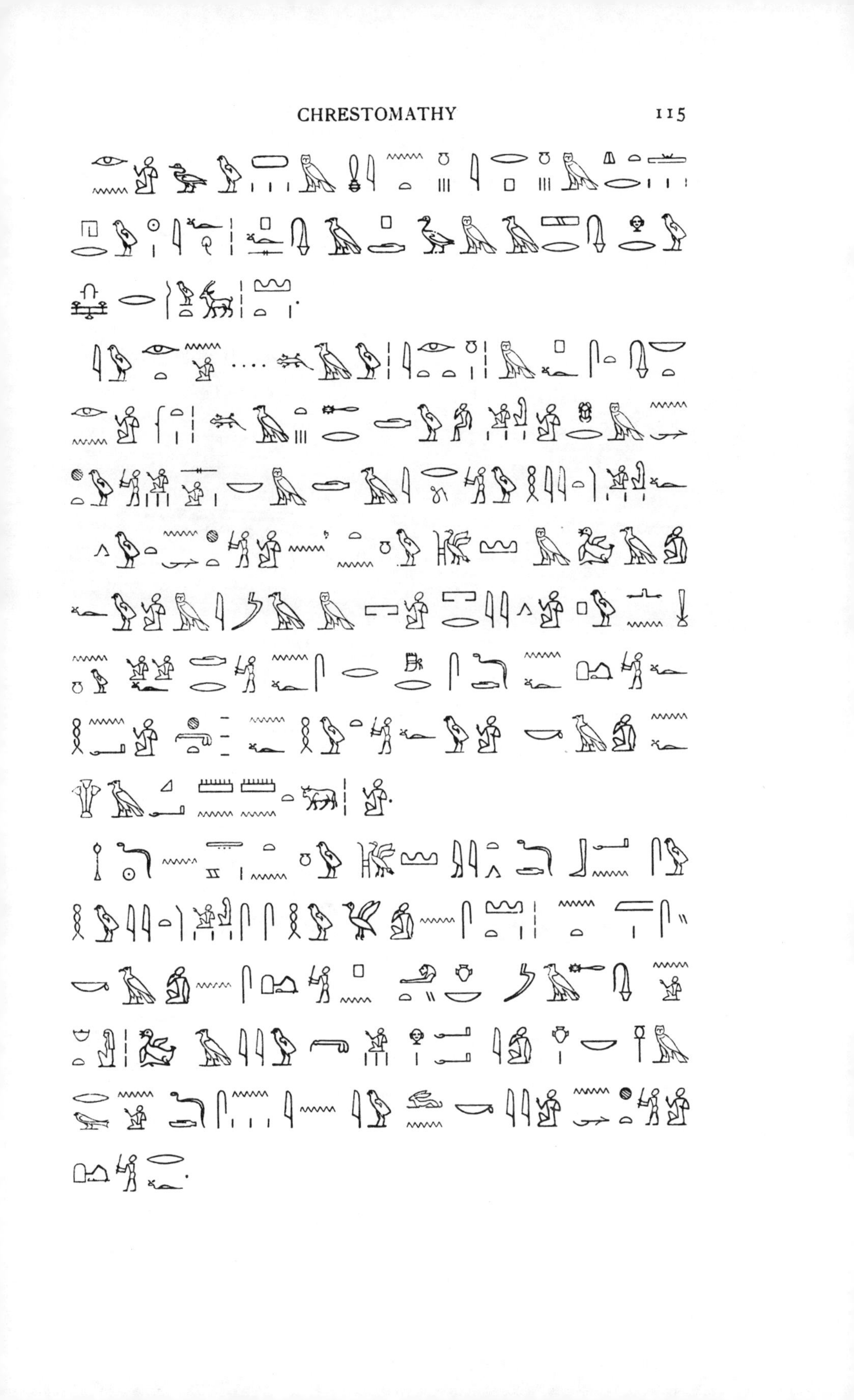

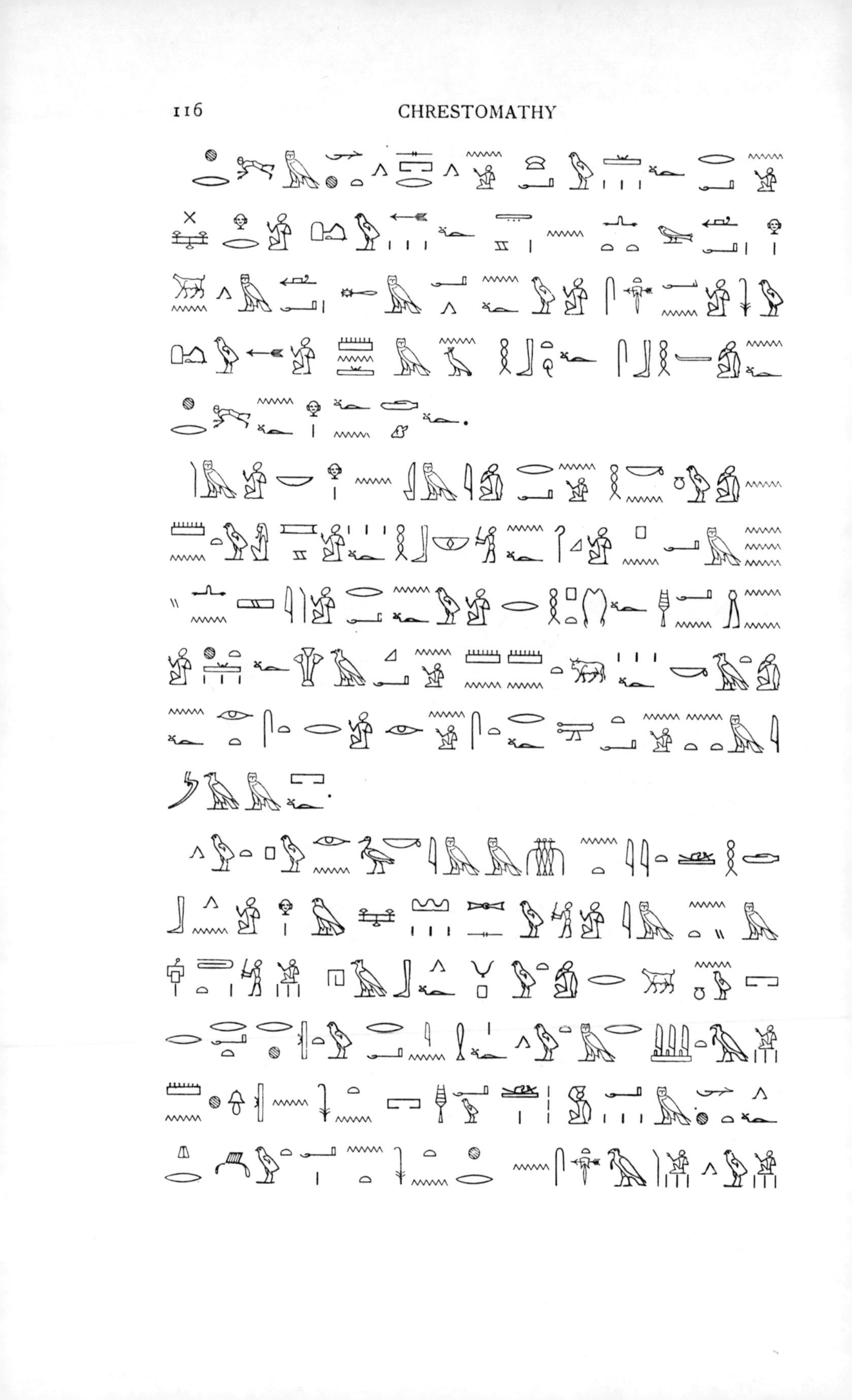

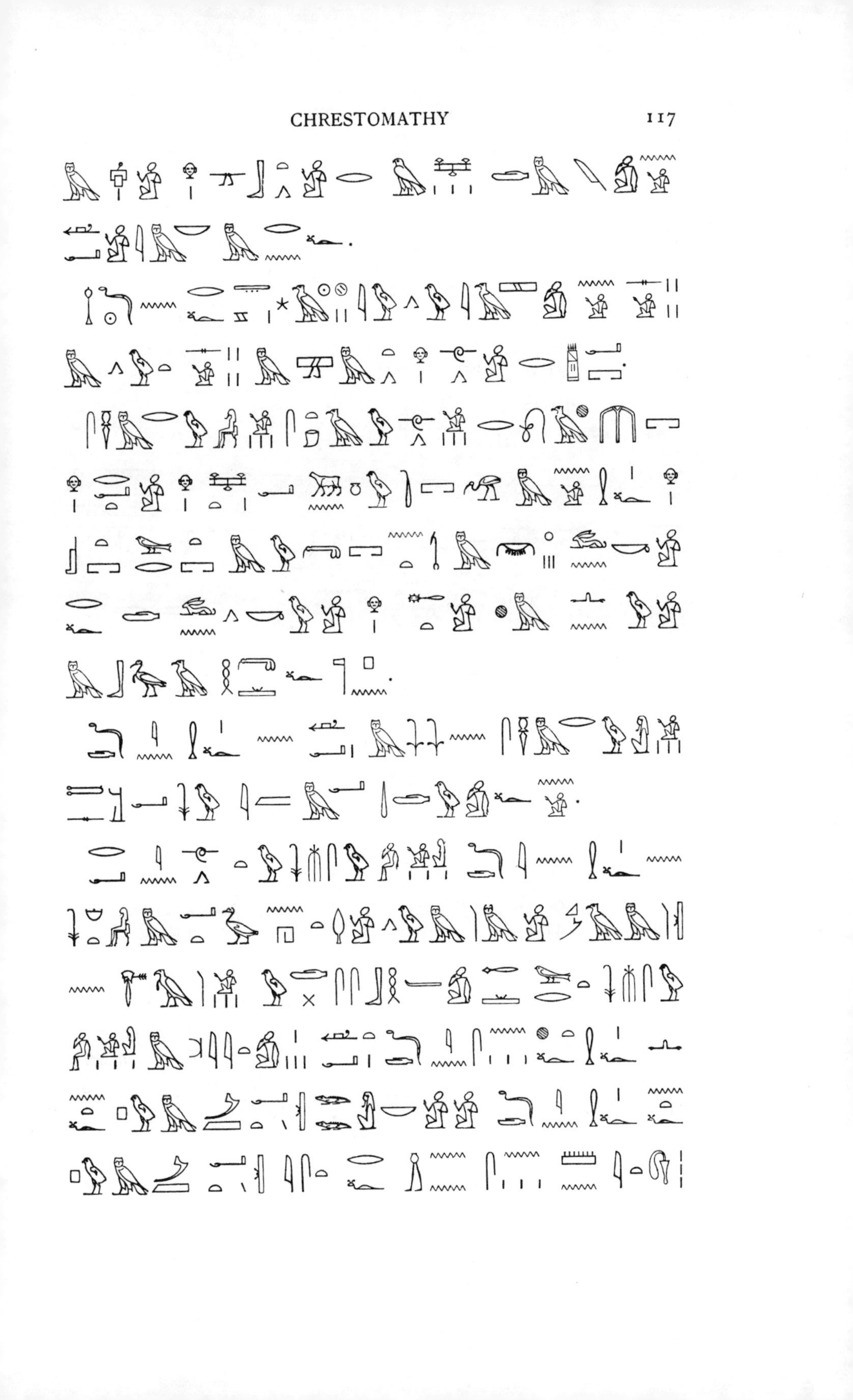

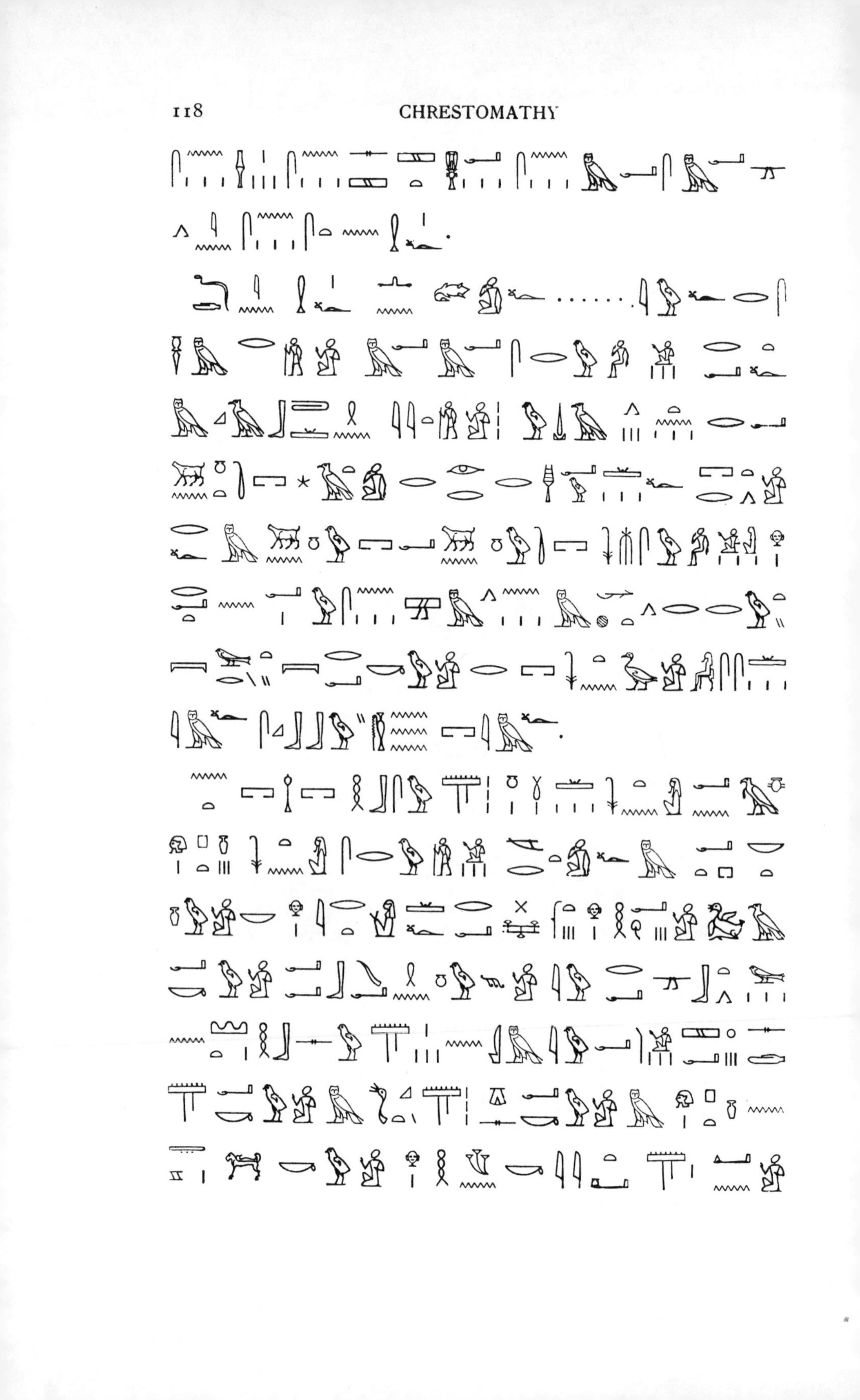

(GARDINER, *Die Erzählung des Sinuhe und die Hirtengeschichte*, Leipzig, 1909.)

VII

*The Tale of the Two Brothers**

I. — 1. [ ] 2. [ ]

* This later text is used because it illustrates the transition from Classical to New Egyptian.

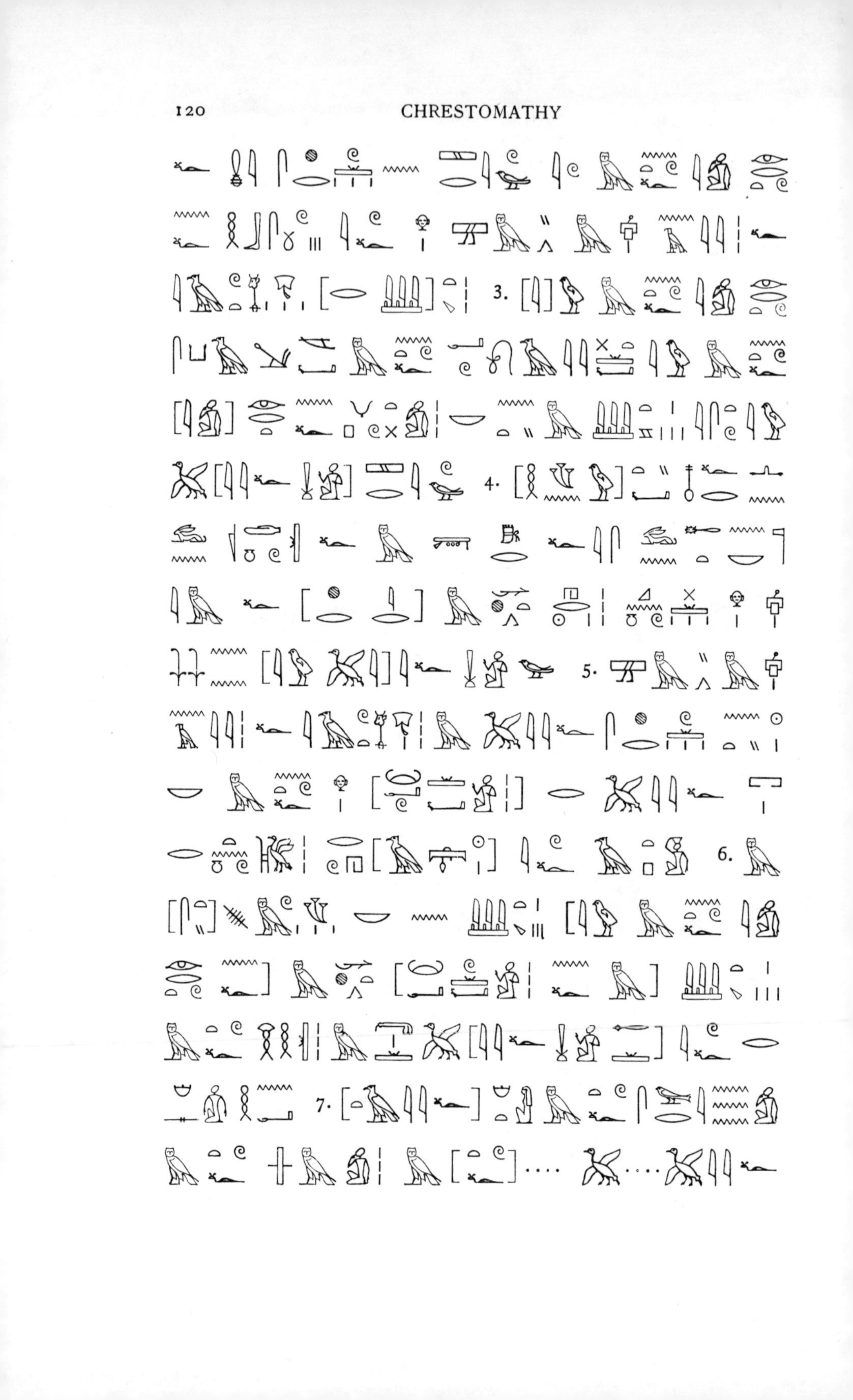

8. . .

. . . . . .

9. (?)

10.

11. — 1.

2.

3.

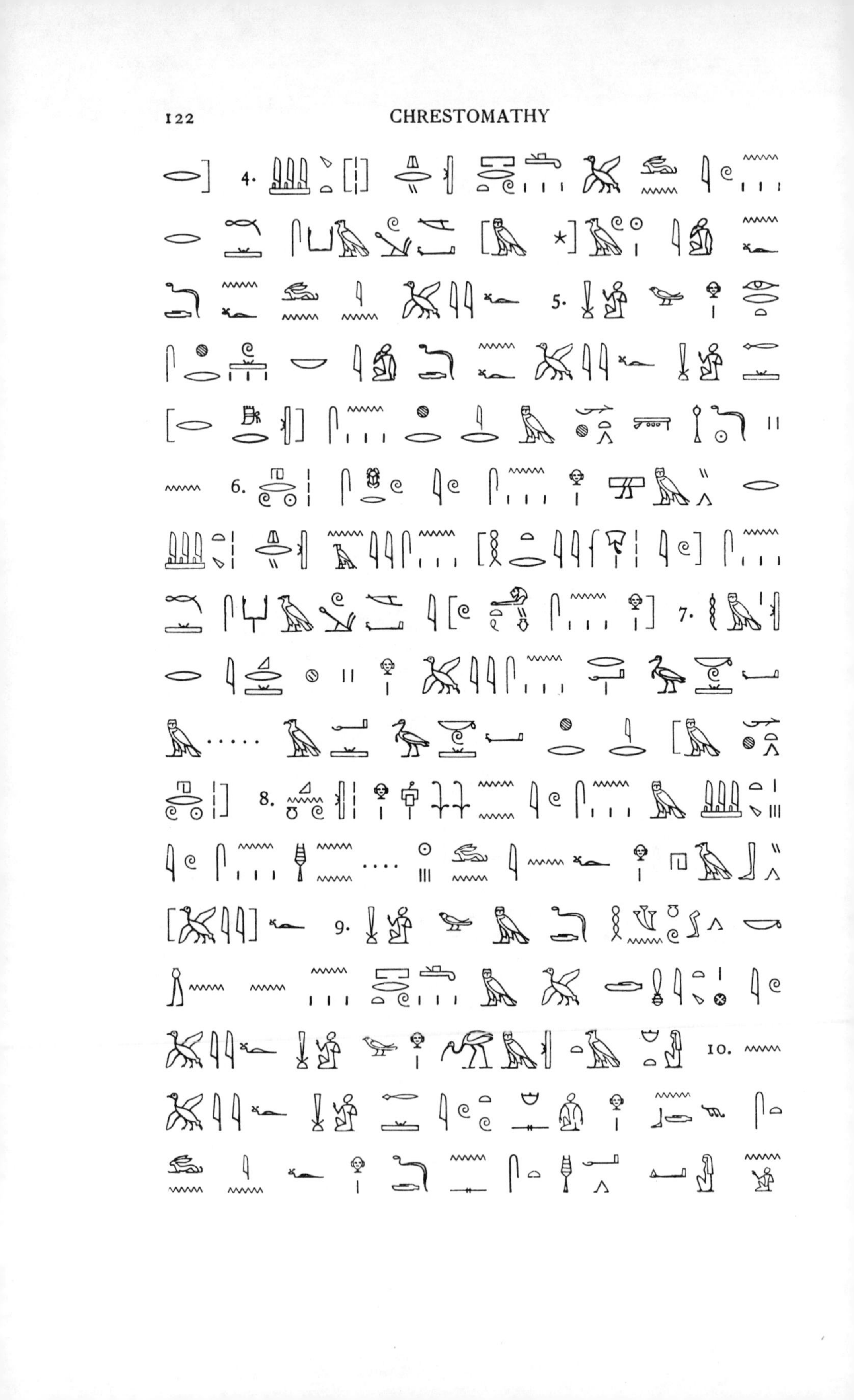

4.

5.

6.

7.

8.

9.

10.

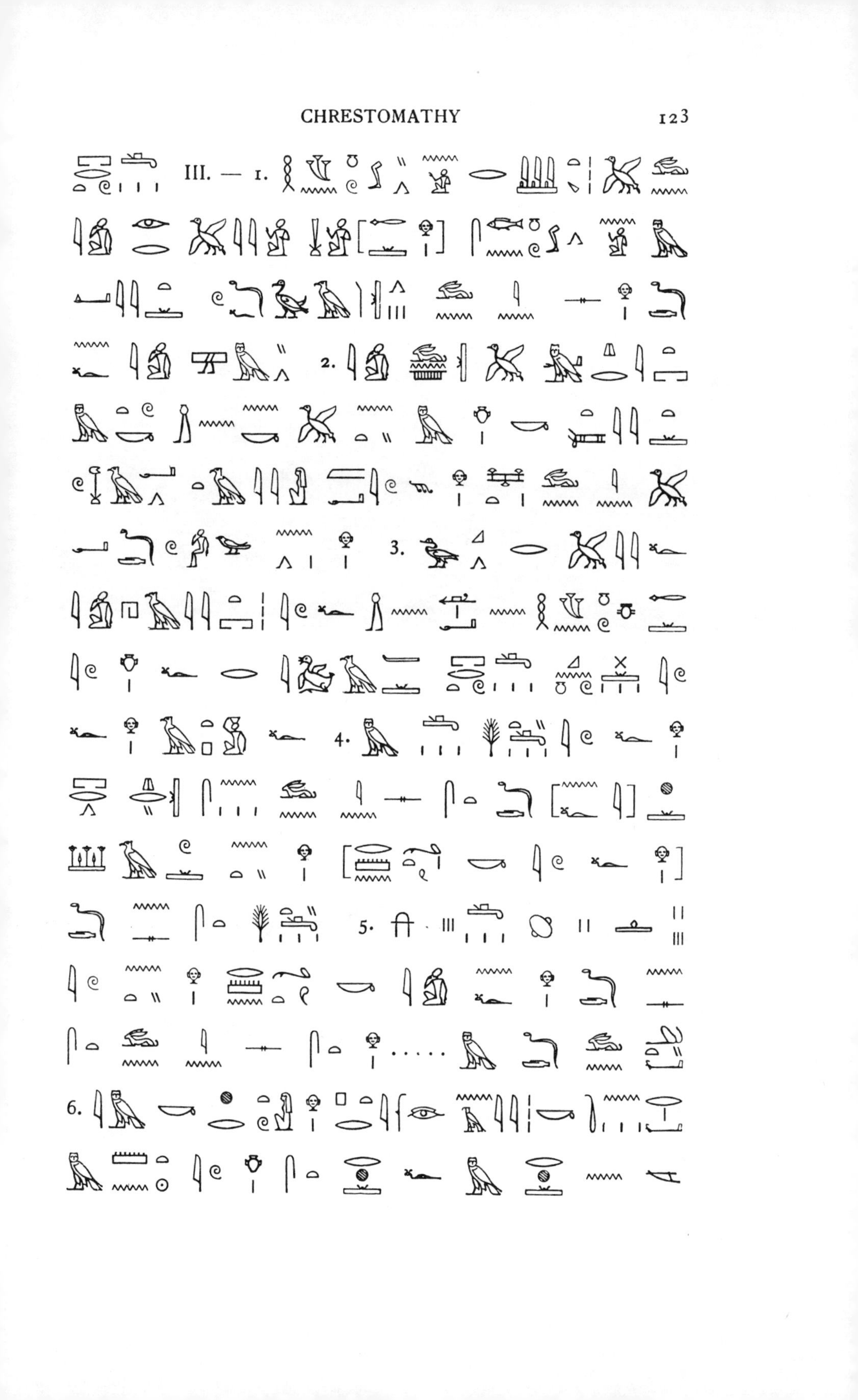

III. — 1.

2.

3.

4.

5.

6.

. . . . . 7.

8.

. . . . . . 9.

10.

IV. — 1.

(?)

2.

(?) 3.

4.

5.

6.

7.

8.

9.

10.

V. — 1.

2.

3.

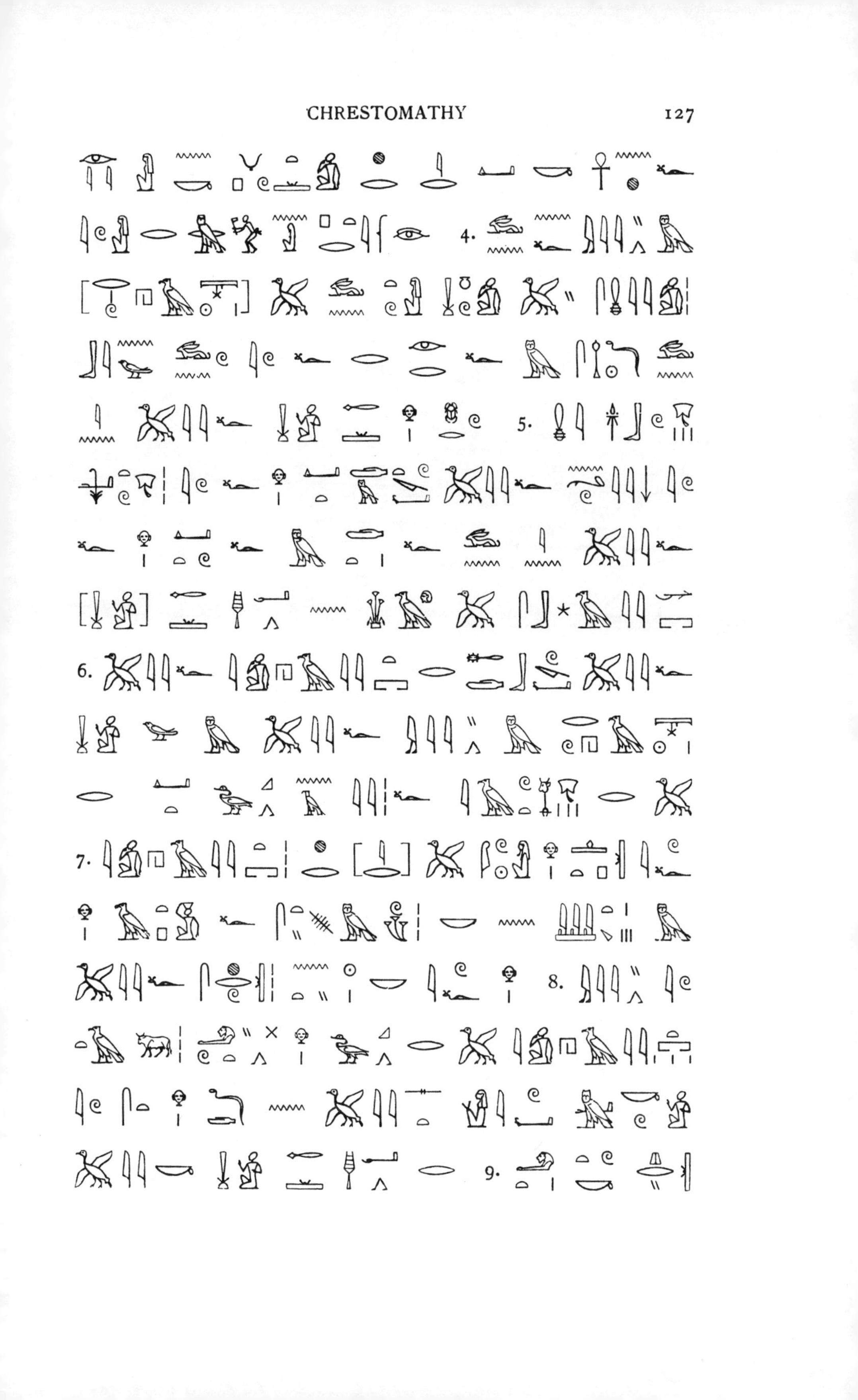

4.

5.

6.

7.

8.

9.

VI. — 1.

2.

3.

4.

5.

6.

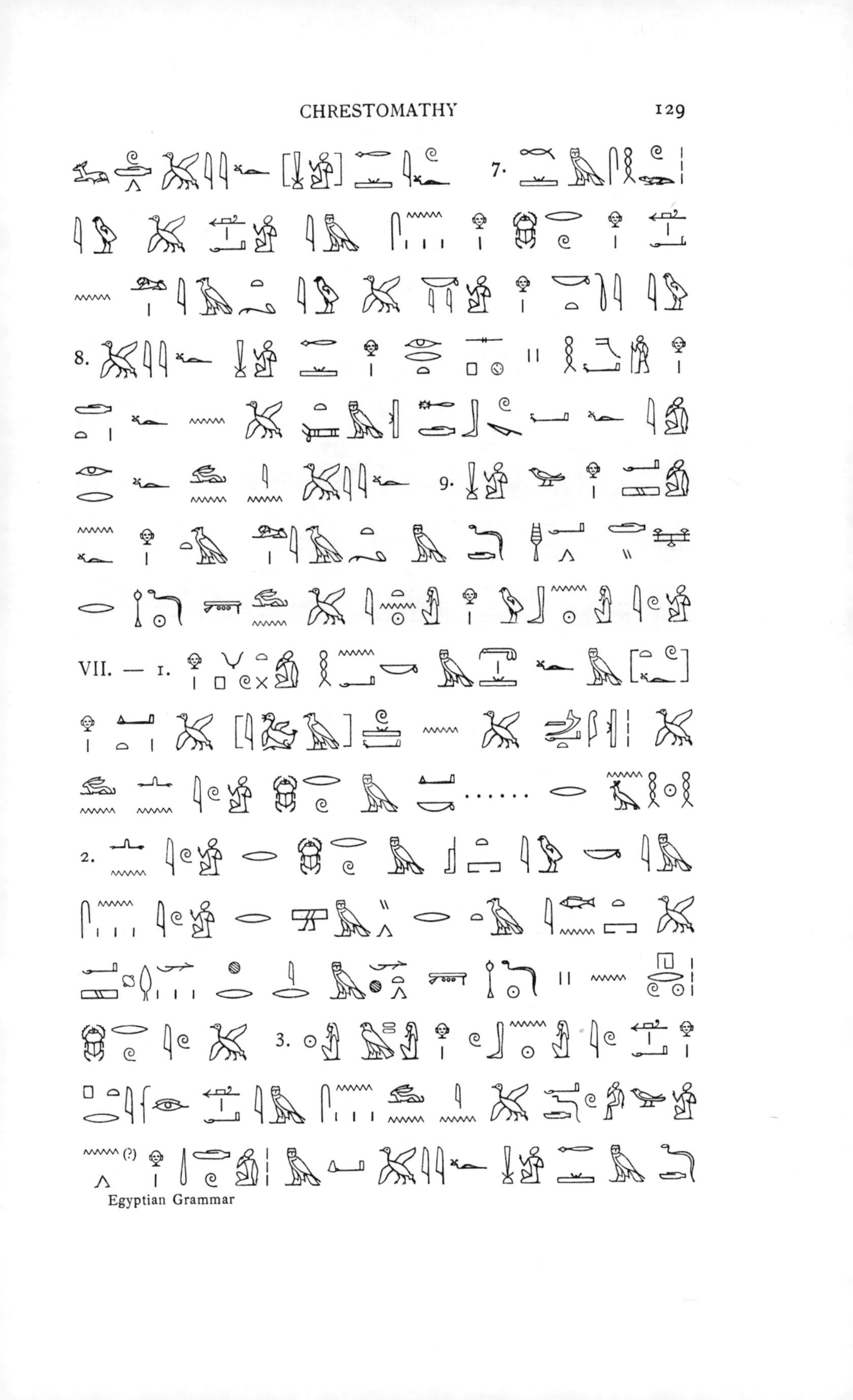

7.

8.

9.

VII. — 1.

2.

3.

(?)

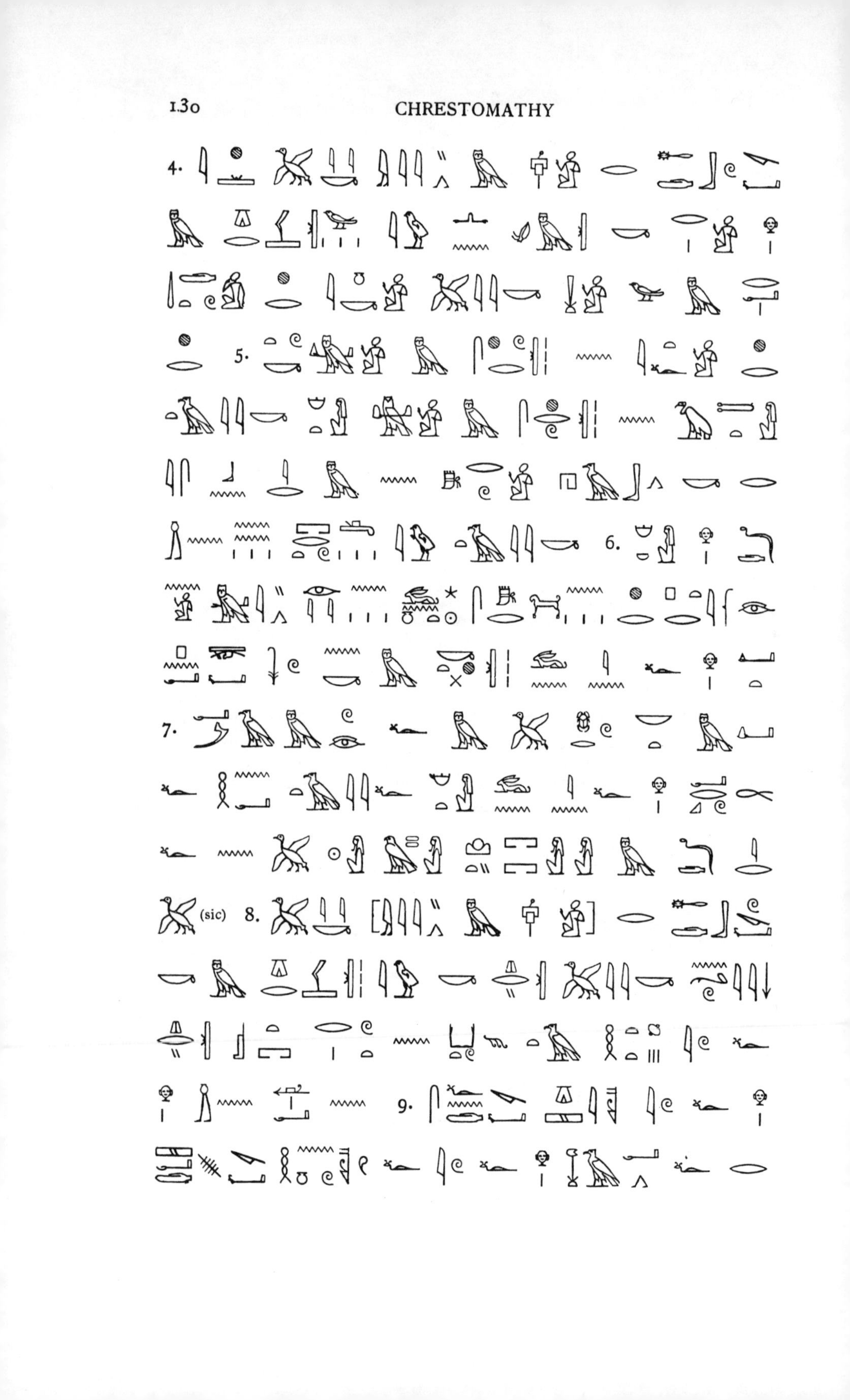

4.

5.

6.

7.

(sic) 8.

9.

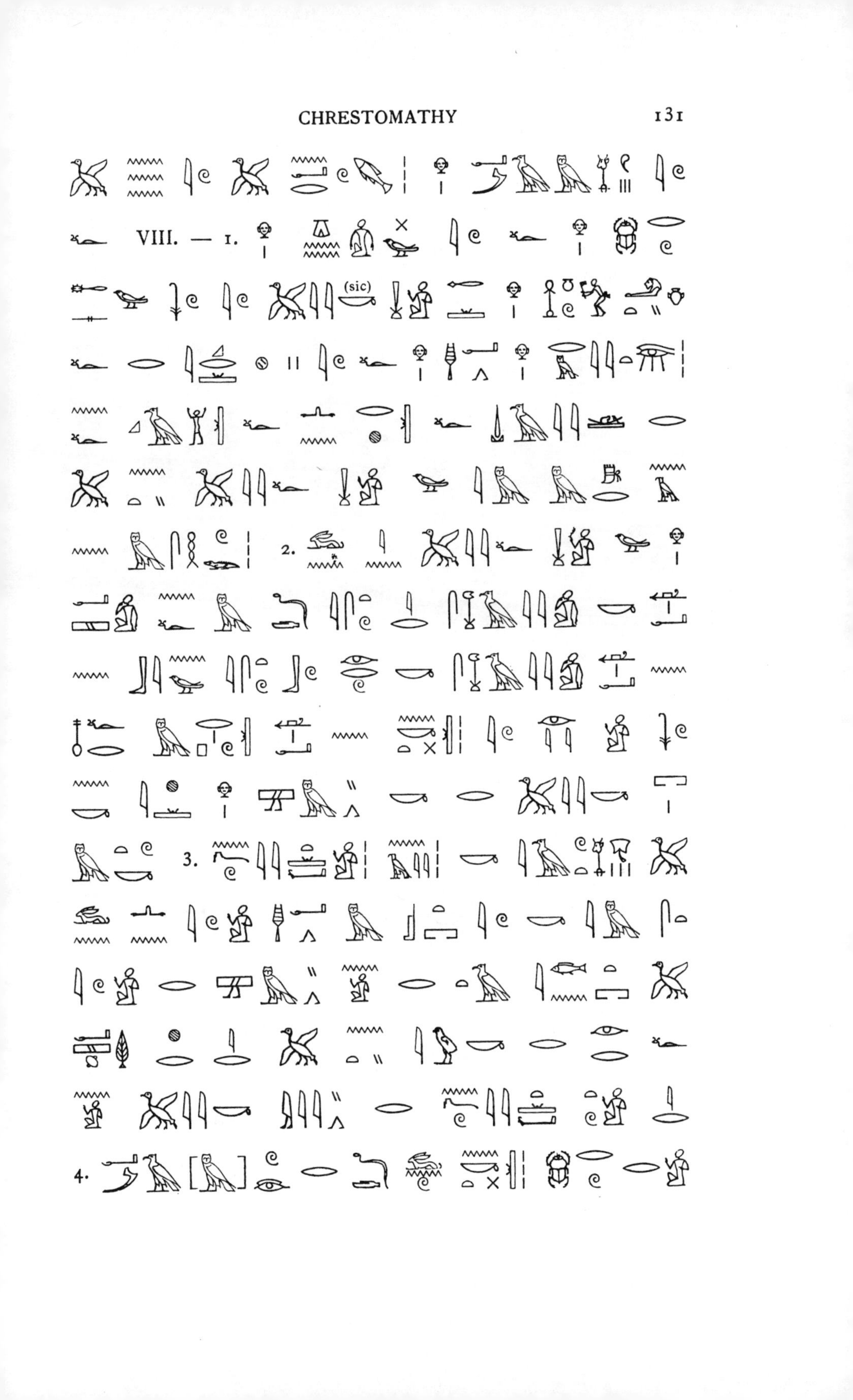

VIII. — 1.

(sic)

2.

3.

4.

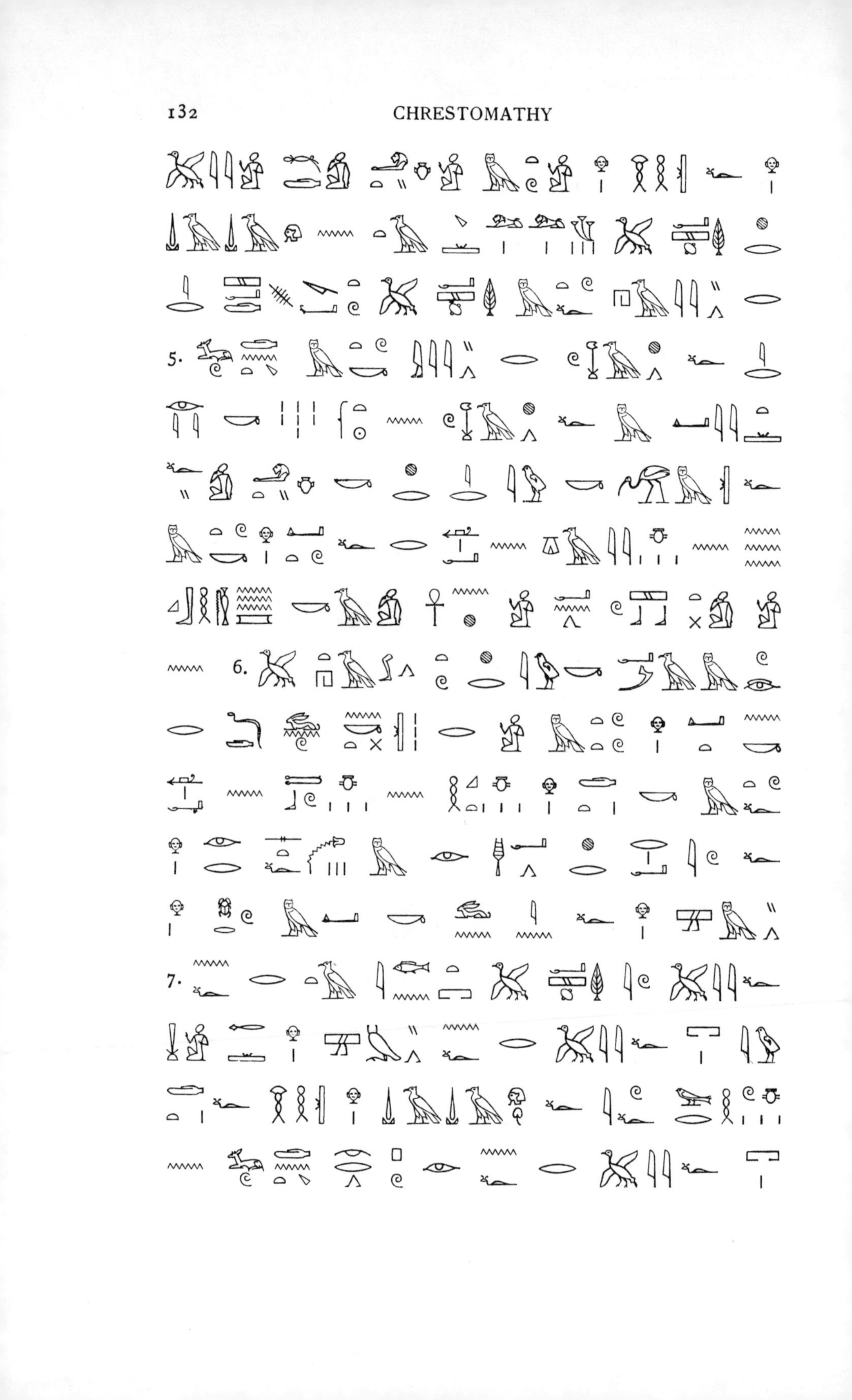

5.

6.

7.

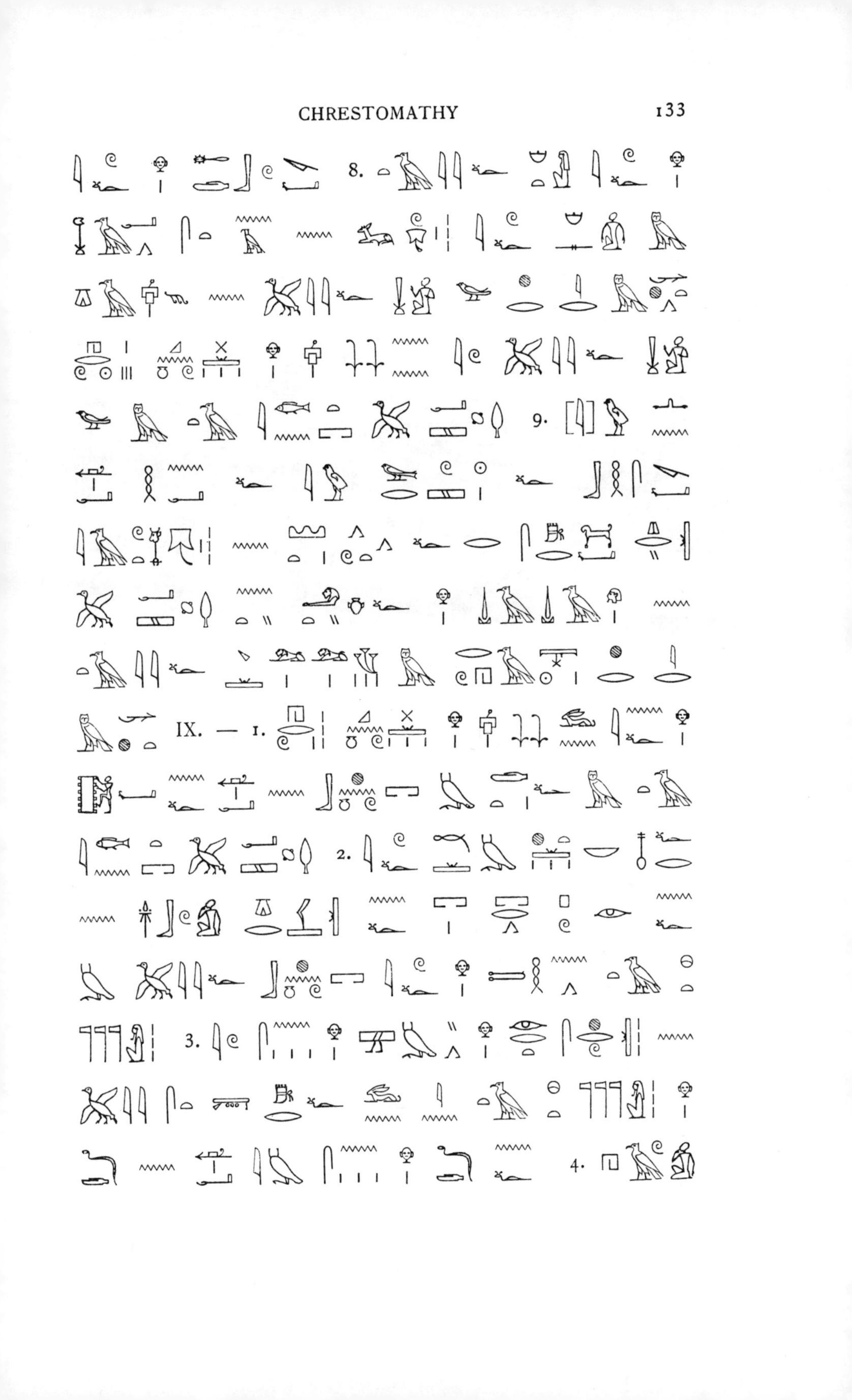

8.

9.

IX. — 1.

2.

3.

4.

5.

6.

7.

8.

9.

X. — 1.

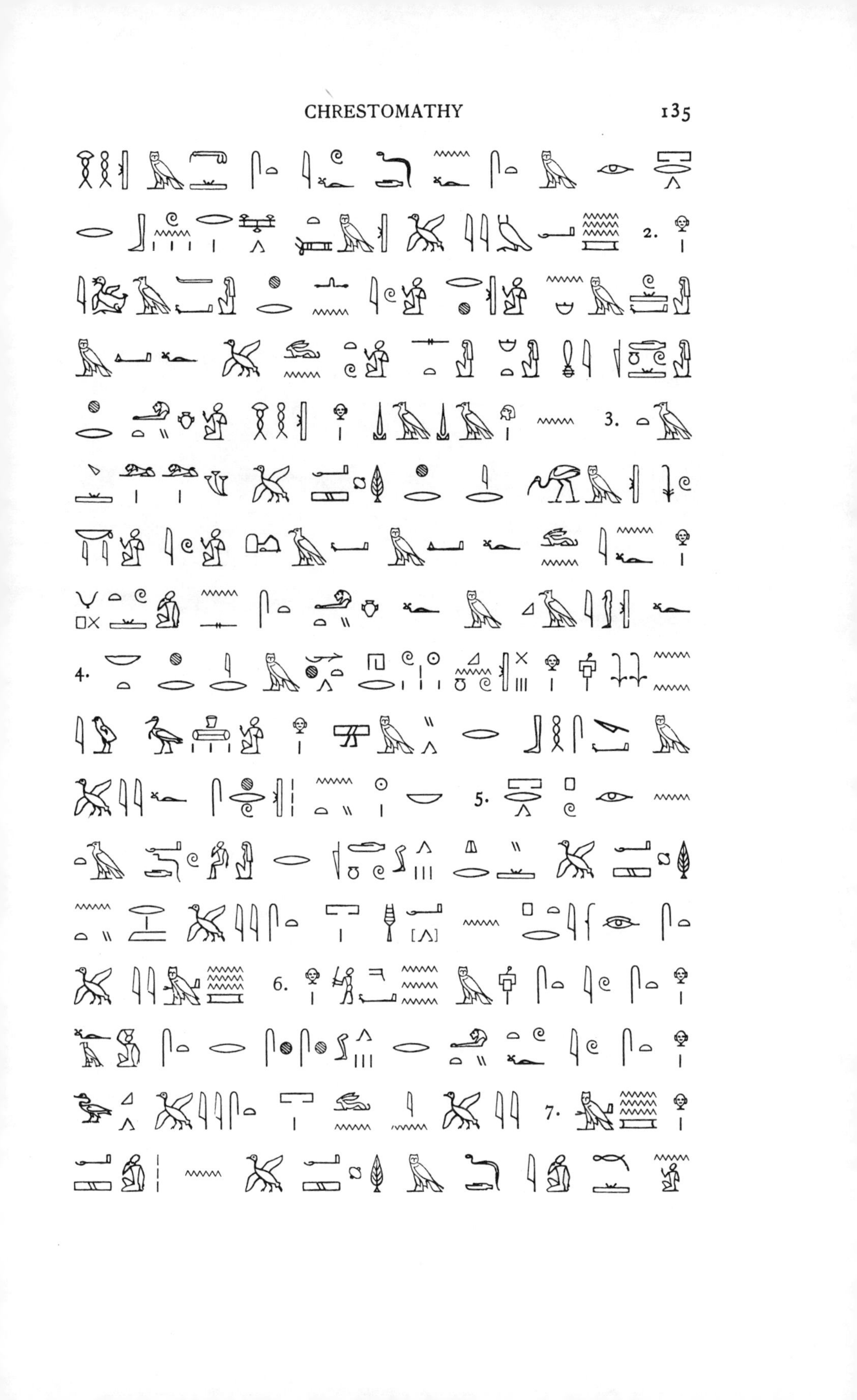

2.

3.

4.

5.

6.

7.

8.

9.

10.

XI. — 1.

2.

3.

4.

5.

6.

7.

8.

9.

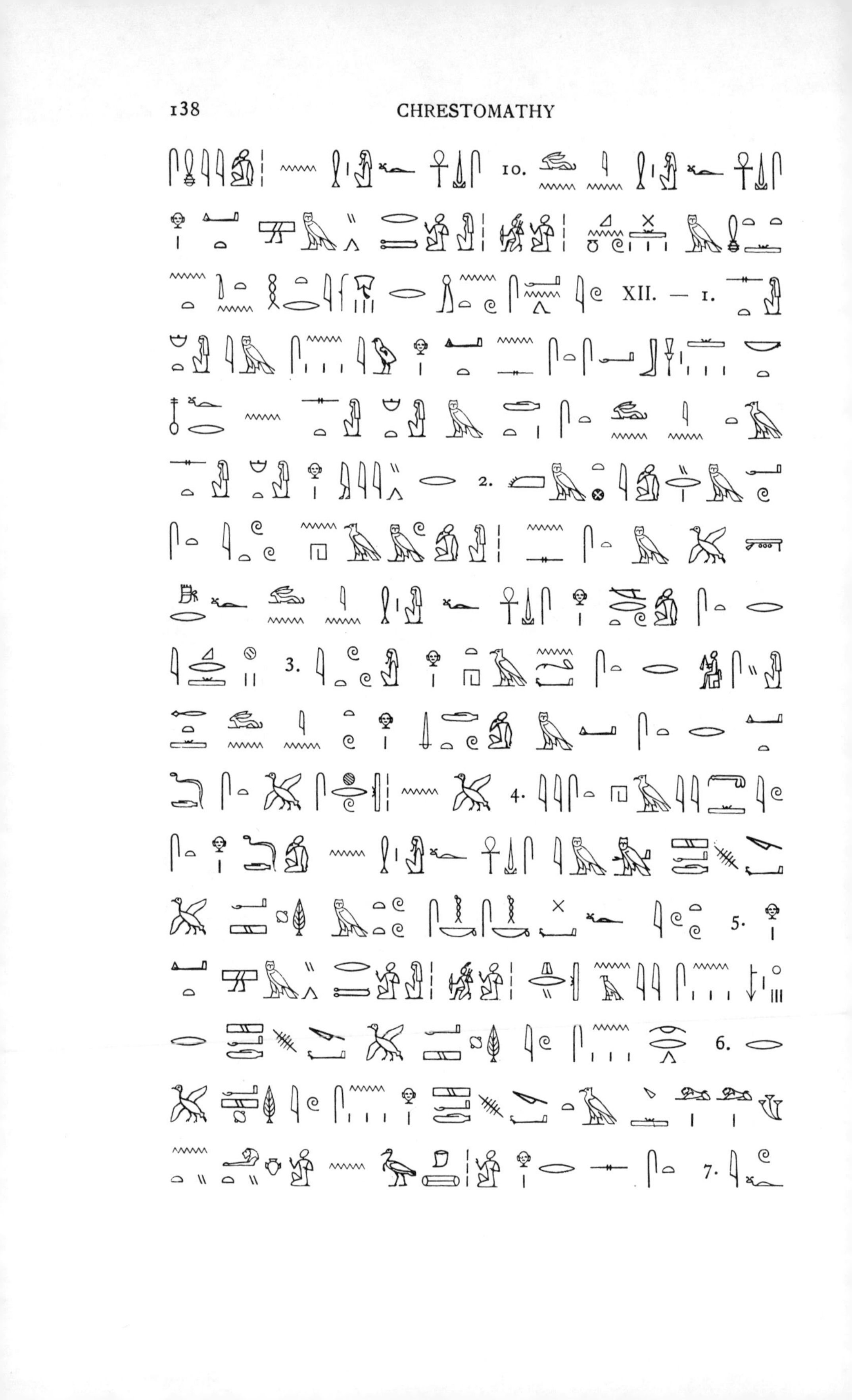

10.

XII. — 1.

2.

3.

4.

5.

6.

7.

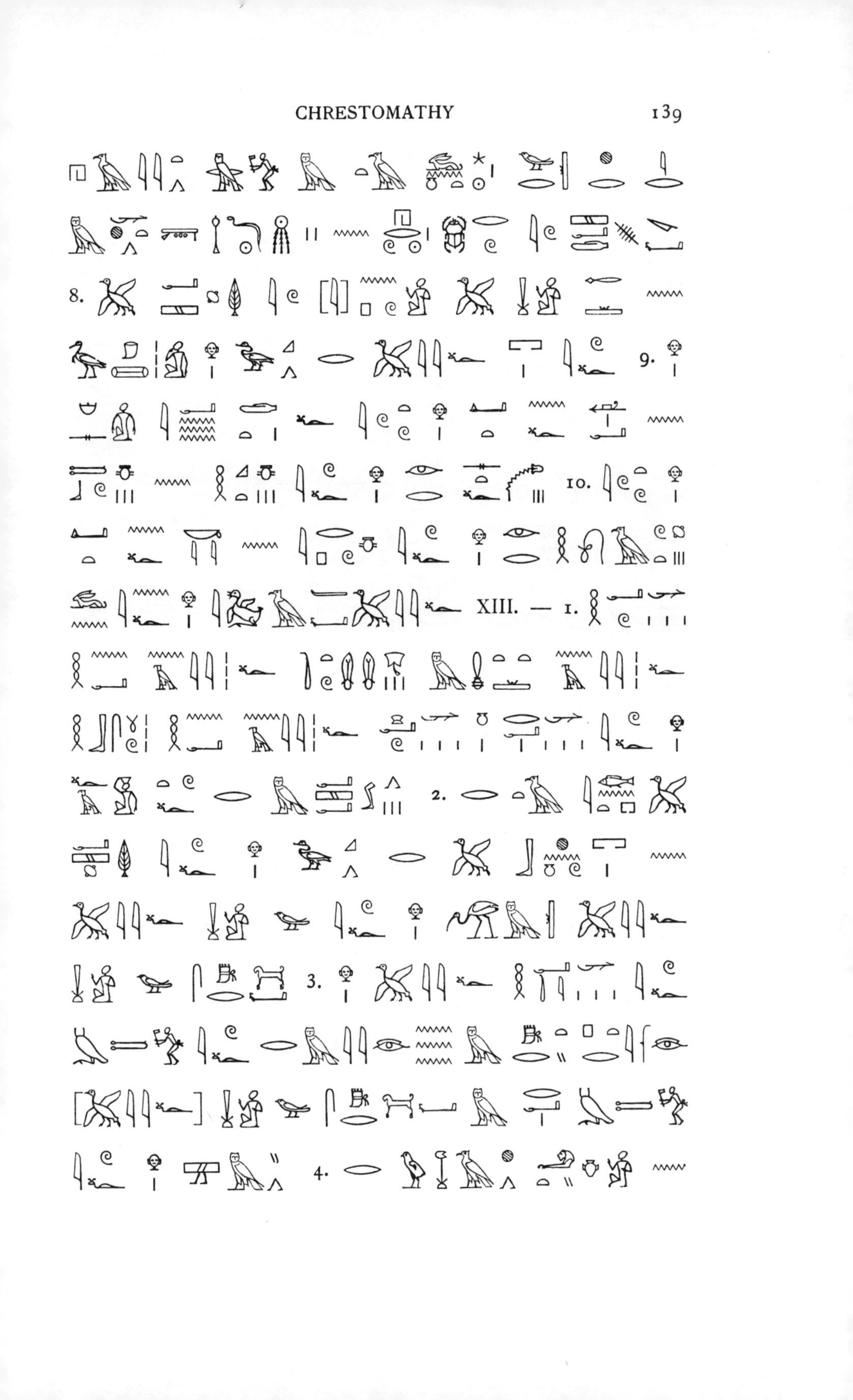

8.

9.

10.

XIII. — 1.

2.

3.

4.

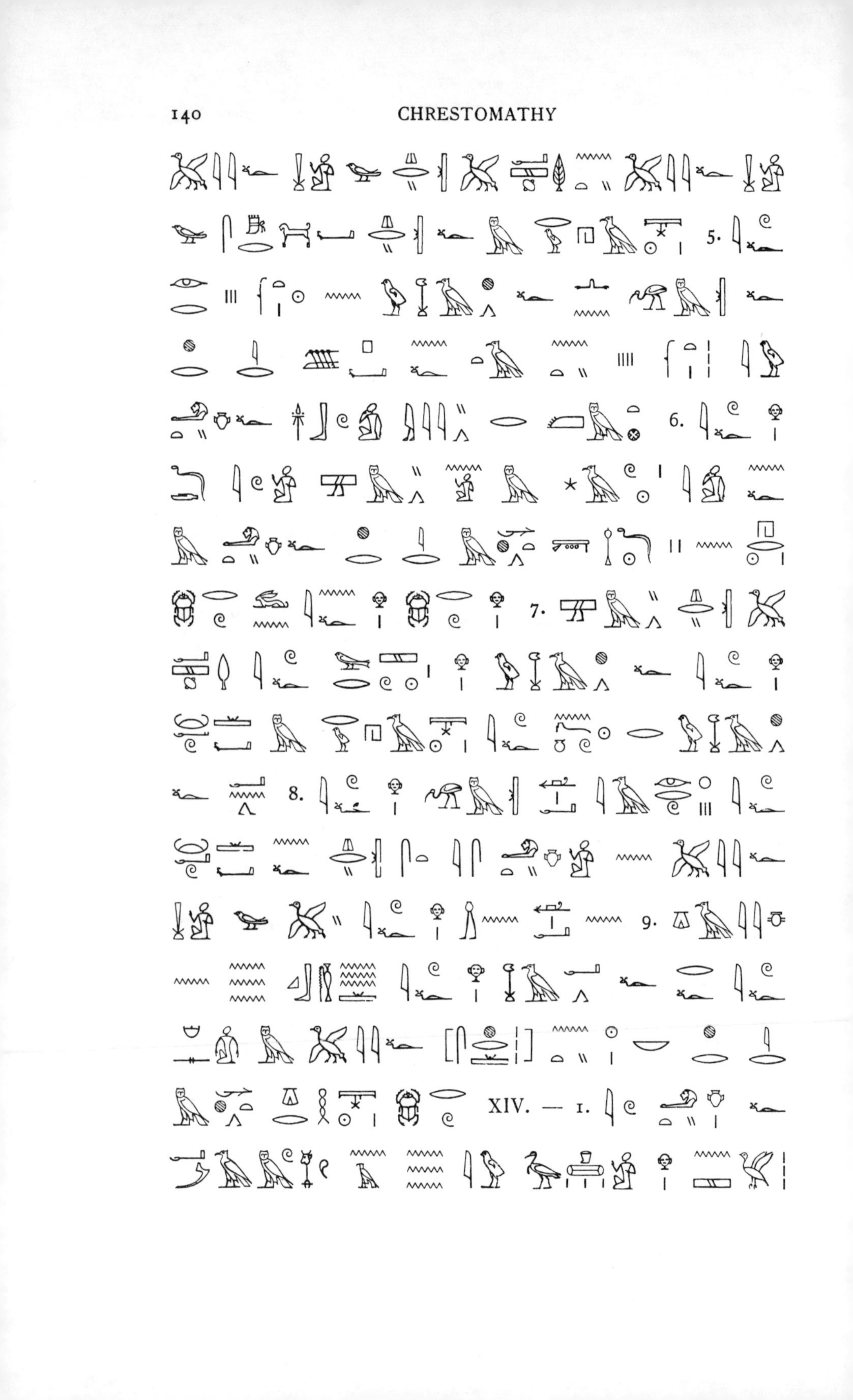

5.

6.

7.

8.

9.

XIV. — 1.

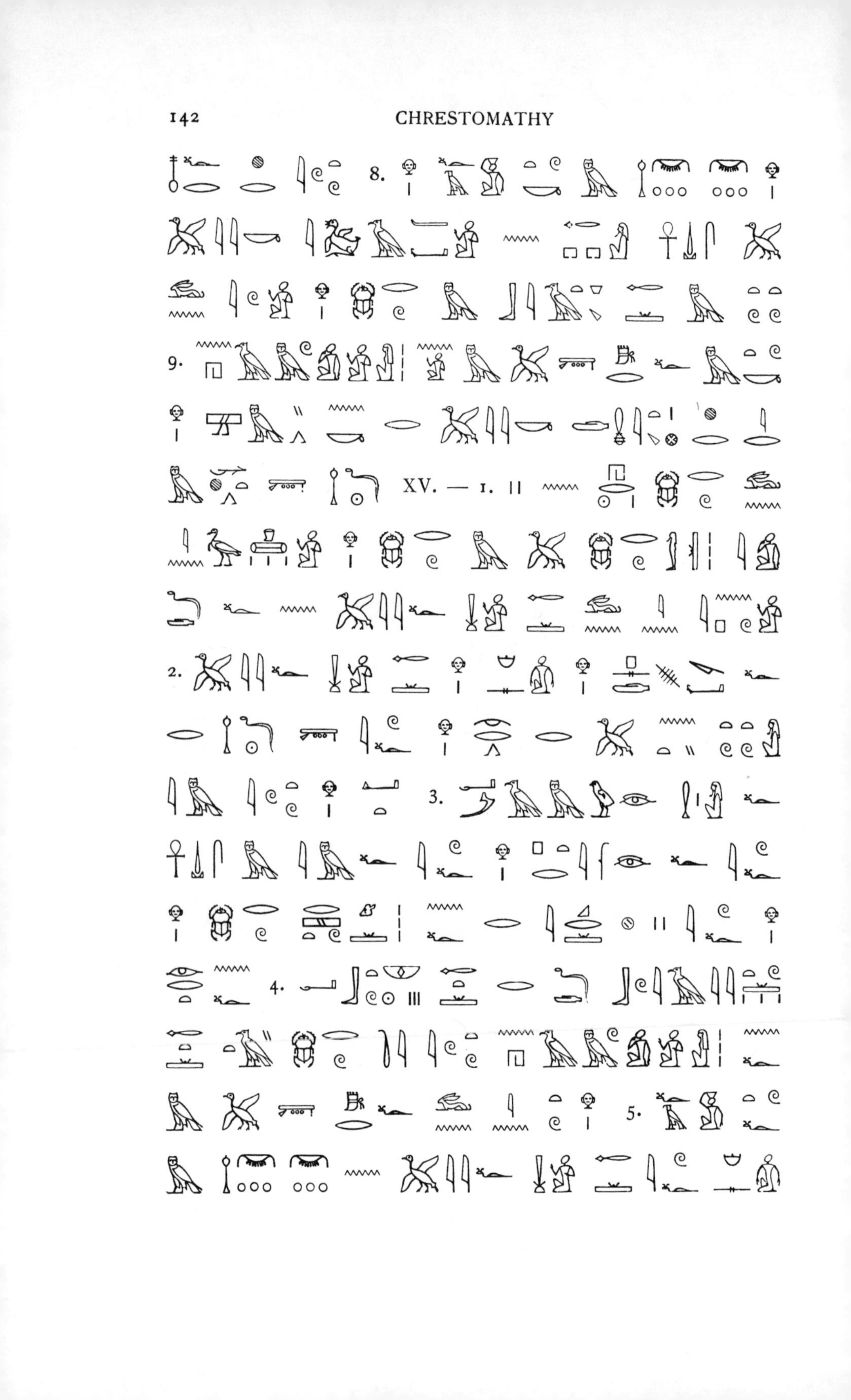

8.

9.

XV. — 1.

2.

3.

4.

5.

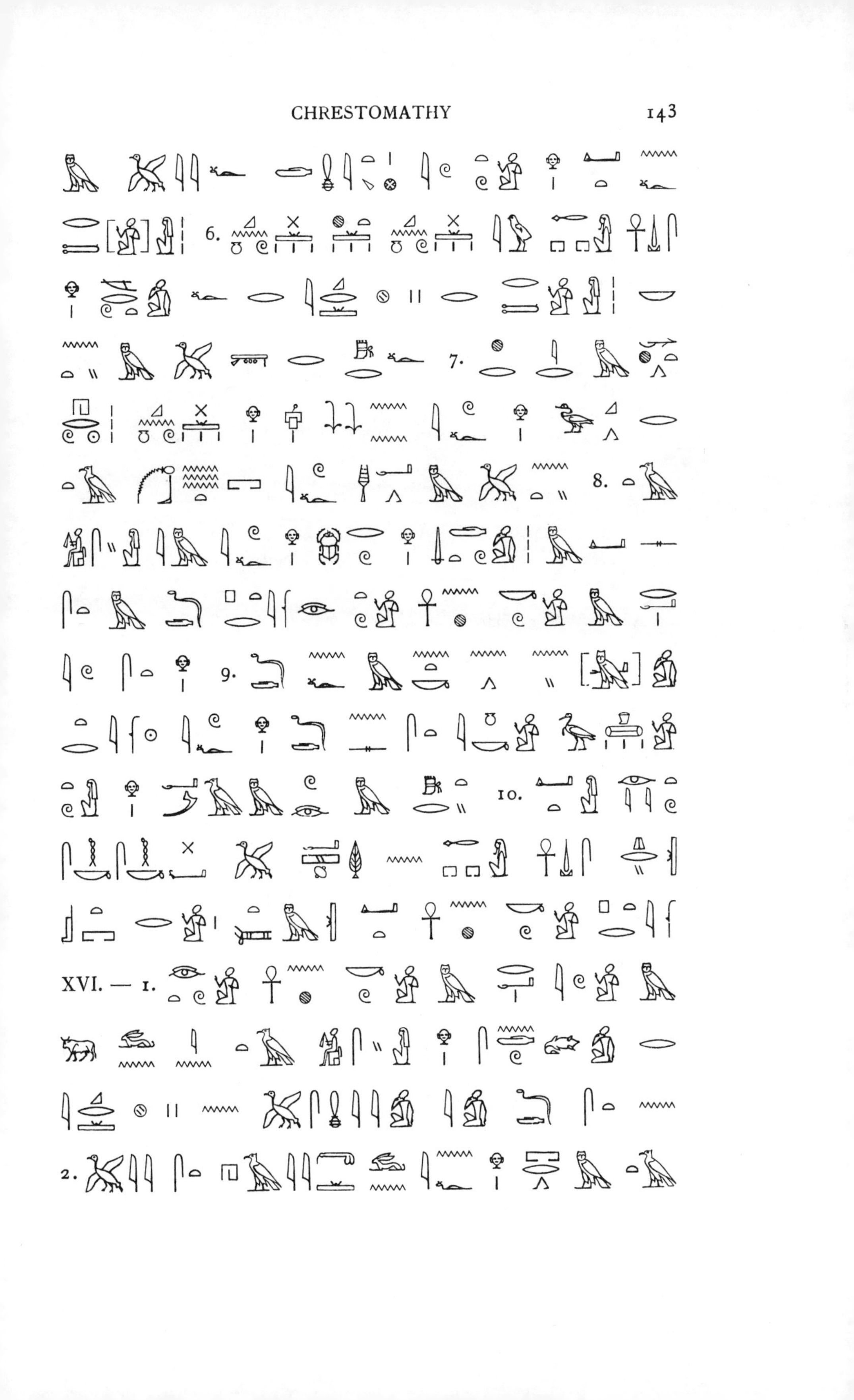

6.

7.

8.

9.

10.

XVI. — 1.

2.

3.

4.

5.

6.

7.

8.

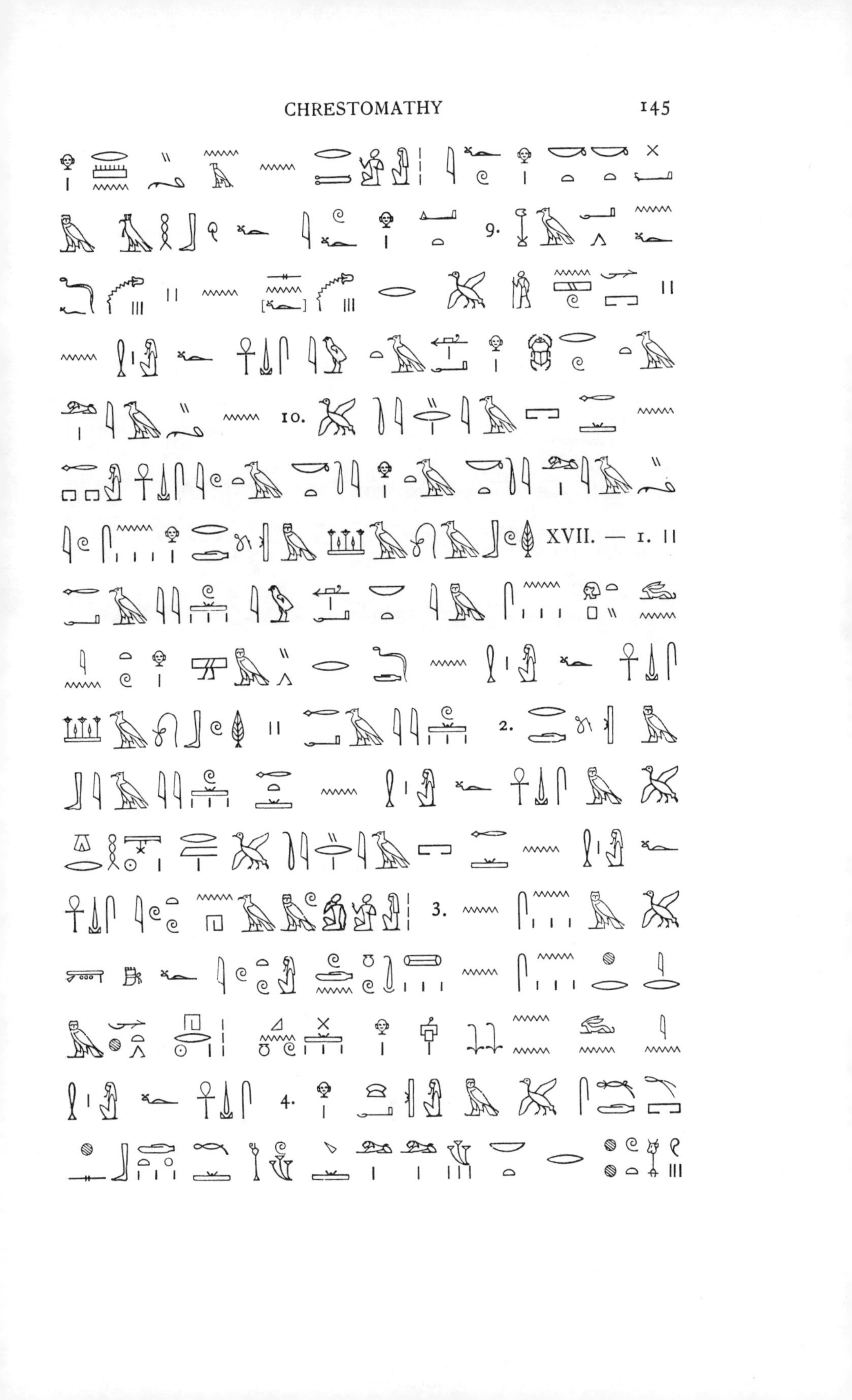

9.

10.

XVII. — 1.

2.

3.

4.

5.

6.

7.

(?)

8.

9.

10.

XVIII. — 1.

2.

3.

4.

5.

6.

7.

8.

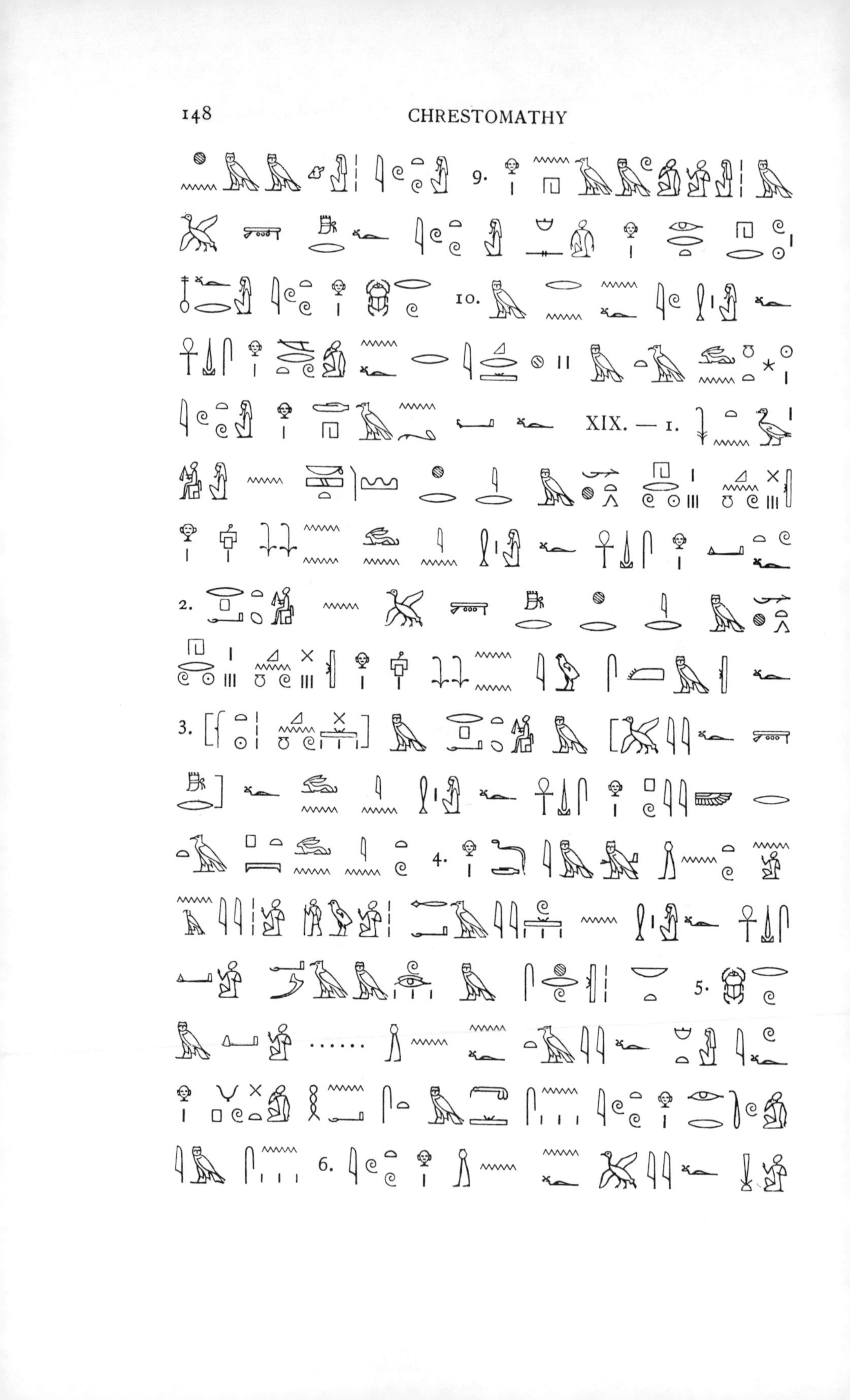

9.

10.

XIX. — 1.

2.

3.

4.

5.

......

6.

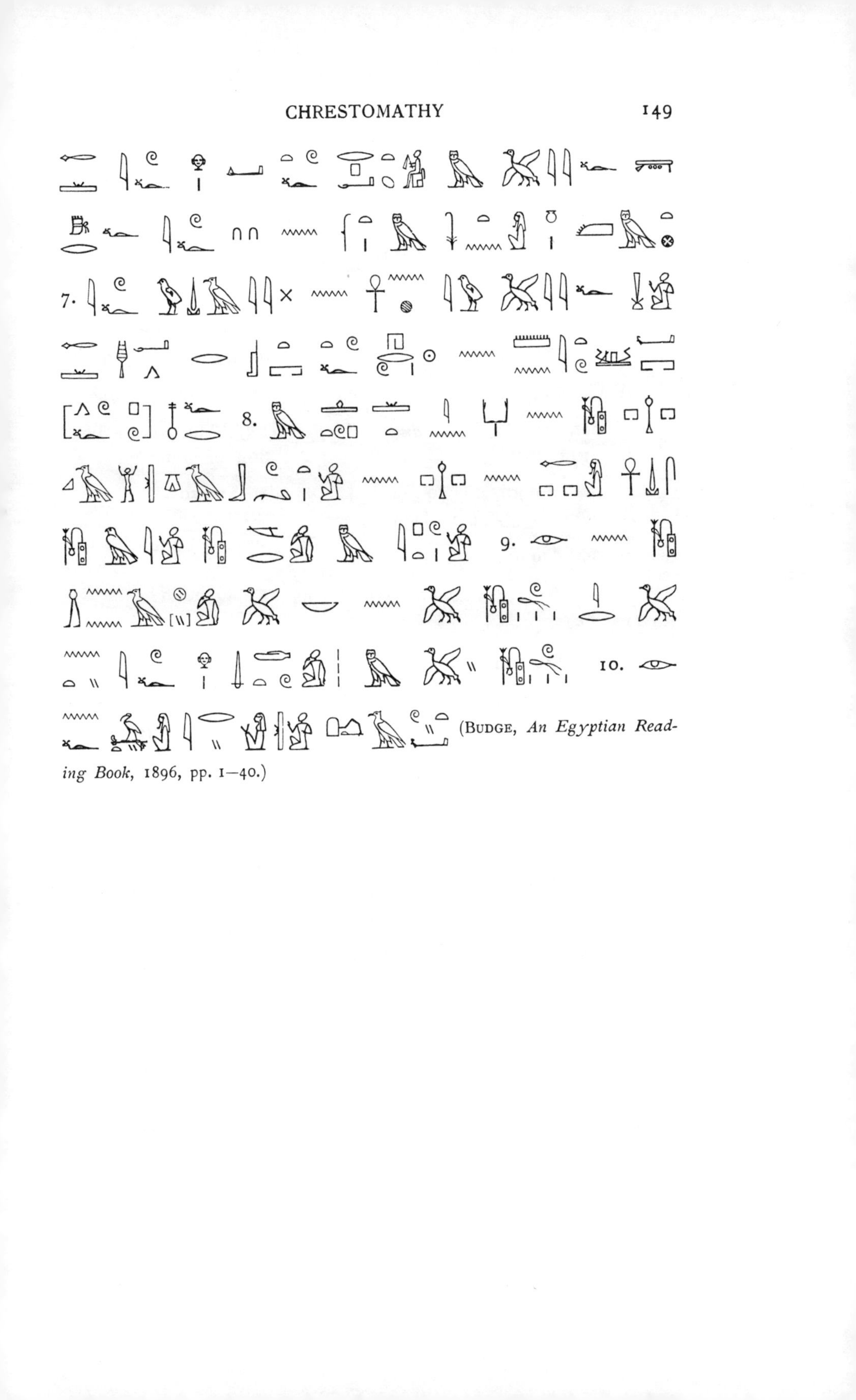

7.

8.

9.

10.

(BUDGE, *An Egyptian Reading Book*, 1896, pp. 1–40.)

SIGN LIST*

A. Men

2 det. "to call"; Interjection; ʿš

5 det. "to worship"; *dwꜣ*, *yꜣw*

8 det. "high," "to rejoice"; *ḳꜣy*, *ḥʿy*, *ḳꜣ*, *ḥʿ*

det. "to fall"

9 det. "to turn around"; *ʿny*

13 det. "to run"; phon. *yn*

15 det. "to dance," "to rejoice"; *ḳśy*

19 det. "to bow"; *ḳśy*

26 det. "dwarf"

27 det. "statue," "mummy," "figure," "death," *twt*

det. "mummy"

ḥwy "to strike"

29 *wr* "great"; *śr* (*śyr*?) "high official"; *śmśw* "old" (confused with 30)

30 det. "old"; *yꜣw*, *śmśw* (confused with 29)

31 det. "to smite"; *ḥw*

45 *nyny* "to pour a libation of water"

47 det. "to sow"

49 *ḳwś* "to build"

51 *ḳd* "to build"

56 *ḳś*

59 det. "statue"

70 det. "king"; *ʾyty* "king" (This figure means "king" also with other kinds of crowns or sceptres)

71 det. "child"; *ẖrd* and other words for "child"; *nn*, *ḥwn*, later *nw*

72 det. "to sit"

80, 79 det. "enemy," "death"; *ḫfty* "enemy"

---

* This Sign List is based upon ERMAN's selection in his *Ägyptische Grammatik*. The abbreviations used are: det. = determinative, phon. = phonogram (alphabetic or syllabic).

82 } det. "soldier"; *mšʿ* "soldier"
83

84 det. "prisoner," "barbarian"

85 det. "prisoner," "barbarian," "death"

88 det. "criminal"

89 det. "man"; suffix 1st pers. sing.

91 det. "to speak," "to think," "to eat," "to drink"

92 det. "to rest"; *wrd* "to rest"

93 det. *hn* "to adore"

94 det. *dwꜣ* "to worship"; "to hide"

95 det. "to hide"; *ymn* "to hide"

98 *swr* "to drink"

"to row"

100 det. "to hide"; *ḥꜣp*, *ymn* "to hide"; cf. O 48

101 *wʿb* "priest," "to clean"; cf. W 25

102 *sꜣṯ* "to dispense water"

105 det. "to load," "to carry," "to build"; *ꜣṯp* "laden," *fꜣy* "to carry," *kꜣ-t* "work"

106 *ḥḥ* (*n rnp·wt*) great number

110 det. "blessed dead"

113 det. "honoured person"; 1st pers. sing. suffix

117 det. "king" (also with different kinds of crowns and sceptres); suffix

120 "king," Osiris

128 *mynw* "shepherd," "watchman"; *sꜣw* "to watch"

"foreigner," Bedouin

129 } *špśy* "honourable"; det. "blessed dead"
131

133 det. "to fall"; *ẖr*

135 det. "to swim"

B. Women

3 "singer," "dancer"

7 det. "woman"; suffix 1st and 2nd pers. sing.

9 det. "blessed dead"

10 det. "woman of position"

12 *yry* "belonging to"

14 det. "pregnant"; *bkꜣ*

15 det. "to give birth to"; *mśy*

16 det. "nurse"; *rnn* "to rear"

C. Gods

1 *wśyr* Osiris

3, 4 *ptḥ* Ptaḥ

7 *ṯnn* Ptaḥ

9 *yn-ḥr·t* Onuris

10 *mnw* Min

11 *ymn* Amon

19 *šw* Show

25 *rʿ* Reʿ

27 *rʿ* Reʿ

31 *sṯḫ* (*śtš*) Set; *bʿr* Baal

32 *ynpw* Anubis

33 *dḥwty* Thot

36 *ẖnmw* Khnum

54 *mȝʿ·t* Maāt; "truth"

D. Parts of Men

Cf. "teeth" V 4; "heart" W 23

1 *tp*, *ḏȝḏȝ* "head"; *tpy* "first"; det. "head," "to nod," *gwȝ*

3 *ḥr* "face"; "upon"; phon. *ḥr*

5 det. "hair," "temples," "colour," "bald," "grief"; *šn* "hair"; *wšr* "bald," "destroyed"

10 *yr·t* "eye"; *yr* "to see" (cf. *wśyr*); phon. *yr*; det. "to see," *ʿn* (*ʿyn*); *yry* "to do"

12 det. "eye," "to see"; det. *ʿn* (*ʿyn*)

13 det. "eye-paint"

14 det. "to weep"; *rmy* "weeping"

15 det. *ʿn* (*ʿyn*)

17 det. "divine eye"; *wḏȝ·t*

cf. U 2

23 det. *mwt* "to die"; *yr* pupil; phon. *yr*

det. *mȝȝ* "to see"

25 det. "eye-brows"

28 *ḫnt* "nose," "before"; det. "nose," "breath," "joy"; *fnḏ* "nose"; *šr·t* "nose"; cf. F 4, 5

29 *rȝ* "mouth"; phon. *rȝ*, *r*

31 *śp·t* "lip"; *śpr* "rib," "to reach"; cf. N 28, 30

32 det. "jaw"

33 det. "to spit," "to flow out" (of the body)

35 *mdw* "staff," "to speak"

det. "back," *pśd*; *yȝ·t* "back"

37 late form of the preceding sign, and of the two following. Also *śm* for M 35

38 det. "to cut up" (cf. the preceding sign), *šʿ*

39 det. "breast," "to suckle"

41 *sẖn*, *ḥpt* "to embrace," "to happen"; det. "to embrace," *pgꜣ*

ḥm-kꜣ "funerary-priest"

46 *kꜣ* "power," "strength," "force"; phon. *kꜣ*

47, 48, 42 *n* (*nn*), *nyw* "not"; *nywty* "not having"; phon. *n*; det. negation

49, 56 *ḏśr* "magnificent"

51 *ẖny* "to row"; phon. *ẖn*

52 *ʿḥꜣ*, *yḥꜣ* "to fight"; phon. *ʿḥꜣ*

58 *ḥwy* "to reign"

59 *ʿ* "arm"; *rdy* "to give"; phon. *ʿ*; det. for D 69 and D 63

60, 62 *mḥ* "ell"; *rmn* "arm"; *rmny* "to carry"; det. "arm," "what is done with the arm"; *grḥ*

63 *rdy*, *dy* "to give"; also used for the following

65 det. "to give"; phon. *my*

66 *ḥnk* "to present," "to distribute"

68 *yʿy* "to wash"

69 det. "that which requires power"; *nḫt* "strength"; "to smite"

72 *ẖrp* "to lead"

76 *ḏr·t* (*ḏꜣ·t*) "hand"; phon. *ḏ*

77 det. "hand"

79 *yꜣdy* "to tow"

82 det. "fist," "to fasten"; *ꜣmm* "to fasten"

84 *ḏbʿ* "finger"; *ḏbʿ* 10,000; cf. T 1 and 6

det. "middle," "correct," *mtr*; *ʿḳꜣ* "right"; *mtr* "middle," "sign"

87 det. "to take," "powder," "fruit"; *ṯꜣy* "to take"; *dḳr*

90 *bꜣḥ* "phallus," "before"; det. "male," "ox," "ass," "to copulate"; *ṯꜣ* "male"; *kꜣ* "ox"

phon. *mt* "man"

93 for Q 12 (T 12)

94 det. "testicles"

95 *ḥm·t* "woman"; phon. *ḥm*; cf. N 70

det. "female"

96 *yw* "to go," *nmt* "to pace"; det. "to go"; *ʿḳ* "to enter"

98 det. "to go back"; *ʿny* "to turn around"; *pry* "to go out"

99 det. "leg," "to step"; *rd* "foot"; *wʿr* "to flee"; phon. *gḥś, wʿr*

100 det. "to step over"; *thy* "to step over"

101 *grg* "to lie in wait for," "to equip," "lie"

102 phon. *ḳ*

det. "to eat"; *wnm* "to eat"

103 phon. *b*

109 det. "meat";

111 *ḥʿ* "limb"; *ywf* "meat"

E. Mammals

2 det. "horse"; *śśm·t*, *ḥtr* "horse"

3 det. "bull"; *yḥ* "ox"; *yw3* "ox"; *k3* "bull"

6 det. "cow"

9 "bound sacrificial animal"

12 det. "calf"; *bḥs* "calf"

13 det. *yb* "buck"; *yby* "to thirst"

14 det. "new-born animal"; phon. *yw*

15 *b3* "sacred ram"; *ẖnm* Khnum; *b3* "soul"; det. "ram"

17 det. "goat," "herd"; *m3-ḥd?*

19 *śʿḥ* "nobleman"

22 *ẖn·t* "leather skin"; *ẖnw* "interior"; phon. *ẖn*

28 det. *ḳnd* "to rage"; "baboon"

36 det. "lion"; *m3y* "lion"

38 phon. *rw*; later *šnʿ* for U 13

44 *nb* "sphinx"; det. "statue"

49 *s3b* "jackal"; *s3b* "judge"; det. *wp-w3·wt* Upwat

52 det. Anubis; *ynpw* Anubis

55 *ynpw* Anubis; later *ḥry-ššt3* (a title)

58 phon. *wn*

65 *śr* "giraffe"; *śr*

66 *stš* (*sth*) Seth; det. "dreadful"; "bad

67 weather"; "ass"; *bʿr*

F. Parts of Mammals

Cf. "lungs" R 20; "tongue" S 37; "heart" Y 9, W 23. 46

3 *yḥ*, instead of E 3

4 wrong for D 28

5 "nose," "to breathe"; see D 28; also *rš*

6 det. "neck," "to swallow"

8 *šfy·t* "appearance"

11, 13 *šš3* "reasonable"

15 *pḥ·t* "power"; *3·t* "head-dress," "moment"

16 *ḥ3·t* "fore-part"; *ḥ3*

30 *3·t* "moment"; cf. F 15

33 *wp·t* "top," "summit"; phon. *wp*

35 *y3w·t* "office"

37 *wp-rnp·t* "New Year"

41 *ʿb* "horn"; phon. *ʿb*; det. "horn"; *db* "horn"

44 *ybḥ* "tooth"; phon. *bḥ*, *ḥw*, *by3*; det. "tooth," "activity of the mouth"

45 late for F 44

46 *mśḏr* "ear"; *śḏm* "to hear"; *ydn* "to represent"; det. "ear," "to hear"; *dng*, *yd*

48 *pḥ* "end," "to reach"; *kf3* "hinder part"; phon. *pḥ*

49 *ḥpš* "thigh," "strength"; det. "thigh"

52 *whm* "to repeat"; det. "leg of an animal"

whm "to repeat"

54 phon. *k3p*, *kp*; later for S 47

58 det. "beast"

59 *ś3b* "coloured"

60 *śṯy* "to shoot"

61 det. "tail," "thorn"

63 *ywʿ* "bone"; *ywʿ* "inheritance"; *yśwy* compensation; det. "meat"

G. Birds

1 phon. *3*, also for G 5

(–), 5 *tyw*

6, 7 phon. *nḥ*

8, 9 *ḥr*, *ḥrw* Horus; det. "falcon"

13 *ḥr-nb·ty* (?), royal title

15 det. "god," "king"

16 *ymn*; old for S 56

17 *ḥry·t-nṯr*; old for R 16

28 det. "holy bird"; *ʿẖm* "divine image"

30 *nr·t* "vulture"; *mw·t* Mut; *mw·t* "mother"; phon. *nr*, *mt*; det. "vulture"

31 *mw·t* Mut

33 *nb·ty* "the protective goddesses of Egypt"

36 phon. *m*

37 *mm*; late for Z 29

38, 39, 40 *my* "take"; *ym* "give"; phon. *m*

44 *mr*, *mt*

46 *gmy* "to find"; phon. *gm*

48 *ḏḥwty* Thot

53 *b3* "soul"; *bk* (*byk*) "to work"; phon. *b3*, *bk*

54 *b3w* "souls"

57, 58 *y3ḫ* "to shine"

60 det. *bnw* "phoenix"

61 *bʿḥ* "to overflow"

64 *dšr* "red"

63, 66 det. *wš3* "to feed"; *ḏf3* "food"; *ḥw*

67 det. "birds," "insects"; *s3* "son"; *3pd* "bird"; phon. *s3*; *gbb* Geb; det. *ḥtm*

rḫty "washer"

70 *śd3* "to tremble"

71 *ʿḳ* "to enter"

73 phon. *p3*; *p3y* "to flee"

75 *ḫny* "to flutter"; det. "to flee"; also for the following

det. *ḳm3*, *ṯn*; cf. T 6

78 *ḏb·t* "brick"

79 phon. *wr*; *wr* "great"

80 det. "small," "bad"; *nḏś* "small"; *šry* "small"

81, 82 *rḫy·t* "people"

83 phon. *w*

87 *ṯ3* "young bird"; phon. *ṯ3*

88 *sš* "nest"

90 *sš* "swamp," "nest"; *ywn* "nest"; det. "nest"

91 *śnḏ* "fear"

92 *b3* "soul"

H. Parts of Birds

1 old for G 67

3 *nr·t* "vulture"; *nr* "male"

5 det. *pḳ*

7 late for G 58

8 det. *mꜣʿ*

12 det. "to fly," "wing"

13 *šw·t* "feather"; phon. *šw*; det. "truth"; *mꜣʿ·t* "truth"

17 see D 62

18 *šꜣ·t* "bird-claw"?

20 for D 84

21 later *sꜣ* "son"; det. "goddess," "queen"

I. Amphibia

2 *ʿšꜣ* "many"

4 det. "crocodile"; *ꜣd* "fury"

yty "king"

det. *śꜣḳ*

7 *śbk* Sobk

8 *km* "black"; phon. *km*

9 det. "frog"; goddess *ḥḳt*

10 *ḥfn* "tadpole"; *ḥfn* 100,000

11, 16 det. "snake"; "goddess"

22 det. "worm"

24 det. "evil being"

26 *ḏ·t* "serpent," "snake"; *ḏ·t* "body"; phon. *ḏ*

27 see Z 9

30 phon. *f*

32 later *pry* "to come out"

33 later *ʿḳ* "to go in"

K. Fish

1 phon. *yn*; *rm* "fish"

ʿnḏ-mr(?) "government title"

4 det. "fish," "disgust"; *bś* "lead in"

6 *spꜣ*

10 *ẖꜣ·t* "body"; phon. *ẖꜣ*

L. Insects

Cf. "mussel" N 72

1 *by·t* "bee," "honey"; *byty* "king of Lower Egypt"

4 *ḫpr* "beetle"; *ḫpr* "to become"

5 det. "flying-sun"

7 *ʿff* "fly"

8 det. "chastity"

9 "scorpion," *śrḳ* "to breathe"; goddess *śrḳ·t*

see I 30

M. Plants

Cf. bundle of reeds Q 32; D 37

1 *y3m* "a tree," "sweet"; det. "tree"; *ḳb*

det. "tree"

9 *ḫt* "wood," "tree"; phon. *ḫt*; det. "wood," "tree"

13 *rnp·t* "year"; *tr* "time"; *ḥ3·t-sp* "year of a reign"; *rnp* "to bloom"; cf. M 15. 17

15 *tr* "time"; det. *ty*, *mry*; cf. 13

16 *rnp·t* "year"; cf. 13

17 *rnp* "to bloom"; cf. 13

22 *nḫb* "leaf"; goddess *Nḫb·t*; city *Nḫb* (el Kab)

phon. *nn*

24 *nswt* (*ny-śwt?*), "king of Upper Egypt"; *rś* "south"; phon. *św*

24, 30 *rś* "south"

26, 27 *šmᶜ* Upper Egypt; "to practice music"

33 phon. *y*

y, *yy*

34 *yy* "to go"

35 *śḫ·t* "field"; *śm* (cf. D 37)

36 *ᶜ3b·t* "offering"

37 *š3* "field"; *3ḫ·t* "inundation"; phon. *š3*

41 phon. *ḥn*; *ysy* "old"; det. "plant"

42 det. "swamp," "north"; phon. *ḫ3*

43 det. "swamp," "north"; *ydḥ* "Delta swamps"; *mḥ·t* "north"

45 det. Upper Egypt

47, 48 *w3ḏ* "green"; phon. *w3ḏ* (later *wḏ*)

50, 47 late for N 39

58 det. "buds"

59 for V 39

63 det. "flower"

67 phon. *wn*; *wnm* "to eat"; cf. R 28

wn-ḏw

68 *ḫ3* 1000; phon. *ḫ3*

70 later form of ; cf. V 6

74, 75, 76 } *ḥḏ* "club," "white"; phon. *ḥḏ*; also for the following

77 old, 73 late } *wḏy* "to command"; phon. *wḏ*

U 32, 79 } *ḥśf* "to ward off"

80 *mśy* "to give birth to," phon. *mś*

82 *bd·t* "spelt"

84 det. "ear of corn"

86 *yt* "barley"

89, 88 } *šnw·t* "barn"

90 det. "wine"

93, 94 } *bnr* "sweet"; "date"; *rd* "to grow"

98 *nḏm* "sweet"

N. Heaven, Earth, Water

1 *p·t* "heaven"; *ḥr·t* "heaven"; *ḥry* "that which is above"; det. "heaven," "above"; *h3y·t* "hall"

2, 3 } det. "night," "evening"; *grḥ* "night"

4 det. "rain," "dew"; *y3d·t* "dew"

5 *tḥn* "lightening," "to shine"; det. "weather," "rain"

7 } *rʿ* "sun," "sun-god"; det. "sun," "time"; *hrw* day; *śśw* "day of the month"

8 see Z 11

11 *rʿ* "sun" (as god)

13 } *ḥnmm·t* "mankind"; det. "rays"; *wbn* "to make light"

14 *śpd·t* triangle; *śpd* "make ready"; *śpd·t* "dog-star"

17 det. "flying-sun"

23 *ḫʿy* "to rise"; phon. *ḫʿ*

26 see X 12

28 *šsp* "span"

28, 30 } *yʿḥ* "moon"; *ybd* "month"; cf. D 31

ybd "month"

35 *śb3* "star"; *dw3* "morning-star"; *dw3·t* "underworld"; *dw3* "to adore"; *wnwt* "hour"; phon. *śb3*, *dw3*

36 late *dw3·t* "underworld"

37 } *t3* "land"; phon. *t3*; det. *ḏ·t*

39 *t3wy* "the two Egypts"

40 *ḫ3ś·t* "foreign country"; *smy·t* "desert," "necropolis"; god *ḥ3*; det. "desert," "foreign country"

42 *ḏw* "mountain"; phon. *ḏw*; later *mn*

44 *3ḫ·t* "horizon"

46 *śp3·t* "district"; *ḥsp* "district"; det. "section of country"

47 det. "land"

X 21 det. "land"; *ydb* "bank"

48 det. "land," "limited time"

49 *w3·t* "way"; det. *w3y* "to be far"; "way"; "place"; *mṯn* "way"; phon. *w3*, *ḥr*

św3 "to go by"

50 *gś* "side"; phon. *ym*, *gś*; later *m*

51, 52 det. "stone"; *ynr* "stone"

53 det. "grain" (of sand, seed, &c.)

55 phon. *n*

mw "water"; phon. *mw*; det. "water"

58 *mr* "canal"; *mry* "to love"; phon. *my*; det. "waters"; cf. N 66

62, 59, 60 *š* "sea"; phon. *š*; det. "sea," "water"; *ḫnt*

for the preceding, and for 58

61 *šm* "to go"

66 *yw* "island"; *3ḫ·t* "horizon"; phon. *yw*; det. "island"

"bread," cf. X 1

Z 20 *sny* "to open," "to pass by," *sn* "similar"

67 *3ḫty* "belonging to the horizon"

70 det. *by3*; cf. D 95

72 phon. *ḫ3*

O. Buildings and their Parts

Cf. "pillar" Q 29. T 41

1 *n·t* "city"; det. "city"

3, 4 *pr* "house"; *pry* "to go out"; phon. *pr*; det. "building"

6 *pr·t-r-ḫrw* "funeral-offering"

7 *pr-ḥḏ* "treasury"

9 phon. *h*

10 *mr* name of Egypt; phon. *mr*, *nm*

12, 22 *ḥ·t* "large house"

15 *ḥ·t nṯr* "temple"

16 *ḥ·t ʿ3·t* "castle"

17 *nb·t-ḥ·t* Nephthys

19 *ḥ·t-ḥr* Hathor

29 *ˁḥˁ* "palace"

32 *wśḫ·t* "palace court"

36 det. "wall"; *ynb* "wall"

37 } det. "to destroy"

41 det. "fortress"

43 det. "gate"

44 *ṯ3yty* title of the Chief Justice

45 *ḳnb* "angle"; *ḳnb·t* "officials"

48 } *ḥ3p* "to hide"; phon.
U 49 } *ḥ3p*, *ḥp*; cf. A 100

52 det. "pyramid," "grave"

53 det. "obelisk"; *tḫn* "obelisk"

54 det. "memorial tablet"; *wḏ* "stela"

61 *ḫkr* "to adorn"; cf. X 19

62 *sḥ* "arbour," "hall"; *sḥ* "counsel"; det. "hall"; later for the following sign

ˁrḳ "to bend"

63 }
64 } *ḥb-śd* "royal jubilee"

65 *ḥb* "feast"; cf. 63 and W 49

68 }
67 } det. "stairs," "to ascend"

69 *ˁ3* "door"; det. "to open"; phon. *ˁ3*

70 phon. *s*

71 *swy* (?) "to go"; *sby* "to go," "to bring"; *ms* "to bring"

73 *ṯsy* "to knot"; phon. *ṯs*

74 *mnw* Min; *ḫm* "holy of holies"

75 *mnw* Min

77 }
Q 34 } phon. *ḳd*

80 *sḥ* "hall"

P. Ships and their Parts

1 } det. "ship," "to journey"; *wy3*; *ḫd* "to move down stream"

det. *pnˁ* "to turn over"

6 *wḥˁ*

14 det. "to sail"; *ḫnty* "to sail up stream"

16 *ṯ3w* "wind," *nf*, *nfw* "breath"; det. "wind," "air"

19 *ˁḥˁ* "to stand"; phon. *ˁḥˁ*

21 det. "rudder"; *ḥm* "rudder"

22 *ḫrw* "voice"; *ḥp·t*; det. "rudder"

23 *ššp* (*sšp*, later *šp*) "to receive"; phon. *ššp* (*sšp*, *šp*)

Q. House Articles

1 *ś·t* "seat"; *ꜣś*; *ꜣś·t* Isis (cf. *wśyr*); phon. *ś*, *ḥtm*

3 det. "armchair"

5 *wṯs* "portable chair"; phon. *wś*; det. "chair"

7
8 det. "to lie," "to sleep," "to die"; *śḏr* "at night"

9 phon. *ś*

ḫmnw "eight"

12 for T 12

15 $\frac{2}{3}$

17 *ḥtp* "offering"; *ḥtp* "to rest"

wdḥw "table for food"

20 *ẖr* "under"

ẖr·t-hrw "daily"

23
25 det. "coffin"; *ḳrśw* "coffin"

26 *yꜣ·t* "place"

28 *ḏbꜣ* "to repair"; phon. *ḏbꜣ*

29 *ywn* "pillar"; phon. *ywn*; later *yn*

31 phon. *ḥn*

32
34 phon. *ys*

37 god *ššm*

39 *mḏr* (later *mḏd*) "to press"

42 det. "clothes"; *mnḫ·t* + *šś* (*ʿrf* V 6–8)

mnḫ·t "clothes"

44 det. *wrś* "pillow"

46 *śry·t* "standard"

47 det. "shade"; *ḫꜣb·t* "shade"

48 det. "balances"

51
52 *wḏʿ* "to set right"

53
54 *wṯs*, *ṯsy*, *ṯs* "to lift up"; det. *ṯs*; cf. T 2

58 *mꜣʿ* "true"

59 stand for images of gods and for district names; cf. G 15. 48, O 75

60 phon. *p*

R. Temple Articles

Cf. F 35, S 47

1 *wdḥw*

2 det. "altar"; *ḫꜣw·t* "altar"

13 *nṯr* "god"; det. "god"

16 *ḫry·t-nṯr* "kingdom of the dead"

18 *ḏd* "holy pillar," "to remain"

20 *smꜣ* "lungs," "to unite"

22 *śn* "two," "brother"; phon. *śn*

26 *yꜣb* "left"; cf. U 31

28 *ymy* "to consist in"; for M 67 in *wnm* "to eat"; phon. *ym*

M 67

29 *śšꜣ·t* "goddess of wisdom"

S. Clothing, Jewelry, Insignia

Cf. Y 11, M 80

1, 24 "wreath"; *mḥ* "wreath"; cf. T 7

3 later phon. *k*

7 *ḫprš* "head-dress"

8 *ḥḏ·t* "crown of Upper Egypt"

11 *n·t* "crown of Lower Egypt," *dšr·t* the same; *byty* "king of Lower Egypt"; phon. later *n*

13 det. *sḫm·t* "crown of Upper and Lower Egypt"

14 see V 1

17 *šw·ty* "feather as head-dress"

28 *yḥwty* "farmer"; phon. *ʿḥ*, *yḥ*

30 det. "skirt"; *šnḏw·t* "skirt"

31 *śṯy·t* name of a country; goddess Sathis; *śṯ*

32, Q 13 det. "clothes"; *ḥbś* "clothes"

37 *nś* "tongue"; *ymy-rꜣ* "foreman"; "death"; phon. *nś*, *mr*

38 *ṯb·t* "sandal"

39 *šn* "circle"; cf. 44

41 *dmḏ* "to unite"

42 Isis

43 *ʿnḫ* "to live"

44 *ḏꜣś·t* (?) "treasure"; det. "seal"; *ḫtm* "seal"

45 *ḏꜣś·t* (?) "treasure"; gentilic: "treasurer"

46 *mny·t* "weight on collar"

47 *kꜣp* "to smoke"; phon. *kꜣp*, *kp*; cf. F 54

ʿ "caravan"

48 *ʿpr* "to provide"; det. "tassel"

50 *śḫm* "mighty"; *ḫrp* "to lead"; *ʿbꜣ* "sceptre"

m-n "to take"

56 *ymn* "right," *ymn·t* "western," *ʿwnmy* "right"

60 *ḫw·t* "fan"

62 *ḥḳꜣ* "to rule"

63 *ʿw·t* "sheep," "pigs," &c.

64 *wꜣś·t* "sceptre"; *ḏʿm* "gold"; *wꜣś*, *ḏʿm*; cf. U 54

65 *wꜣś·t* Thebes

66 *wśr* "strong"

75 *nḫꜣḫꜣ*

76 god *bꜣbꜣ*

T. Arms and War Articles

Cf. M 74–76; U 45, 38; R 22; V 27; Z 29, 30

6, 1 det. "foreign"; *ʿꜣm* "Asiatic," *ṯḥn* "Libyan," *nḥśy* "negro"; *ḏʿ*; *ḳmꜣ* "to throw," "to create"; *ṯny* "to lift up oneself"; cf. G 75, T 2, 13, S 63

2 *rś* "to grow"

3 *sḫn* "support"

7 *mdḥ* "to cut"; det. "axe"

9 *tpy* "first"

10 *ḫpš* "crescent-sword"

12, 20 *śšm* "butcher"; *śšm* "to lead"; cf. Q 12, D 93

13 det. *mny* "to land," "to graze"

14, 15 det. "to cut"; *dm* "to sharpen," "to name"

21 *pḏ·t* "bow"; det. "bow"

26, 31 *sty* Nubia

28 *pḏ·t* "bow"; *pḏ* "to broaden out"

33 *šśr* "arrow"; *śḫr* "to milk," *swn*

38 *śꜣ* "back," "behind"; phon. *śꜣ*

41 *ʿꜣ* "great"; phon. *ʿꜣ*

43 *ẖ·t*, *ẖꜣ·t* "body"; phon. *ẖ*

45 det. "war-chariot"; *wrry·t* "war-chariot"

U. Tools and Agricultural Implements

Cf. M 79; V 15; W 6; X 17

1 ḫnr "to confine"

late for *m*

2 *ty·t* "part"; cf. D 17

3 *śtp* "to select"

5, 4 phon. *nw*

7 det. "to smite"; *ḥwy* "to smite"

8 phon. *m3*

m3ᶜ

12 *mry* "to love"; phon. *mr*; det. "to hoe"

šnᶜ "to ward off"; "warehouse"

13 *hb* "plough"; *pr·t* "fruit"; phon. *hb*; det. "to plough"; also for the preceding *šnᶜ*

14 *tm* "to complete"; *ytm* Atum; phon. *tm*

by3 "ore," "to be astonished"

18 *ḥk3* corn-measure

19 phon. *ty*

20 det. "weight," "mineral"; *śmn*; *ḥsmn* "a metal," "natron"

21 phon. *d̲3*

24 *mr* "sick," "pyramid"; phon. *mr*; *3b* (U 31)

27 *mnḫ* "to saw," "excellent"

28 *ḥm* "handwork"

29 *wb3* "to open"

31 phon. *3b*

32 see M 79, *ḥśf*

36, 35 *nd̲* "to paint"

38, 37 *wᶜ* "one"; phon. *wᶜ*

40, V 20 *nrt* Neith

41 det. "to sheer"

42 *šmś* "to follow"

45 *ḳś* (*ḳrś*?) "bone"; *ḳrś* "to bury"; phon. *ḳś*, *ḳrś*; det. "bone"; "tube"; *gnw·t*

mśnty (?) "sculptor"

47 see V 4

48 *ś3ḥ*

49 see O 48; *ḥp* (*ḥ3p*)

50 *nb* "gold"

53 *ḥd̲* "silver"

54 *ḏʿm* "gold"

55 *śḫt* "net"

śḫt "to weave"

V. Wicker-work

Cf. M 77, 73; O 73; Q 9

1 det. "cord"; *šnṯ*; *šꜣ·t* "hundred"; "to fasten"; phon. late *w*; cf. S 14

2 *śṯꜣ* "to draw"; det. *ꜣś*

4 / U 47 *śꜣḥ* "toe," "to land"

5 phon. *ꜣw*; *ꜣwy* "wide"

ymꜣḫ "dignity"

6 phon. *šś*; det. "cord," "to bind"; cf. V 8

wgꜣ

phon. *šn*; cf. M 70

8 det. "sack"; *ʿrf* "bag"; phon. *gb*

10 det. "to bind," "to loose"; "book"; *ʿrḳ* "to end"

13 late for V 10

15 / 18 *mḥ* "to fill"; phon. *mḥ*

17 *šd* "to take"; phon. *šd*

20 see U 40

21 *ʿnd* (*ʿꜣḏ*?) "to be well"; phon. *ʿnḏ* (*ʿꜣḏ*?)

25 *śnṯ* "foundation"

26 phon. *wꜣ*

27 *rwḏ* (*rḏ*) "to grow"; det. *ꜣy*, *ꜣr*

28 *sꜣ* "protection"

29 *sꜣ* "protection"

30 phon. *ḥ*

34 phon. *śk*; cf. V 38

37 *wꜣḥ* "to lay"; cf. V 38

38 for V 34, 37

39 / 40 *wdn* "offering"; cf. M 59

41 *pḫr* "to surround"; *dbn* "to surround," "weight"; *wḏb* "to turn back"; *ḳꜣb* "interior"

43 phon. *ṯ*

44 *yṯy* "to seize"

45 *wt* "to wrap up"; det. "to embalm," "death," "smell," "to reckon"; *ḥśb* "to reckon"; cf. Y 3

46 det. "smell"

W. Vessels

Cf. V 8; E 22; V 17

1 *bꜣś·t* name of a city; goddess Bast; det. "oil"; *mrḥ·t* "oil"

4 *ḥsy* "to praise"

5 det. "cold"; *ḳbb*, *ḳbḥ* "to be cool"

6 *ḥm* "majesty," "servant"

8, 9 *ḫnt* "before"

11 *ḫnm* "to unite"; Khnum

13, 23, 17, 21 det. "vessel," "liquid"; *ḥḳ·t* "beer"; *dpw*; *wbꜣ* "servant"

14 det. "milk"

20 det. "wine"

21 phon. *nw*, *yn* (?); det. *ḳd*, *nḏ*; "vessel," "liquid"; *ẖnw* "interior"

22 *yny* "to bring"; phon. *yn*

23 *yb* "heart"; det. "heart"

det. "stone vessel," "ivory"; *mꜣwṯ*

25 *wꜥb* "clean," "priest"; cf. A 101

27 *ꜥb*, *wꜥb* "clean"

29 *my* (old *mr*) "as," "like"; phon. *my*

31 *wśḫ* "wide"; *ḥnw·t* "lady"; phon. *ꜥb*; det. "vessel"

33 see X 1

38, 37 det. "fire"; *nśr*

39 *bꜣ*

40 *ḏr* "border"; phon. *ḏr*

42 *nś·t* "throne"; phon. *g*

43 *nb* "lord," "all"; phon. *nb*

44 phon. *k*

46 *kꜣ·t* "female beast"

49 det. "feast"; *ḥb* "feast"; cf. O 65

50 *ẖry-ḥb* "priest"

53 *yt* "barley," "corn-measure"; det. "grain"

Z 27 late for 53

57 *ydr* "flock"

59 *ḥmt* "copper"; det. "metal"

60 *tꜣ* "hot"; phon. *tꜣ*

X. Offerings

1, N 66 det. "bread"

3 *nḫn* el Kab

W 35, W 33, 5, 19 *tꜣ* "bread"; phon. *tꜣ*; *yt* "father"

10, 11 *pꜣw·t* "bread for offering"; *pꜣw·t* "antiquity"; det. "bread"

N 26, 12 — *pśḏ·t* "ninefold"

14 — *sp* "heap of corn"; *sp* "times"; cf. 3

15 — old form of 14

17 — phon. *ẖ*

21 — cf. N 47

22 — *rdy* "to give"

Y. Writing, Music, and Game Articles

1 — *sẖ* (*sš*) "to write"; *nʿʿ* "mottled"; *śnʿʿ* "to polish"

2 — *mḏ3·t* "book"; det. abstract idea; *dmḏ* "together"

3 — *g3w* "sack"; *mśn*; det. *g3w*

8, 6 — *sšš·t* "sistrum," "clapper"; cf. S 50 *śẖm*

9 — *nfr* "good"

11 — *śy3* "to recognize"

12 — *mn* "to remain"; phon. *mn*

14 — *yb3* man at draughts

Z. Strokes and Doubtful Signs

5 — determinative of the dual; phon. *y*

7 — det. "to divide," "to reckon," "to break"; *šbn* "to be different"; *św3* "to go by"; cf. N 49

9 — *mḏ* "ten"

I 27 — *mḏ·t* "depth"

10 — det. "furniture," "basket"; *ḥry·t* "fear"

11 — *dny*; det. "to divide"

N 8 — det. "circle"; *ḳd*

12 — phon. *t*

15 — *ḳn* "to finish"; det. *ḏ3ḏ3·t*

19 — "cartouche"; *rn* "name"

20 — see N 66

22 — *śḳr* "to smite"

25 — *yp·t* "harem"

29, 30 — phon. *nm*

GLOSSARY

ꜣ

ꜣw length.
ꜣwy to be long, to be wide, to be happy, glad.
ꜣwy-yb to make glad.
ꜣw·t length.
ꜣw·t-ʿ present, gift.
ꜣb to cease.
ꜣby to desire, to wish, to love.
ꜣby (*ꜣbw*) panther.
ꜣbḫ (*y*?) to mix.
ꜣbd hen.
ꜣbḏw city of Abydos.
ꜣpd goose, duck, fowl.
ꜣmm to grasp, to hold.
ꜣh to consent, to be beautiful.
ꜣḥ·t land, field, estate.
ꜣḫ glorious.
ꜣḫw splendour, the blessed ones.
ꜣḫ·t glory, horizon; two horizons as title of Harmachis.
ꜣśy to hasten.
ꜣśy·w quickly.
ꜣś·t goddess Isis.
ꜣś·t place.
ꜣś·t-ḥr direction.
ꜣšr to roast.
ꜣḳ to diminish.
ꜣgby flood.
ꜣ·t moment.
ꜣtp (*ꜣṯp*) to fill, to load.
ꜣḏꜣ splinter.

y

y Oh! behold, he who, that which.
yꜣꜣ name of a district.
yꜣꜣy·t branch.
yꜣw worship, adoration, to praise.
yꜣwy old age.
yꜣw·t office, a noble, old man; cattle.
yꜣb·ty eastern.
yꜣrr·t fruit, grapes, wine.
yꜣḫw glorified, profitable.
yꜣḫ·t horizon.
yꜣš to call, to summons.
yꜣk·t herb, bulblike.
yꜣ·t place, holy place.
yy to come.
yy-wy welcome!
yywyꜣ father of Queen Tiy.
yʿy to wash.
yʿḥmś Ahmose.
yw to come, to go, to arrive, to travel; and, but, for, then, when; island; dog.
ywꜣ cow.
ywy I; to separate.
ywʿ to reward, heir.
ywʿw inheritance.
ywf meat.
yw·f he.
ywnw Heliopolis.
ywr conception.
ywh to take.
yw(*t*) to come.
yw·tw one, he, she, it; there is, there was; with det. of deity = Pharaoh.
ywtn ground, mud.
yb heart; to think, to believe.
yb-yʿy restorer.
ybḥ tooth.
ybd month.

yp to count; grief.
ypd plank (?).
yf (*ywf*) meat.
yfd linen.
yfdy bed.
ym = *m*; in, to, there, therefore.
ym river, sea.
ym3 tent.
ym3ḫ honour, reputation, worthy.
ym3ḫy worthy.
ymy to give, to put, to make, to allow; come!; be not; during, in.
ymy-ḥ3·t old time.
ymy·t during, in.
ymn god Amon.
ymn-mś Amenmes.
ymn·ty west, western, right.
ymnt·t western.
ymr to be deaf.
ym(?)·*t* graciousness.
yn by, when, is not?, pray!, "said he," introduces a question.
yny to bring, to summons, to take, to take possession.
ynw gifts, offerings.
ynb wall.
ynpw god Anubis; name of a person.
yn-m who?
ynn3 name of a person.
ynr stone, shell.
yn-rf therefore.
ynḥ to surround, to enclose; eyebrow.
yn·t fish; valley.
yntf Intef.
(*y*)*nḏ-ḥr* hail!; homage, praise.
yr now.
yry to do, to make; belonging to, of such a nature, companion.
yry-yḫ·t offerings.
yry-ʿ·t officer.
yry-mʿw with, in company with.
yry-ḥ3·t pilot.
yrp wine, beer.
yr-p3 verily.
yr = *r* to, than.
yrnṯ river Orontes.
yr·t eye.
yrṯ·t milk.
yhw (*yhy·t*) stable.
yhm·t bank (of a river).
yḥ cow, ox.
yḥw weakness, childishness.
yḫ how!, what?, Ah!, let me.
yḫm (*ḫm*) not to know.
yḫ·t thing; wealth, goods.
yḫ-tm lest.
ys to go.
ysy hasten.
yś behold, that (particle), interrogative.
yśr tamarisk; *yśry* belonging to the tamarisk.
yśśy Isosi.
yś·t place.
yśt behold.
yśtn to surround.
yśtw behold.
yśtw-yr whilst.
yś·t-r·f now, therefore.
yḳ beef.
yḳr to be wise, to be fine, exceedingly.
yt = *ytf* = *tf* father; corn, barley, grain.
yty to take; king, prince.
ytm god Atum.
ytn to quarrel with.
yt-nṯr "father of the god" = title of a priest.
ytrw stream.
ytḥ to drag.
yṯ3 to carry off, to lead, to take away; thief, crooked.
yṯy to take, to take to, to seize.

ytn sun; Aton.
ydb·wy two borders.
ydnw assistant of.

ʿ

ʿ arm, hand, side, place.
ʿꜣ ass, door, here, great.
ʿꜣy to be great, to beat.
ʿꜣ·w very much.
ʿꜣb to be astonished (?)
ʿꜣm Asiatic, Syrian.
ʿꜣ-ḫpr·w-rʿ Thutmose III.
ʿyn lime-stone.
ʿʿy to speak, to utter a cry, foreign language.
ʿʿb to comb.
ʿwꜣ to decay, to stink; to steal.
ʿwꜣy to steal, to rob; robber; to harvest.
ʿwn-yb caprice.
ʿw·t-ḫꜣś·t game.
ʿb horn.
ʿbꜣ sceptre.
ʿbt (ḥb) feast.
ʿfn·t hair.
ʿm to understand, to give heed; to absorb, to devour.
ʿmwynnsy name of a person.
ʿn again.
ʿny to return, to retreat, to repeat, to turn around, to look around.
ʿnḫ to live, life.
ʿnḫwy ears.
ʿntyw perfumes.
ʿrf bag.
ʿrrw·t office of administration.
ʿrḳ to swear an oath.
ʿrḳy last.
ʿḥꜣ to fight, strife, combat.
ʿḥꜣw weapon, shaft.
ʿḥꜣwty combat.
ʿḥʿ to stand; then; palace; cargo-boat; life, time of life, duration of life.
ʿḥʿw time; rank.
ʿhʿ·t grave.
ʿẖnwty royal chamber or cabinet.
ʿš to call, to cry; cedar.
ʿšꜣ to be many, numerous.
ʿḳ to enter, to come to.
ʿḳw food, bread.
ʿ·t door, chamber; limb, member of body.
ʿḏꜣ evil, evil-doer, violence.
ʿḏy fat, greece.
ʿḏd young man.
ʿḏd·t young woman.

w

w (?) place, district.
wꜣy to bow, to be inclined to, to be about to.
wꜣy-r to be far from.
wꜣw wave.
wꜣb persea (tree)?
wꜣḥ to place, to set, to lie down, to lay down, to last; to be happy; fortunate.
wꜣḫ hypostyle hall.
wꜣḫy hall, pillared hall, hypostyle hall.
wꜣś sceptre; happiness, good fortune.
wꜣśy to go to ruin, to be decayed.
wꜣś·t Thebes.
wꜣgy to make festival.
wꜣ·t way, road, side.
wꜣ·t-ḥr name of a place.
wꜣḏ to be green, green, young.
wꜣḏ-wr sea.
wʿ one.
wʿb to be clean, clean; priest; to purify, purification.

wʿb·t place of purification.
wʿf to fetter, to bind.
wʿ-nb each one.
wʿr to come out.
wʿr·t coffer.
wʿ·t sole.
wʿ·ty sole, only, altogether.
wb3 to enter.
wb3·t servant.
wbn to rise, to arise.
wpy to judge, to plead, to open.
wpw (*ypw*) messenger.
wp-w3·wt god Upuat, title of Osiris.
wpw-ḥr except.
wpw·t (*ypw·t*) messenger, work, knowledge, tidings, report.
wmt·t room.
wn to open.
wny name of a person.
wnw·t hour.
wnm (*wm*) to eat, food.
wn-p3 when.
wnn existence, lifetime.
wnn-nfr Osiris.
wnḫ to clothe, to put on, to tie up (hair).
wr to be great, great, prince, chief, oldest (son); evil.
wrry·t war-chariot.
wrḥ to anoint, to smear, to daub.
wrš to pass time, to watch; by day.
wršy·t watchman.
wrḏ to rest.
whn to renew, to report.
wḥy·t tribe.
wḥʿ to return home.
wḫ3 to seek; to shake out, to fall.
wśyr Osiris.
wśm electrum.
wśr to be mighty, mighty, wisdom.
wśr-rf a proper name.
wśḫ to be wide, width.
wśḫ·t punt, ferry, raft.
wšb to reply, answer.
wg3 evil, shame, feebleness.
w·t name of a town.
wtṯ to beget.
wdy to utter.
wdn to make offerings, offering.
wdḥw libation table.
wḏ to command, to entrust.
wḏ3 to go, to pass away, to come; to be well, to be whole, to be happy, to be glad; good fortune.
wḏʿ to cut off; divorced person.
wḏw garland.
wḏb shore.
wḏf to delay.

b

b3 to be happy, fortunate; to hack up.
b3w might.
b3ḳ oil.
b3k servant.
b3·t bush, stalk.
b3t3w name of a person.
by3 fortress; mine in Sinai.
by3y·t a wonder, miracle.
by3·t character, person.
byn evil.
byk to work, servant.
by·t honey.
byty-d3s·t high official who carries the seal of the king.
bʿl god Baal.
bʿḥ to flood.
bw place; not.

bw-nb all men, everyone.
bw-n-rꜣ "place of the mouth" = outside.
bw ẖr place at which.
bb·t (*bꜣbꜣ·t*) whirlpool (?).
bn not.
bnw·t black granite.
bnr sweet.
bn·t harp.
bhꜣ to flee.
bḥś to hunt.
bẖn (*bẖnw*) house.
bšy to be sick, to be soiled.
bšṯ to revolt.
btꜣw evil, squalor.
bdš become discouraged, to retreat.
bd·t (*bd·ty*) wheat, barley.

p

pꜣ to fly.
pꜣ-wn for, because.
pꜣw·t beginning.
pꜣw·ty cycle (of the gods).
pꜣw·t nṯrw cycle of the gods, nine-fold gods.
pꜣ-nty anyone.
pꜣ-śmy because of.
pꜥ·t tribe.
pwy demonstr. this.
pfś (*fśy*) to boil, to cook.
pnꜥ to upset, to turn around.
pry to go out, to ascend; hero.
pr-ꜥꜣ pharaoh.
pr-ffy an unknown place.
pr-ḥḏ treasury, double white house.
pr·ṭ Spring; grain.
pr·t-r-ẖrw funeral offerings.
pḥ to reach.
pḥwy hinder-part.
pḥ·ty strength, energy.
pẖr to penetrate.
pẖr·t remedy; troops.
pśy (*fśy*) to bake, to boil.
pśš to divide.
pśḏ back.
pśḏ·t the nine-fold gods.
pḳ·t fine linen.
p·t heaven.
ptny proper name.
ptr to see, to watch, to behold.
ptr (*pty*) what?
pḏ·t pśḏ the nine-bow people.

f

fꜣy to bring to, to give to, to carry, to take up, to start.
fy old abs. pron.
fnḏ nose, nostril.
fẖ to set forth.
fśy to cook, to bake, to boil.

m

m in, with, against.
mꜣꜥ (?) to slaughter, to offer (sacrifice).
mꜣꜥś·t liver (?).
mꜣꜥ·t truth, justly.
mꜣꜥ·t-kꜣ-rꜥ Hatshepsut.
mꜣwy to renew.
mꜣwṯ red granite.
mꜣḥ garland.
mꜣ-ḥsꜣ (*mꜣ-ḥs*) lion.
mꜣꜥ-ẖrw to justify, blessed, justified.
mꜣẖ to burn.
my like, as, that, when.
my (*mꜥy*) come!
myny to die.
my-śẖrw-n like, in the condition of.
my-ḳy after the manner of the whole.
my-ḳd like, quite.
mytt then.

mʿ by, from, with, because, then, behold; for emphasis.
mʿyw hair.
mʿbꜣ 30
mʿhry·t (*mẖry·t*) granary.
mʿḥʿ·t tomb.
mʿt (*mṯ*) behold.
mw (*myw*) water.
mwt to die, to perish, to kill, the dead.
mw·t mother.
m-bꜣḥ before, in the presence of.
m-m (*mʿ-mʿ*) among.
m-mʿ with, together with.
m-myt·t likewise, as well as.
m-mn·t daily.
mn to remain.
mn (*myny*) to be sick, to die, to land.
mny (*myny*) to die, to land, to rest, to depend; to marry.
mn-yb brave.
mny·t castanets.
mnʿ·t nurse.
mnw monument.
mnw god Min.
mnw·t dove.
mnfy·t army, staff.
mnmn to quake.
mnmn·t herd.
mnḫ to be pleasant, to be favourable, excellent.
mn-ḫpr-rʿ Thutmose III.
mnḫ·t linen, clothes.
mn·t anything.
mntw·f it, he.
mnṯw god Mont.
m-n-ḏrw when.
mr to grieve, to be anxious, to have pity for, grief, sorrowful; master, overseer, director, general; woman (?); canal; pyramid.
m-rꜣ-ʿ nevertheless, as though.
mry to love, to desire, beloved.
mry·t river-bank.
m-rʿ-ḫr but.
mrw-ynśy name of a man.
m-r-pw or.
mrmyptw name of a person.
mrḥ·t oil.
mr·t serving man.
mḥ to fill, to begin; ell.
m-ḥꜣ·t before.
mḥꜣ·t door.
m-ḥr-n to.
mḥ·ty north, northward.
m-ḫt after, afterwards, hereafter, behind, together.
m-ḫd northward.
m-ḫnw in, into, within, among, thereon.
m-ḫr·t-hrw daily.
msḥ crocodile.
mś child; for emphasis.
m-śꜣ after, behind, with.
mśy to give birth to, to be born.
mśy·t supper.
mśw·t childbirth.
mśḫn·t goddess of birth.
mśḏy to hate.
m·śḏm·t paint, black paint.
mšʿ to walk, soldier, army.
mšw dagger.
m-ḳꜣb among, in the midst of.
mk lest.
mk (*mʿk*) behold.
mky (*mʿky*) to protect.
m-grg falsley.
mt- conjunctive prefix.
mty director.
mtw- conjunctive prefix.
mtw·k thou.
mtw·tw one, it; when.

m·tn behold (ye).
mtr to bear witness.
mṯꜣ to defy.
mṯn (*mꜥṯn*) way.
m-dy from.
mdw to speak, to cry, word, voice; staff of authority, authority.
mdnyt name of a place.
md·t word, matter.
m-ḏr because of.
m-ḏrty when.

n

n of, to, by (in swearing); not.
nꜣy·f his.
ny to belong to (*ny-śy mr-pr* it belongs to the master of the house).
nyw·ty·t (*nyw·ty, nyw·tt*) not, no, that which does not exist, not having.
nyś (*nysbḏ* [?]) to call, to proclaim.
n-ꜥꜣ·t-n because.
nꜥy to journey, to sail.
nꜥr a kind of fish.
nw to see, to look; time; axe.
nwy to care for; flood; knife.
n-wr-n because of.
nw·t goddess Nut; town, city, residence.
nb each; gold; lord.
nb-mꜣꜥ·t-rꜥ Amenophis III.
nb-kꜣw-rꜥ name of a king.
nb·t lady.
nb·ty (?) "the two goddesses of the land," title of a king.
nbt-ḥt goddess Nephthys.
nbd to plait hair, lock of hair.
n-pꜣ but.
nfw (*ṯꜣw*) breath; *nfrw* grain
nfr good; beauty; breath; *nfrw* grain.
nfry·t-r until.
nm (*nym*) who.
nmy to low, to shout.
nmyw-šꜥyw name of nomads.
nmw payment.
nmḥ weak.
nmt to wander, wandering.
nn this, those.
n-nym-try who.
nry to fear.
nrw strength.
nrr to bow (?).
nr·t mankind.
nhw to despair; anything.
nhm to rejoice.
nhrn Naharina (Mesopotamia).
nhśy Nubian, negro.
nḥb·t neck.
nḥm to deliver, to escape, to take away, to rob.
nḥḥ for ever.
nḥw·t lamentation.
nḫb·t Nekhbet, name of a king; colour (?).
nḫn to be young; town Nechen.
nḫt to be strong, to be mighty, strength; victory.
nḫty name of a man.
nswy·t (?) kingdom.
nswt (?) king.
nś to belong to, according to measure.
nś·t throne.
nś·t-tꜣ·wy Karnak.
nš to tremble; portal (?), step (?).
nkt thing.
ngꜣw bull; town of Nagau.
n·t city, town.
nty·t that which is, being, thing.
ntf it.
nt-ḥtr cavalry.
nṯr god.

nṯry divinity, divine.
nṯry·t godly, divinity.
nṯr nfr "good god" = the king.
nṯ-ḥtr charioteer.
nṯr·t goddess.
ndw to deliver, to set free.
nḏ to avenge.
nḏy·t pettiness.
nḏm to be sweet, to be glad, to please, to be well, to rejoice; sweet.
nḏnḏ to ask, to discourse.
nḏry to seize.
nḏ-ḥr homage.
nḏś to be small, little one.
n-ḏrtw when.

r to, since.
rꜣ mouth, voice, entrance, to talk; charm.
rꜣ-ꜣw a place-Tura.
rꜣ-yt door.
rꜣ-ꜥwy work.
r-ꜣw (*n-ꜣw*) throughout.
rꜣ-pw or.
rꜣ-pr temple.
rꜣ-ḥḏ treasure-house.
rꜣ-śṯꜣ-w Sakkara.
rꜥ day; the god Reꜥ.
rꜥ-wśr Wsr-rꜥ, name of a man.
rꜥ-bꜣk work.
rꜥ-ḥr-ꜣḫty Harmakhis.
r-ꜥḳꜣ opposite.
rwyy to flee, to escape.
rwy·t side.
rwhꜣ evening.
rwty double gate.
rpꜥ·t (*rpꜥ·ty*) prince, heir-apparent.
rf for emphasis.
rm fish.
rmy to weep.
r-my·ty·t in like manner.
rmn shoulder, arm, side.
rmṯ mankind.
rn name.
rnpy·t fruit, flowers.
rnp·t fruit; year.
rnn to suckle, to bring up.
r-nty·t introduces a final clause.
rḫ to know, to be learned, wisdom.
rḫy·t mankind, people.
r-ḫft before.
rḫty laundryman.
rś south.
rśy southern.
ršw to rejoice.
ršw·t joy.
ršrš to be glad, to be pleased, to enjoy.
rk time.
r-gś near, by the side of.
r-tw place (?).
rd to grow up, to develop; foot, leg.
rdy to give.
rdḏdt name of a woman.
r-ḏr whole.
r-ḏd that, introduces a final clause.

h

hꜣ hail!
hꜣy to go away, to advance, to descend, to pour in, to overthrow, to embark; husband.
hꜣw near; Oh!
hꜣb to send.
hy to rejoice; husband.
hb to labour.
hp law.
hmy to be ignorant.
hnw to shout for joy; pots.
hry to be satisfied.

hrw to be content; day.
hd hero.
hdhd to attack.

ḥ

ḥꜣ Oh!; behold.
ḥꜣ (*n-ḥꜣ*) behind.
ḥꜣw naked.
ḥꜣw-nb foreign countries.
ḥ(ꜣ)pw·ty spy.
ḥꜣ-ny Oh, that (in respect to me).
ḥꜣḳ to seize.
ḥꜣty heart.
ḥꜣ·ty before.
ḥꜣty-ʿ beginning.
ḥꜣ·ty-ʿ count, prince.
ḥꜣ·t-sp year of reign.
ḥʿ flesh, body, limb.
ḥʿy to rejoice.
ḥʿw staff.
ḥʿpy Nile.
ḥʿt bed.
ḥw nourishment.
ḥwꜣ to be spoiled, to stink, to be annoyed.
ḥwy to smite, to beat, to pursue; Oh!
ḥwy·t rain.
ḥwn-n-n-nswt Herakleopolis.
ḥwtf to despoil.
ḥb to lament over (?), feast.
ḥbꜣbꜣ to waddle (of a goose).
ḥbś linen, garment, clothes.
ḥpt the arms.
ḥfꜣw snake, dragon.
ḥm male-servant; majesty.
ḥmꜣy·t salt.
ḥmw poor; rudder; 40.
ḥmw·t workshops.
ḥmw·ty workmen.
ḥm-nṯr prophet, priest.
ḥmśy to sit, to set, to place; sitting.
ḥm-kꜣ priest of the dead.
ḥm·t woman, wife, lady.
ḥn (*ḥnnw*) to go; to bar.
ḥnw goods, property; vase, jar.
ḥnw·t lady.
ḥnwty farmer.
ḥnwtt name of a lady.
ḥnmm·t mankind, people.
ḥnn (*ḥnnw*) phallus.
ḥnś narrow.
ḥnky·t bed.
ḥnk·t gift.
ḥr upon, to, because; overseer; Horus.
ḥry withdrawn; chief; name of a person.
ḥry-yb dwelling in.
ḥry·w-šʿ sand-dwellers.
ḥry·t terror; the upper.
ḥry-tp chief.
ḥry-ḏꜣḏꜣ chief.
ḥrw upper path.
ḥrw-r except, in addition to.
ḥr-m why!
ḥr-mʿ in front of.
ḥr-nhw-n for the sake of.
ḥr-ntt because, as it is.
ḥrr·t flower.
ḥr-śꜣ after.
ḥr-śhm·t-rʿ-ʿnḫ name of a king.
ḥr·t grave, necropolis.
ḥḥ for ever; million.
ḥs to arrive.
ḥsy to praise; praiseworthy; singing.
ḥsw·t favour, love, honour.
ḥsmn natron.
ḥs·t praise, favour.
ḥśy to sing, singer; an offering.

ḥśb to reckon; measures.

ḥśḳ to cut off.

ḥḳȝ prince, ruler.

ḥḳȝ·t lordship.

ḥḳr hungry.

ḥḳ·t beer, ale; goddess Ḥeḳt.

ḥkȝ (in plural) magic.

ḥknw praise, thanksgiving.

ḥkr hungry.

ḥ·t fortress, castle, wall.

ḥtp to rest, to sit down, to set free, to satisfy; a measure, basket; offering.

ḥtp-dy-nswt an offering which the king gives.

ḥtpw-nṯr offering, oblation.

ḥtp-nfr-ḥk-wȝś·t-ymn Amenophis II.

ḥtp-ḥk-wȝś·t-ymn Amenophis III.

ḥtp·t food, offerings.

ḥtm to cease, to go to ruins.

ḥ·t-nṯr temple.

ḥtr team, cavalry.

ḥ·t-ḥr Hathor.

ḥtt shameful deed.

ḥdb to arrive, to pass time.

ḥd·t white crown, crown of Upper Egypt.

ḥḏ to be bright, white, silver.

ḥḏy to be unusable.

ḥḏ·t white crown of Upper Egypt.

ḥḏ-tȝ the earth becomes bright = sunrise.

ḫ

ḫȝ 1000.

ḫȝy·t slaughter.

ḫȝʿ to fall, to throw, to leave.

ḫȝwy night.

ḫȝw·t altar.

ḫȝrw Syria.

ḫȝr·t widow.

ḫȝś·t foreign land, desert, land, bank.

ḫȝś·ty foreigner, Bedouin.

ḫʿy to shine, to adorn.

ḫʿw shining, splendour; crown; tools; weapon, javelin.

ḫʿw-nw-rȝ-ʿ-ḫt weapons.

ḫʿr to rage.

ḫʿ-kȝ·w-rʿ Sesostris III.

ḫwś to build.

ḫbȝ to ill-treat.

ḫby to dance.

ḫbśw·t (*ḫbsw·t*) beard.

ḫpy·t death.

ḫpr to come into being; a figure.

ḫpry sun-god.

ḫprw forms, being.

ḫpš strength.

ḫft to, before, just as, according to.

ḫfty enemy.

ḫft-ḥr before, in the presence of.

ḫm (*šmm*) to be hot, dry.

ḫmy not to do, not to know, to loose consciousness.

ḫmt to propose, to think.

ḫmt third.

ḫn to dance.

ḫnw·t musician.

ḫnmś friend, friendship.

ḫnm·t waiting women.

ḫn-n-md·t speech, discourse, proverb.

ḫnr (*ḫny*) prisoner.

ḫnr·t (?) prison.

ḫnt forehead.

ḫnty to journey southward, southward; first.

ḫnty-ymn·tyw "First of the Westerners" = a title of Osiris as god of the dead.
ḫnd to tread; throne.
ḫndw throne.
ḫr to fall; hostile prince; and, but; among, near, with, when, then, until.
ḫry belonging to.
ḫr-yr now, when, yet.
ḫr-yr-ḥr when, after.
ḫrw voice, sound; army.
ḫrp to bring, to conduct, to advance; stela, tombstone.
ḫrpw mallet.
ḫr-n for.
ḫr-rʿ when.
ḫr-św-m Oh!
ḫr·t thing belonging to.
ḫrtw "they say."
ḫḫ neck, throat.
ḫsf to protect, to draw near.
ḫsḏ to mould.
ḫśbḏ lapis-lazuli.
ḫśf to drive away, to defend, to prosecute.
ḫt tree.
ḫ·t thing.
ḫtꜣ Ḫeta, Hittite country.
ḫty to inscribe.
ḫtf according as.
ḫtm to close, to lock, to seal; seal.
ḫdy to sail down stream, northward.

ẖ

ẖꜣb·t "wire" of the crown.
ẖꜣr a bin.
ẖpꜣ umbilical cord.
ẖmʿ to fall upon.
ẖmś to bend.
ẖn to enter into.
ẖny·t sailor.
ẖnw inside; abode, residence, palace.
ẖnw-ʿ to embrace, in arms.
ẖnm to unite oneself.
ẖnmw god Khnum.
ẖnm·t-ḥꜣ·t-špś·wt-ymn Hatshepsut.
ẖr under, with.
ẖry·t possession.
ẖry·t-nt̠r underworld.
ẖr-ḥꜣ at the head of.
ẖr-ḥꜣ·t before, old time.
ẖrd child.
ẖsy to be weak, to be faint, miserable, despised, wretched.
ẖsy·t despised.
ẖ·t body, belly; people.
ẖdb to slay.
ẖdr misery (?).

s

s (*ꜣ*?) man.
sꜣ son; priesthood.
sꜣw to beware, guardian; Nḫn, title of an official.
sꜣb jackal; judge.
sꜣnht Sinuhe.
sꜣ·t daughter.
sꜣt̠ (*sꜣt*) to froth over.
s·ʿḳ to cause to go.
swnw name of a place.
swn·t sale.
swr (*swy*) to drink.
sb (*sby*) to go, to pass by, to follow.
sp time, example.
spꜣ·t district.
spy to remain over.
sp-pw is it the time?, is it worth while?
sf to be gracious.
sf·t (*sft̠*) knife.
smꜣy to unite.
smꜣ-tꜣ neck or strip of land.
smy tidings.
smy·t desert.
sny to open, to spread out.

snf blood.
shs (*śḫśḫ*) to run.
sḫr leadership.
sḫs (*śḫśḫ*) flight.
ssm horse.
sš to write, scribe, book, writing.
sš see *sny*.
sšn blossom of the lotus.
sšš·t sistrum.
s·t woman.
sd tail.

ś

ś3 back.
ś33 to recognize.
ś3y to satisfy; fierce-eyed.
ś3b judge.
ś3r woe.
ś3ḥ to reach, to approach, to present with.
ś3ḫbw proper name.
ś3ḳ to gather together.
śy3ḫ to glorify.
śyny to await.
śʿb trinkets.
śʿḥ nobility, freedom.
św the sun, light.
św3y to pass, to go by.
św3ḥ to continue.
św3š to worship, to praise.
śwḥ·t egg.
śwt (= *św*) 3 per. mas. sing. per. pron.
śwḏ to inherit, to provision.
śwḏ to command.
śwḏ3 to refresh, to give health to.
śb3 door.
śbḥ to laugh, to cry, to call out.
śbk god Sebek.
śpr to come, to go, to arrive, to reach; to bewail, to lament, lamentation.
śpry to let go forth.
śpdd to make ready, to be.
śf yesterday.
śm (*śmw*, *śtmw*) vegetables.
śm3 to kill, to do battle.
śm3ʿ to pray, to cry; forehead.
śm3ʿ to justify.
śmy to report; because of.
śmwn truly.
śmn goose.
ś·mnḫ to beautify.
śmr friend, companion.
śmḥy left, east.
śn brother.
śny to curse.
śnw to complain.
śnb to be well, health.
śn-nw a second, a companion.
śnḫbḫb to draw back (?).
śn·t sister.
śn·ty both sisters.
śnṯr incense.
śnḏ to be afraid, fear.
śnḏ3r3 country of Sendar.
śnḏm to dwell, to sit.
śr (*śyr*) prince, high official, burgher, princely.
śrw princes.
śrḫ throne.
śrḫy to announce to.
śḥw to assemble.
śḥry to take oneself away.
śḥtm to destroy.
śḥḏ to make bright, to clear up, to manifest.
śḫ3 to remember, to bethink, to think.
śḫ3ḫ to assist, to hasten.
śḫpr to cause to exist.
śḫm to be powerful, might; double crown, sceptre.

śẖr to overthrow; counsel, manner, nature, thing; according to the manner of, according to.

śẖśẖ to run, to pursue.

śḫ·t field.

śḫ·ty peasant, fellah, farmer.

śẖd stand on head, upside down.

śẖr to overlay.

śẖ·ty peasant.

śśpd to be in good order.

śśm·t a mare.

śśn to smell, to breathe.

śšm to lead, to fashion (?).

śšmw guide, leader, fashioner.

śšt3 to enchant.

śšd diadem.

śḳbbwy bath-room.

śḳr-ᶜnḫ prisoner.

śḳd rower.

śḳdy to sail.

śk behold.

śk3 to plough.

śkm to finish.

śkśk to destroy.

śgnn ointment.

śgr silence.

ś·t (*yś·t*) place.

śt3 to lift, to take away; to make light, fire.

śty to discharge a bow; Nubia; smell.

śtyw (*śṯtyw*) Asiatics, bedouin.

ś·t-yry right place, in (their season).

ś·t-wr·t throne.

śtp to choose.

śtpw the best, the choise.

śṯ when.

śṯ3 to lead.

śṯp to choose.

śṯp·t oblation, offering of flesh.

śṯ·ty Syrian.

śd to clothe; tail.

śḏf3 to supply with, supply.

śḏm to hear.

śḏr to lie down, to sleep, to spend the night.

š

š pond.

š3 tree, garden.

š3ᶜ-m since.

š3w weight, quantity.

š3b victuals.

š3ś to go, to hasten.

š3śy to go.

š3·t-dw3 150.

š3d to dig.

šᶜ (*šᶜy*) sand.

šᶜ·t book.

šᶜd to cut, cut off, cut down.

šw sun.

šw3 common man, poor man.

šwy to be dry.

šwy-m empty = without.

šw·ty double feather (king's crown).

špś monument, stela.

špśy holy, fine; Sacred Lady, Principal Favourite.

špśś wealth.

šfy·t strength.

šm to go.

šmy to go.

šmᶜ south; dancing.

šmᶜy·t dancing girl.

šmᶜ-sp·t district of Upper Egypt.

šmw wheat.

šmm to be hot, to be dry.

šmśy to serve, to follow.

šmśw follower, servant, bodyguard; following.

šmś-ḥr servants of Horus, Kings of antiquity.

šn to be sick, to be grieved, to suffer.
šny to encircle.
šny (*šnw*) hair.
šnʿ to avert; edge of a path.
šnw·t courtiers.
šnb·t skin, body.
šnḏw·t skirt, clothing.
šry small, younger (of persons).
šry·t young person; daughter.
šś linen.
šsp to receive, to take, to begin, to conceive; statue of a god.
šś wardrobe; alabaster.
šś3 ability.
šdy to read; to suckle.

ḳ

ḳ3y to leap; to raise.
ḳ3y·t high.
ḳ3ḳ3w a ship.
ḳ3g3b name of a man.
ḳy fulness.
ḳby to increase.
ḳbb to be cool, to refresh.
ḳm3 to create; form, figure, person.
ḳmy ointment, salve.
ḳmʿtw southern.
ḳn to be many, many.
ḳny to be strong, to be brave, to carry; porter.
ḳny·t strength.
ḳnḳn to beat.
ḳn·t domain.
ḳnd rage.
ḳnd·t rage.
ḳry thunder.
ḳrśw coffin.
ḳr·t (?) bolt.
ḳś to be sick; bone.
ḳśn foolish.
ḳḳ3 to rule over.
ḳd to build; figure, likeness, character; like.
ḳdy to walk.
ḳdnwm name of a place.
ḳdtr dirty.

k

k3 soul (" Ka "); bull; behold, verily, in truth.
k3y to speak, to say aloud, to think, to desire, to plan, to forsee.
k3wty workman.
k3-nḫt-ḫʿ-m-w3ś·t Thutmose III.
k3ry Nubian country.
k3š Kush.
k3·t work; wife, woman.
k3tw hidden.
ky (*kyy*) another.
kwkw darkness.
kw·ty thou.
kf3 to uncover.
km to finish.
km·t Egypt.
kśy to bow.
kśw crouched position.
kš Nubia.
kšt Kush.
kkw darkness.
kty another.
kty-yḫ·t another matter, others.
ktkt to twitch.
kdšw Kadesh.

g

g3y vase, vessel.
g3ś3 grief.
gb (*gbb*) god Geb.
gb3 arm, side.
gbgb to cast down, to fall.
gmy to find.
gmḥ to see, to perceive.
gmḥ·t crown.
gmgm to creek.
gnn (*g3nn*) to be weak, helpless.
gr to be silent.

grḥ to rest, to be calm.

grg to found, to build, to take, to provide for, to lay a trap.

grg faithless, false; baseness, falsehood.

gr·t but.

gś side, half; to anoint, to perfume.

gšy dagger.

t

tꜣ bread, earth.

tꜣ-wnw·t at once.

tꜣ-mry Egypt.

tꜣš border, frontier.

tꜣ-ḏśr cemetery.

tyy Queen Tiy.

tyw yes.

tywy belonging to thee.

ty-rꜣ-yꜣ door.

tw- late Egyptian prefix.

tw "one," thou, thee.

twt image, statue; unite, be together.

tp head, first.

tpy first, beginning, chief; to breathe.

tpy-ʿ ancestor.

tpy·t fine oil.

tp-ʿ before.

tp-m before.

tp-ḥśb exactness.

tpty fine oil, fine.

tf (*yt*) father.

tm to stop, not to do.

tm (see *ytm*).

tmyt lest.

tny old age.

tnw name of a place, Tnw = Rtnw (?).

tnnw each; weakness (?).

tr (*ty*) time.

try pray! to mark a question.

tr-n during, while.

thy to err, to transgress, to attack.

thmy (*thy*) to drive out.

thn to proclaim.

tḫn obelisk.

tkn to consort with.

tty King Tety.

ṯ

ṯꜣ chicken.

ṯꜣy to seize, to shave; man, male.

ṯꜣw wind (see *nfw*).

ṯꜣ·ty vizier.

ṯʿw to run.

ṯwyꜣ mother of Queen Tiy.

ṯb vessel.

ṯb·t sandal.

ṯpḥ·t cavern.

ṯny sheikh (?); town This; Thinis district.

ṯnrʿ mighty deeds.

ṯnṯꜣ·t throne.

ṯḥwḥw to rejoice.

ṯḥn to draw nigh, to collide.

ṯs proverb.

ṯsy to raise, to lift up, to exalt.

ṯsw to command, a general.

ṯtw (*ṯb·t*) sandals.

d

d (*dy*) to put; here; there.

dꜣy (*dꜣr*) to rule.

dꜣb fig.

dy to give; *dy-ʿnḫ* "given life."

dwꜣ to adore, to praise, to instruct (?), to become morning; early, to-morrow.

dwꜣy·t morning.

dwn to throw down, to lie down, to stretch out.

dbꜣ to give back.

dbn to search.

dbḥ to beseech.

dp bushel.

dp·t ship, boat; taste.

df drop (?).
dm to sharpen; to name.
dmy to arrive at, to come after, to be related to; city, town, village, place.
dmy·t city.
dm·t knife.
dny to take part.
dr to vanquish, to destroy, to drive away.
drp to present, to make libation, to offer sacrifice.
dhny to name.
dḥwty god Thot.
dḥr leather.
dśr grave.
dḳr fruit.
d·t hand.
ddy Dedy (a person).
ddwn Dedwn (a person).

ḏ

ḏȝy to cross, to cross the water.
ḏȝmw generation.
ḏȝḏȝ head; college of priests.
ḏȝḏȝ-m to.
ḏȝḏȝ·t college.
ḏʿ storm.
ḏʿm gold.
ḏw mountain; evil (*ḏw·t*).
ḏbȝ to stop, to pay, payment, wages.
ḏbʿ·t seal.
ḏb·t brick, tile.
ḏfȝ food.
ḏr extremity, whole; since.
ḏrw boundary, limit.
ḏr·t hand.
ḏḥwty god Thot.
ḏḥwty-mś-nfr-ḫprw Thutmose III.
ḏḫwty-nḫt proper name.
ḏśr-mnw-ymn name of a door.
ḏśr-kȝ-rʿ Amenophis I.
ḏ·t eternity, for ever; serf.
ḏd to speak; to last; account.
ḏdw city Busiris.
ḏdb to collect.
ḏd·t endurance, duration, stability.